_AU'S DOG

David Edmonds is, and John Eidinow was, an award-winning journalist with the BBC. Their hugely acclaimed debut, *Wittgenstein's Poker*, has been published in eighteen languages and was shortlisted for the *Guardian* First Book Award. *Bobby Fischer Goes to War*, their second book, was described as 'a fascinating story, admirably told' in the *Daily Telegraph* and praised by the *Sunday Times* as 'a gripping read'.

ROUSSEAU'S DOG

Two Great Thinkers at War in the Age of Enlightenment

DAVID EDMONDS AND
JOHN EIDINOW

faber and faber

First published in 2006
by Faber and Faber Limited
3 Queen Square London WC1N 3AU
This paperback edition first published in 2007

Typeset by Faber and Faber
Printed in England by Mackays of Chatham

A CIP record for this book
is available from the British Library

ISBN 978-0-571-22406-7

2 4 6 8 10 9 7 5 3 1

To clan Oppenheimer
and to
Elisabeth, Sam, Esther and Hannah Eidinow

Love: To regard with the affection of a friend.
Dr Johnson

He who has not lived before 1789 has not experienced
the true sweetness of life.
Talleyrand

Contents

I
Fear and Flight

Patron and exile, captured by Allan Ramsey in 1766

On the evening of 10 January 1766, the weather in the English Channel was foul – stormy, wet and cold. That night, after being held in harbour by unfavourable winds, a packet boat beat its way, rolling and plunging, from Calais to Dover. Among the passengers were two men who had met for the first time some three weeks earlier in Paris, a British diplomat and a Swiss refugee. The refugee was accompanied by his beloved dog, Sultan, small and brown with a curly tail. The diplomat stayed below, tormented by sea sickness. The refugee remained on deck all night; the frozen sailors marvelled at his hardiness.

If the ship had foundered, she would have carried to the bottom of the Channel two of the most influential thinkers of the eighteenth century.

The diplomat was David Hume. His contributions to philosophy – on induction, causation, necessity, personal identity, morality, and theism – are of such enduring importance that his name belongs in the league of the most elite philosophers, the league that would also include Plato, Aristotle, Descartes, Kant and Wittgenstein. A contemporary and friend of Adam Smith's, he paved the way to modern economics; he also modernized historiography.

The refugee was Jean-Jacques Rousseau. His intellectual range and achievements were equally staggering. He made epochal contributions to political theory, literature and education. His autobiography, the *Confessions,* was a stunningly original work, one that has spawned countless successors but still sets the standard for a narrative of self-revelation and artistic development. *Émile*, his educational tract, transformed the debate about the upbringing of children and was instrumental in altering our perceptions of childhood. *On the Social Contract*, his most significant political publication, has been cited as an inspiration for generations of revolutionaries. More fundamentally, Rousseau altered the way we view ourselves, our emotions and our relationship to society and to the natural world.

The circumstances in which they travelled together could not have differed more. David Hume was returning to London at the end of his service as secretary of the British embassy in Paris. His twenty-six months in office had been a triumph, perhaps the happiest time of his life. He had been the darling of the Paris salons, the hothouses of the French Enlightenment, winning acclaim for his decency as well as his intellect. He was awarded the appellation *le bon David* in tribute to his nobility of character.

Hume's generosity towards a stranger in distress seemed at one with his good nature. He had accepted the burden of arranging refuge in England for the fifty-three-year-old Rousseau, whose books and pamphlets had aroused such intense religious and political opposition that he had been driven from domicile in France and then from asylum in his native Switzerland, where a mob, whipped up by a priest, had stoned his house. Recognizing the lethal potency of his pen, the local authorities were determined to rid themselves of so subversive a figure.

For ten years, Rousseau had sensed himself a man under siege. Convinced of plots against him, with his freedom threatened by the French and Swiss authorities, with his inability to find a permanent resting place, driven from one refuge to another,

Rousseau had come to regard persecution as his lot, even his badge of honour. It fitted with his resolution, taken long before, to live alone, away from the world of men. This solitary life did not preclude friendship, but for Rousseau friendship had to be engaged in unequivocally – it involved the total transparency of one person's heart to another's. It was possible only between equals and was incompatible with any form of servitude.

However, Rousseau was now dependent on Hume for survival in a country where he knew no one and could not speak the language. He had left behind, in Switzerland, Thérèse Le Vasseur, the former scullery maid who was his steadfast companion, acting as his *gouvernante* or housekeeper, for over thirty years. Rousseau was immensely fond of her, needing her by his side and longing for her when they were separated. Sultan, at least, was with him. Rousseau's emotions about Sultan were sufficiently intense to amaze onlookers. The one-time dog-owning Hume said, 'His affection for that creature is above all expression or conception.'

For much of his adult life, a second creature had kept Rousseau company.

'It seems plain', said Friedrich Grimm, the self-appointed cultural correspondent to the courts of Europe, 'that [Rousseau] takes with him a companion who will not suffer him to rest in peace.' This agitated companion, just as inseparable from Rousseau as Sultan and forever growling at his heels, was the writer's deeply rooted belief that the world was hostile and treacherous, ready at any moment to betray him.

The boat docked at Dover at midday on 11 January. Setting foot on English soil, Rousseau embraced Hume, not uttering a word, and covered Hume's face with kisses and tears. Just after the travellers arrived in London, Hume wrote to his brother, 'I think I could live with [Rousseau] all my life in mutual friendship and esteem.' Blithely, the letter continued, 'I believe that one great source of our concord is that neither he nor I are disputatious.'

In Paris, Hume had communed with many of the intellectual luminaries and leading hostesses of the age. Yet, even during the French Enlightenment, with received notions, institutions and cultures under challenge from radical thinkers in every area of life, no other radical thinker was quite like Rousseau. In all his benevolence, had Hume, *le bon David*, any real idea of what he had taken on?

2

Simple Soul

Mme de Warens: she brought young men into the bosom of
the Catholic Church

Issues from the hand of God the simple soul.
T. S. Eliot, *Animula*

'My birth was the first of my misfortunes,' Jean-Jacques Rousseau wrote in the *Confessions*. He was born in Geneva on 28 June 1712, the second son of Isaac Rousseau, a watchmaker, and Susan Bernard, the daughter of a Genevan Calvinist minister. His mother died ten days later. Although he remarried, recorded Rousseau, his father never fully recovered from his wife's death. Because he saw her in his infant second son, his embraces of Jean-Jacques were always grief-laden. A half-century later, Rousseau vividly recalled how, when his father suggested that they should talk about the mother, he replied, 'Very well, Father, but we are sure to cry.'

For a child suffering from devastating loss and its concomitant anger and yearning, such demands must have been traumatic. Little wonder if Rousseau carried into adulthood a craving for unconditional love, combined with an expectation of betrayal and a lack of trust in others. Little wonder if he lived with a sense of innocence lost, regret for a life of happiness just missed, and a preoccupation with his inner self: an inner self that was in some ways more reliable than the external world. He might get the facts wrong, 'but I cannot go wrong about what I felt'.

Rousseau was not a robust boy: he had an embarrassing and painful complaint that would torment him all his life – a congenital malformation of his urinary tract. He passed water slowly and with difficulty, while his bladder felt as if it was only half emptying its contents.

Aged ten, having lost his mother, the child lost his father: Isaac quarrelled with a French captain who thereupon accused him of drawing his sword in the city, a crime under Genevan law. Rather than go to prison, his father chose to exile himself from Geneva. Rousseau was taken in by his uncle, who sent him and his own son, Rousseau's cousin Bernard, to stay in the country with a pastor who taught them Latin. Later, Rousseau recalled a time of bucolic bliss and commented on a theme that would forever preoccupy him, friendship: 'The simplicity of this rural existence brought me one invaluable benefit; it opened my heart to friendship.' He also discovered a sexual proclivity at the hands of the pastor's sister. When he was naughty, she beat him. But this only aroused him sexually and he could not wait to offend again.

Geneva was a small, walled city-state of just over twenty thousand inhabitants, secured by mountainous frontiers. Doubly cut off from its environs, yet still threatened by the powerful surrounding Catholic monarchies, Geneva retained a distinctive culture and ambience, coloured particularly by Calvinism. Calvin had written its constitution in 1541, designing it to bring about his Godly vision. Rousseau always took pride in calling himself a 'Citizen of Geneva' (his friends wrote to him as 'Dear Citizen') and his growing up there moulded his thinking, particularly about politics, democratic participation and individual responsibility.

But, on Sunday, 14 March 1728, Rousseau suffered his third wrenching separation, and bade his childhood a definitive farewell. By this time, he was back in the city as a sixteen-year-old apprentice to an engraver. While walking with some comrades outside the walls, he heard the distant signal announcing the evening locking of the gates. Running desperately towards them, he saw the first drawbridge rising when he was only twenty paces away. He had already been punished twice for being caught beyond the walls, and now he determined not to return to his master and to leave Geneva altogether. His cousin Bernard came out of the city to supply him with a few presents for his journey, including a small sword. In the first of his conjectured plots, Rousseau suspected his uncle and aunt had entrusted Bernard with the gifts to rid themselves of their troublesome nephew rather than urge his homecoming. He walked off in the direction of Savoy.

One week later, in Annecy, he received an introduction to a woman who would have a decisive impact on his life. Mme de Warens, just under thirty, and with 'a ravishing complexion', was a Swiss baroness and Catholic convert. Her principal hobby is said to have been rescuing Protestant souls, particularly those lodged in the bodies of handsome young men. She took in the homeless boy, and within five years she and her charge were lovers. In the meantime, on the advice of a priest, she dispatched Rousseau to Turin, where he embraced Catholicism and spent a short period at a religious hospice (in which he was subjected to unwanted male sexual attention, narrated in physical detail in the *Confessions*), and worked as a domestic valet.

He remained with Mme de Warens – the woman he would always refer to as 'mamma', while she nicknamed him 'little one' – on and off until April 1740. Then, following his return from a trip, he discovered that she had taken up with another young blood, the son of a local high official. (According to Rousseau, 'a tall, pale, silly youth, tolerably well built with a face as dull as his wits.') It must have felt like another betrayal.

This precipitated a move to Lyon, where Rousseau would encounter his first '*philosophe*' – the label given to the prime instigators of the French Enlightenment. The *philosophes*, a group of scientists, artists, writers and statesmen, believed in the construction of a rational order and in truth arrived at through reason. Holding received ideas up to critical scrutiny, they were sceptical of tradition and authority, particularly religious authority. They saw themselves as part of a loose, yet nonetheless unified, cosmopolitan culture of progress. In Lyon, Rousseau took the post of tutor to the children of the city's chief provost, M. de Mably, two of whose brothers were *philosophes*. The family gave Rousseau vital introductions for the next stage of his career.

Music would be a constant in that career, a vocation to which Rousseau devoted much of his spare time. He was an accomplished player of several instruments, including the flute and the violin. He said of himself, 'J.J. was born for music.' Throughout his life, he was to earn an income as a music copyist, and he also nursed ambitions to become a composer. In Lyon, beside teaching (and pilfering his employer's wine and bread), he began to construct a radical new system for musical notation, the fundamental idea being to substitute numbers for visual symbols.

So, in 1741, armed with his newly acquired contacts, his notation project, and a theatrical comedy, he was ready to seek his fame and fortune in the capital of culture.

Fame, combined with a moderate fortune, was indeed to follow, but not yet. For the moment, Paris dismissed the young Genevan as an inarticulate provincial; the musical authorities scornfully rejected his notation.

While he watched his money run out, Rousseau tried his hand at both drama and ballet, and whiled the empty hours away in a café, where he battled at chess against the dazzling player and fellow composer, François-André Philidor. He also fell into conversation with a young man of much the same age and circumstances, Denis Diderot.

Diderot had come to Paris with high literary aspirations, and the energy and talent to match. A born controversialist, ebullient, free-thinking, subversive, he would publish a cascade of political, philosophical and scientific works, as well as novels and plays. But he is most renowned for being one of the founding editors of the *Encyclopédie*, to which he devoted twenty-five years of his life. This gargantuan project required thousands upon thousands of entries and illustrations for an enterprise that called on all the foremost thinkers of the day. Exemplifying and focusing the French Enlightenment, the *Encyclopédie* was intended not merely to document and disseminate knowledge, but also to act as a stimulus to political and social debate. Rousseau earned some money writing the musical entries for the *Encyclopédie* – over two hundred of them in all – though he was also responsible for one of the most prominent political articles, 'Économie Politique', presaging his later critique of property.

For all that activity, Rousseau had really been marking time for eight years, before his life reached its turning point in 1749.

He was on his way to Vincennes prison to see Diderot. His friend had been locked up under a *lettre de cachet*, the notorious royal warrant for imprisonment without legal process, for *Letter on the Blind for the Use of Those Who See,* containing what the censors deemed impious, atheistic views. With publication of the first volume of the *Encyclopédie* imminent, Diderot was in dire need of company to bolster his spirits; his dearest friend (of the moment), Rousseau, was the most regular of visitors, going every other day: 'I was certainly the one who had most sympathy for his sufferings. I thought I should also be the one whose presence would be the most consoling.'

Vincennes was six miles from Paris, and the impoverished Rousseau walked there through the heat and dust of summer. On one occasion, pausing under a roadside tree, he began flipping through the literary journal he had brought along. In it was a notice of an essay competition from the Académie de Dijon. The question was: 'Has the progress of the sciences or the arts done more to corrupt or improve morals?' Rousseau had a revelation: 'From the moment I read those words, I beheld another universe and became another man.' By the time he reached Vincennes, he 'was in a state of agitation bordering upon madness'.

His enemies would say it was a state from which he would never fully depart – and Rousseau would not disagree. From that moment I was lost. All the rest of my life and my misfortunes followed inevitably as a result of that moment's madness.'

He worked feverishly, wrestling with his thoughts during sleepless nights, then scribbling them down in the morning, as would become his habit. The result, in which he provocatively railed against the corrupting influence of civilization, won first prize (a gold medal valued at three hundred *livres*). Published as *Discourse on the Sciences and the Arts*, it caused a national sensation. From being a thirty-eight-year-old failed musician and dramatist, overnight he was now fêted by the coterie of Parisian intellectuals in 'the Republic of Letters' – the sobriquet given to the private world of wit, debate, literature and philosophical inquiry, the salon. It was a world that existed in parallel with the stultifying traditional culture of the royal court.

Although his ideas evolved and mutated over the next two decades, Rousseau established his blueprint with this puncturing of the Enlightenment notion of human development: compared to the past we were less free, less equal, less content, less sincere, more dependent, more alienated, more self-obsessed, more suspicious. It is impossible to exaggerate the seismic shock this caused at a time when thinkers had an axiomatic confidence in progress. Many regarded Rousseau's reflections as perverse. Others appeared to relish being at the receiving end of a philosophical flagellation. Diderot was tireless in promoting Rousseau's brilliant polemic, though it contradicted many of his own ideas, and in essence mocked his worldly aspirations.

Rousseau's personal life was also in transformation. Around 1745, he had entered upon the one close relationship that would endure until his death. Twenty-year-old Thérèse Le Vasseur waited on table in the hotel where Rousseau lodged, near the Sorbonne. An uneducated skivvy, a kitchen and laundry maid, she was the sole support of her unemployed and bankrupt parents. Rousseau was immediately struck by her 'modest behaviour' and 'lively and gentle looks'. He believed that he saw in her a girl with honest feelings, 'a simple girl without coquetry'. 'Thanks to her, I lived happily, as far as the course of events permitted.' He declared to Thérèse that he would never forsake her, but that he would never marry her. Although beneath him in the social order, she was far closer to him in class than the refined denizens of the capital's gilded drawing rooms, to which he would soon gain easy access but in which he would never feel at ease.

The first of their five children was born the following year. All five would be abandoned at the Foundling Hospital in Paris. Baldly stated, this sounds inexcusably callous, though at a time when the arrival of a child could spell disaster, the practice was not regarded as heinous. For the vast majority of its 600,000 inhabitants, the capital was a foul and grisly pit: sewage flowed in the alleys and lanes down to the river where drinking water was drawn. Rousseau recalled his initial impression of the capital in the *Confessions*. 'I saw nothing but dirty and stinking little streets, ugly black houses, a general air of slovenliness and poverty, beggars, carters, menders of old clothes, criers of decoctions and old hats.' Life was a struggle for survival against smallpox and venereal disease. With some thirty thousand practitioners, prostitution was a major industry. In 1750 alone, 3,785 children were deposited at the Hospice des Enfants-Trouvés. There was not much hope for them: most died before their first birthday. Rousseau confesses to having had to use all his rhetorical powers to persuade Mlle Le Vasseur into letting her children go. Because marriage was out of the question, it was 'the sole means of saving her honour'. However, he and Le Vasseur were in a full-time relationship, and that he did not even note down his abandoned children's admission numbers is revealing. He never escaped the charge of inhumanity.

In 1752, the forty-year-old Rousseau triumphed again, and in the most prominent of venues. His opera, *Le Devin du village* ('The Village Soothsayer') was performed before Louis XV in the Court at Fontainebleau, and the King loved it. In his private apartments, he sang the songs and hummed the music. Rousseau, who had watched the opera in his working clothes, with a rough beard and uncombed wig, was nonetheless summoned to an audience with the King. Terrified that his bladder would let him down, he fled back to Paris. Louis would even have bestowed a pension on Rousseau had he not deserted the scene hot-foot. Diderot rebuked him for forfeiting the income and not thinking more of Le Vasseur and her mother. Rousseau agonized that in pocketing the King's sous he would inevitably have been compromised: 'I should have to flatter or be silent . . . Farewell, truth, liberty and courage!'

In 1754, Rousseau returned to Geneva for four months, reconverted to Calvinism and reclaimed his citizenship. He was now toiling over a second competition essay for the Dijon Academy. Dedicated to the city of Geneva, Rousseau's discourse, *On the Origins of Inequality among Men*, was completed in May. It is perhaps his most radical work, highlighting the gap between the rich and powerful on the one hand and the poor and weak on the other, and the spurious attempts that were made to rationalize the disparities. Humans, thought Rousseau, were mired in a condition of servitude, though they had originally been free, and he offered a historical sketch of how this tragic state of affairs had come about, stressing the creation and pernicious impact of private property. He did not win the prize, but the essay boosted his reputation further. He sent a copy to François-Marie Arouet, better known as Voltaire, who responded with double-edged thanks, precipitating a relatively civil, if cool, exchange of letters: 'I have received, Monsieur, your new book against the human race . . . Never has so much intelligence been deployed in an effort to make us beasts.'

The watchmaker's son from Geneva now seemed destined for a life of riches, with entrée guaranteed to the most prestigious salons in the Republic of Letters. With all that within his grasp, he chose instead to seek seclusion in the countryside, amazing his friends and surprising a swelling pack of enemies.

3

Always a Qualified Success

Hume – too rational for his own good

M. Hume is comparable to a brook, clear and limpid,
which flows always evenly and serenely.
Friedrich Grimm, 1759

At a dinner given in Edinburgh, when Hume was a child, the dog Pod was accused of making a foul smell. Cried young David, 'Oh do not hurt the beast. It is not Pod, it is me!' Recording the incident in her memoir, Lady Anne Lindsay commended the child's generosity. 'How very few people would take the evil odour of a stinking conduct from a guiltless Pod to wear it on their own rightful shoulders.'

Lady Lindsay was the first of many to extol Hume's singular goodness. In his account of Hume's final days, Hume's dear friend, the economist Adam Smith, stressed the older man's exemplary character in phrases that likened him to Plato's description of Socrates: 'I have always considered him, both in his lifetime and since his death, as approaching nearly to the idea of a perfectly wise and virtuous man as perhaps the nature of human frailty will permit.' At sixty-six, stricken by terminal bowel cancer, Hume himself would look back on a life of such unrelenting virtues:

> I am, or rather was (for that is the style I must now use in speaking of myself, which emboldens me the more to speak my sentiments) I was, I say, a man of mild disposition, of command of temper, of an open, social, and cheerful humour, capable of attachment, but little susceptible of enmity, and of great moderation in all my passions. Even my love of literary fame, my ruling passion, never soured my temper, notwithstanding my frequent disappointments . . .

'Frequent disappointments' was no exaggeration. Whatever the encomia, Hume's career (we should really say careers) was far from smooth or successful. Indeed, when he and Rousseau first became acquainted, Hume was only just beginning to receive the acclaim that we now regard (and he regarded) as justly his.

David Hume was born in Edinburgh on 26 April 1711 into a moderately wealthy family, though, as a younger son, he could expect to have to make his own way in the world. His father was a comfortably well-off lawyer, Joseph Home of Ninewells, descended from the line of the Earls of Home; his mother, Catherine, was also from an established family. Joseph Home died in 1713, leaving three children: the eldest, John; a daughter, Katherine, and David. David alone later changed the spelling of his name, because 'thae glaekit English buddies' made it rhyme with combe.

As a young man, Hume was briefly a student of law, but found his attention compulsively drawn to philosophy:

> When I was about eighteen years of age, there seemed to be opened up to me a new scene of thought, which transported me beyond measure, & made me, with an ardour natural to young men, throw up every other pleasure or business to apply entirely to it. The law, which was the business I designed to follow, appeared nauseous to me, & I could think of no other way of pushing my fortune in the world but that of a scholar and philosopher.

He studied so hard that he became physically ill with what was diagnosed in 1730 as the 'disease of the learned'. Whatever the disorder, it dogged him for five years; possibly, he never fully recovered – psychologically at least – from its impact. His search for a cure and a vocation took him briefly to a shipping firm in Bristol and, when that did not work out, to France, living first in Rheims, then in Anjou. His two-year visit yielded a manuscript he entitled *Treatise of Human Nature.*

On his return in 1737 to London, the Scot was quick to compare England adversely to France, and the reception of the three-volume *Treatise*, published in 1738, would not have made him better disposed to the English. He borrowed a line from Alexander Pope to mourn what is now universally hailed as a masterpiece: 'It fell dead born from the press.' (Pope: 'All, all but truth, drops dead-born from the press/Like the last Gazette, or the last address.')

Hume had expected a real financial return from the *Treatise* against his investment of time and intellectual energy. The commercial flop meant that, despite his exertions, he had advanced only down a career cul-de-sac. Putting philosophy aside, he returned to the family home at Ninewells and took up essay-writing. He might not be acknowledged yet as a philosopher, but he could at least live by cultivating literary pursuits, essays, reviews, histories. He had a new calling: man of letters. And here, at last, he had a modicum of success: *Essays Moral and Political* (1742) sold out in London.

Yet, if Hume could turn his back on the *Treatise* so easily, others would not. In 1744, the Chair of Ethics and Pneumatical Philosophy fell vacant in Edinburgh. Hume was baulked by clerical opposition to the *Treatise,* on the ground that he was unfit to teach the young. (The same hostility dashed his hopes of the Glasgow Chair of Moral Philosophy in 1751, which went to Adam Smith.)

His next career move was distinctly less elevated, but he was still struggling for money, and men of letters must eat. In 1745, he became tutor to the violent, mad teenage Marquess of Annandale and spent an unhappy, though profitable, year at St Albans. He was already toiling away on what would become *An Enquiry Concerning Human Understanding*, but in April

1746, when he gladly parted from Annandale and his devious entourage, the future, professionally and financially, was uncertain.

However, on Sunday 18 May, an unheralded invitation came to join a military expedition departing on 21 May. Hume jumped at it. He owed the opportunity to a distant relative, Lieutenant-General James St Clair, whose secretary he became. Britain was battling France in the final phase of the War of the Austrian Succession and St Clair's mission was the conquest of French Canada. Later, his orders were changed to an invasion of Brittany, for which no maps or charts were available. The (undeliverable) objective was to draw French forces back from the Low Countries. It was here that Hume witnessed action, soldiers slaughtered, sailors drowned; an officer, convinced he had failed in his duty, killed himself with what Hume saw as Roman dignity. As least military cuisine seems to have agreed with him: he emerged from the campaign inflated into the vast figure that has entered history.

In 1747, St Clair recruited Hume again, this time as secretary on a military mission to Vienna and Turin. In Vienna, protocol demanded that diplomats should curtsy when presented to the Empress of Austria, Maria Theresa. On seeing Hume's waddling approach, she excused them. Hume wrote self-deprecatingly to his brother: 'We esteemed ourselves very much obliged to her for this attention, especially my companions, who were desperately afraid of my falling on them & crushing them.' Then it was on to the northern Italian city of Mantua, where Hume kissed the soil that had produced Virgil, and Turin, where the mission ground to a halt once peace was declared.

At this point we have a portrait of Hume from the future Lord Charlemont, the seventeen-year-old James Caulfeild, who qualified his physical description with the observation that,

'Nature, I believe, never formed any man more unlike his real character than David Hume':

> His face was broad and fat, his mouth wide, and without any other expression than that of imbecility. His eyes vacant and spiritless, and the corpulence of his whole person was far better fitted to communicate the idea of a turtle-eating alderman than of a refined philosopher. His speech in English was rendered ridiculous by the broadest Scottish accent, and his French was, if possible, still more laughable.

He also recorded for posterity Hume in love, though his account reads suspiciously like a Restoration comedy. Hume, allegedly, adored to distraction a beautiful married countess, who led him on for her amusement. She hid Charlemont behind a curtain in her boudoir so that he could enjoy her toying with the obese, infatuated swain as he heaved himself down at her feet, fruitlessly protesting his devotion. Interestingly, given the later image of the plain man, Hume's companions noted, with some mirth, how he adored his military uniform – all lace and gold braid – though Charlemont thought he looked like a trainband grocer.

Hume and St Clair returned to England in time for Christmas 1748. At last, aged thirty-seven, Hume was financially independent and able to pursue his vocation as a writer. In 1749, he departed London for Scotland, and entered a decade of prolific literary output.

Hume put down roots in Edinburgh, where he lived a hard-working but convivial existence, always careful with his money. He dined out as much as he could – four or five times a week – but never tipped (gave a 'veil'). The servants appeared not to mind as he made their masters and mistresses so happy. He ate well, and drank in moderation. He held little suppers: roasted hen and minced collops, washed down with a bottle of punch. He had his own house and a 'regular family; consisting of a head, viz. myself, and two inferior members, a maid, Peggy, and a cat. My sister has since joined me, and keeps me company.'

He published his twelve *Political Discourses*, 'the only work of mine that was successful on the first publication'. A miscellany of history, politics and economics, it reached three editions in two years. But there was also *An Enquiry Concerning the Principles of Morals*, 'which, in my own opinion, (who ought not to judge on that subject) is of all my writings, historical, philosophical, or literary, incomparably the best. It came unnoticed and unobserved into the world.' This was an exaggeration. Reviewers castigated the ideas, but admired the clarity.

In 1752, Hume received some compensation for his failure to win the Glasgow chair, gaining an appointment that carried public esteem in his home city. On 28 January, he became keeper of the Library (librarian) of the Faculty of Advocates ('a petty office of forty or fifty guineas a year', he quibbled). It made him master of thirty thousand volumes, and re-channelled his ambition from essayist to historian – the step that would finally assure his contemporary reputation. While philosophy could rarely move the passions, he reflected, historians were 'the true friends of virtue'.

Edinburgh in the middle of the century was the best of all possible worlds for Hume. Scotland's union with England in 1707 had brought economic prosperity and a cultural awakening, and with it a lively company of newspapers, journals, clubs and improvement societies populated by lawyers, clerics, academics, doctors, and gentlemen who could now afford to leave their estates to live in their tightly knit capital.

Although by disposition happier in small groups, Hume

became more gregarious. The Poker Club, whose subject was politics and object the consumption of claret, assembled at Fortune's Tavern every Friday. When in the city, Hume kept up his attendance until eight months before his death. And, from 1754, the Select Society, of which Hume, Adam Smith and the portrait painter Allan Ramsay were founders, staged debates for men of rank. It had broad interests and extensive cultural influences. Hume's first choice of subject for debate was: 'Whether the difference of national characters be chiefly owing to the nature of different climates, or to moral and political causes?'

Edinburgh's men of rank included many of Hume's regular correspondents: a cousin, the Reverend John Home, author of a tragedy, *Douglas*, and private secretary to George III's Scottish favourite John Stuart, Earl of Bute; Dr William Robertson, a historian whose reputation rivalled Hume's own; Adam Smith, moral philosopher and economist; the Reverend Hugh Blair, minister of the High Church in Edinburgh, and the first Professor of Rhetoric and Belles-lettres at the University; the Reverend Adam Ferguson, Professor of Philosophy at Edinburgh University. It was said that if you stood at the Cross of Edinburgh, within a few minutes you could take fifty men of genius and learning by the hand.

Hume, while on clubbable terms with the ornaments of the Scottish Enlightenment, fitted less snugly into the official culture. In April 1754, his appointment as librarian was soured when three of the curators of the Faculty struck out some French books ordered by Hume from London, describing them as 'indecent, and unworthy of a place in a learned library'. (They included La Fontaine's fables.) In future, all his choices would be vetted, they ruled. However humiliating the insult, Hume needed the library for his researches, and so he came up with the stratagem of keeping the title while handing over his duties. He gave his salary to the blind poet, Thomas Blacklock. Nevertheless, Hume resigned precipitately in January 1757, possibly to secure the post for his friend Adam Ferguson.

A morsel of humble pie was worth it. His epic four-part, six-volume *History of England* appeared between 1754 and 1762, and the series became among the most popular works of history ever published.

Hume wrote his studies in reverse chronological order, beginning with the Stuart monarchs, moving to the House of Tudor, and ending with the earlier periods from Julius Caesar. He made at least £3,200 on the whole history at a time when a man could consider himself well to do on £80 p.a.. As well as financial rewards, there was public and private acclaim. Voltaire called it 'perhaps the best ever written in any language'.

Hume had identified a gap in the thriving book market. Although novels abounded, booksellers stocked little history. In Hume's wake came other, widely praised, histories of England, but his work outran them all, maintaining its classic status into the nineteenth century, by the end of which it had gone through more than a hundred editions. In the United States, the last student version was printed in 1910. That he was a *philosophical* historian distinguished him from his predecessors and contemporaries. In 1762, the *Critical Review* enthused that

> [his] work may be regarded as a table of the human passions, stripped of all disguise, laid naked to the eye, and dissected by the masterly hand of a curious artist. We see actions traced up to their first springs and actuating principles, in so natural a manner, that we cannot avoid giving our assent to Mr Hume's conclusions, even when they disagree with those we should have formed from a perusal of the simple facts.

But this eulogy was a few years in the waiting. The first volume of the *History*, covering the reigns of James I and Charles I, was a commercial dud. Hume, who expected much from his even-handed dealing with the issues of king and parliament, prerogative and liberty, church and state, England and the other British nations, was assailed on all sides. As he noted, 'English, Scotch, and Irish, Whig and Tory, Churchman and Sectary, Freethinker and Religionist, Patriot and Courtier, united in their rage . . . I scarcely, indeed, heard of one man in the three kingdoms, considerable for rank or letters, that could endure the book.'

He diagnosed several causes: the spirit of irreligion in the work, Whig ministers decrying it and London booksellers conspiring against him because it was published by an Edinburgh bookseller. The *Monthly Review* (vol. XII, 1755) gave it a twenty-three-page appraisal, opening with a condescending thrust: 'The history of his own country is the last he ought to have attempted.' The reviewer praised Hume's orderly and elegant narration and command of character, but questioned his impartiality, and ended with a stern rebuke: '[On religion] he seems to be of the opinion, that there are but two species of it in all nature, superstition and fanaticism; and under one or other of these, he gives us to understand, the whole of the Christian profession is, and ever was, included.'

The year 1756 saw Hume choose a London bookseller to publish the second part of the *History,* covering the period from the execution of Charles I to the 1688 revolution. The *Monthly Review* thought it more satisfying: it had none of those indecent excursions on the subject of religion which must have given offence to every candid reader.

In the summer of 1758, Hume departed for London to stay with Annie and Peggy Elliot, who ran a boarding house for Scottish gentlemen in quiet, narrow Lisle Street, near what is now Leicester Square. Socially, London proved frostier than cosy Edinburgh for this Scottish purveyor of contentious theological and political opinions. Samuel Johnson snubbed him. David Garrick introduced him to Edmund Burke, who claimed he had spoken to Hume only because the present liberal state of society required it.

Hume also ventured into political high society, meeting a number of Whig grandees. With some significant politicians he did not get on well, among them George Grenville, soon to be prime minister. Grenville and his Whig allies were all enemies of Bute, then the influential tutor to the future George III, who described the Scottish earl as his 'dearest friend'. The Whig belief that Bute was imbuing George with dangerous ideas of monarchical government stoked anti-Scottish sentiment. This probably contributed to the antagonism towards Hume, who, furthermore, was seen as a Tory sympathizer.

Hume completed the two volumes of the *History of the House of Tudor* in 1759. 'The clamour against this performance was almost equal to that against the *History* of the first two Stuarts.' Horace Walpole thought it 'hasty', inaccurate and careless. Dividing his time between London and Edinburgh, Hume then laboured until November 1761 on what would prove to be the final part of his marathon series, covering the period from Julius Caesar to Henry VII.

The *History* series, ultimately, if belatedly, brought Hume respect, rewards and renown. Certainly his command of prose and his philosophical insight combined to present history as it had never been presented hitherto. He could move the reader with his set pieces and penetrating character studies while deploying his gifts as a philosophic historian to explain the wider significance and motive of what was narrated. His use of satire, parody, irony, his ability to shift effortlessly from factual statements to cleverly observed description, his command of language to create effect – all these enabled him to turn historical events and analysis into a seamless and compelling narrative. His compassionate portrayal of the death of Charles I made readers weep; his near-burlesque vision of Archbishop Laud at Communion made them cry with laughter.

Controversy was inevitable, however. For Hume had involved himself in a fundamental political divide. What attitude should be taken to the Stuart kings and their overthrow? And, historically, had the governance of England been based on an absolute or a limited monarchy? Tories believed, broadly, in an absolutist inheritance of English government grounded in and exercising power through the royal prerogative. Equally broadly, the Whig concept was of a prerogative conventionally limited by the traditional liberties of the people expressed through parliament.

Hume congratulated himself on arriving at a balance between both interpretations. 'My views of things are more conformable to Whig principles; my representations of persons to Tory prejudices.' But, as Hume also understood, his readers were more influenced by his character studies, and so saw him as writing from a Tory viewpoint: 'Nothing can so much prove that men commonly regard more persons than things, as to find that I am commonly numbered among the Tories.'

However, Hume always regarded himself as standing above political divisions, and in his writings Whigs could detect support. At the end of the *History*, while stressing the fragility and flux of the constitution, he claimed that the Glorious Revolution broke irrevocably with the past. 'It gave such an ascendant to popular principles as has put the nature of the English constitution beyond all controversy . . . We, in this island, have ever since enjoyed, if not the best system of government, at least the most entire system of liberty, that ever was known amongst mankind.'

The *History* made Hume moderately prosperous. On Whit Sunday 1762, he announced his purchase of the third storey facing south (and the sixth facing north, as it was built on a slope) of James's Court in Edinburgh, with magnificent views over Edinburgh and across the Firth of Forth. Katherine Home and the maid Peggy joined him, and he bought a chaise.

With the last volume of the *History*, Hume had come to the end of his creative work; from now, he would be dealing only with the devious behaviour of his booksellers, re-editing and revising.

How had Hume's latest career petered out and his intellectual output dried up? To the Earl of Shelburne, an Irish intellectual and future prime minister, Hume likened himself to a Hottentot who flees the cultivated life and returns to his companions in the woods. A man accustomed to retreat and study, he told the Earl, was unfit for the commerce of the great world and it was wise for him to shun it. But behind the rational phrases lay umbrage and bile. Although he now had an enviable reputation and a circle of friends in London, Hume was bitter at the scant regard given to men of letters by men of riches and power. Literature was appreciated in Scotland. This was not so among 'the barbarians who inhabit the Banks of the Thames'.

Indeed, he seems to have returned to Edinburgh estranged from the English, almost seeking refuge. The London 'barbarians' were rife with anti-Scottish prejudice. In September 1764, Gilbert Elliot, an old Edinburgh chum and MP, wrote to Hume, then in Paris, exhorting him to 'love the French as much as you will; but above all continue still an Englishman'. In his resentful reply, Hume mused on his future:

> I believe, taking the continent of Europe from Petersburg to Lisbon, and from Bergen to Naples, there is not one who ever heard of my name, who has not heard of it with advan-

tage, both in point of morals and genius. I do not believe there is one Englishman in fifty who if he heard I had broke my neck tonight would be sorry. Some because I am not a Whig; some because I am not a Christian; and all because I am a Scotsman. Can you seriously talk of my continuing an Englishman?

He contemplated taking the reigns of William of Orange and Anne as his next subject. None the less, he told Andrew Millar, his publisher, 'I have an aversion to appear in the capital till I see that more justice is done me with regard to the preceding volumes . . . The general rage against the Scots is an additional discouragement. I think the Scotch Minister [Bute] is obliged to make me some compensation for this.'

This might have been a pleasantry. If he was genuinely expressing his hopes of a government pension or post, he was in for another disappointment. Bute was indeed thinking of public office for a Scottish historian – but not for Hume. William Robertson was appointed Historiographer Royal for Scotland on 25 July 1763 with an increased stipend of £200. Hume was put out: 'I have been accustomed to meet with nothing but insults and indignities from my native country: But if it continues so, *ingrata patria, ne ossa quidem habebis.*' In the words of the victorious Roman general Scipio Africanus, 'Ungrateful fatherland, you shall not even have my bones.'

Thus in 1763 we find Hume at the height of his literary powers and acknowledged as one of the finest minds of his generation. He has broken new ground in philosophy, politics, economics, historiography. Yet his considerable achievements have not brought him unalloyed success, contentment, or even peace of mind. Rather, at each step of the way, success has been dogged by failure, setbacks, and public hostility. Only the beneficence of his character has won widespread recognition.

At the age of fifty-two, he is about to embark on another change of career and become a diplomat in the European capital of culture. It was much more than a new job; it was an escape to Elysium.

4
Plots, Alarums and Excursions

Mme d'Épinay lent Rousseau a country home – but could she
expect his gratitude?

*No character in human society is more dangerous than
that of the fanatic.*
David Hume

⌈*Cities are the abyss of the human species.*⌉
Jean-Jacques Rousseau

Earlier, while David Hume was still in Edinburgh writing his
History in the Advocates Library and making merry at the
Poker Club, Jean-Jacques Rousseau had resolved on an escape
to solitude.

However baffling it was to his contemporaries, Rousseau
had determined to put Paris behind him. In 1756, aged forty-
four, he accepted the hospitality of Louise-Florence
d'Épinay, a wealthy noblewoman whose family château
stood on the edge of the forest of Montmorency to the north
of Paris. She had rejected her husband, a philandering, dissolute 'tax-farmer' (a role in which, under the archaic tax-
system, serious wealth could be amassed by businessmen
collecting taxes for the king). In her diary she described
Rousseau as seeming 'ignorant of the ways of society, but it
is clear enough that he is exceedingly able. His complexion is
dark and his face is lit up by very burning eyes. When he
talks he appears good-looking. But when one recalls his face
afterwards one thinks of him as plain.' Rousseau was always
lucky in his patrons: Mme d'Épinay would become, for a
time, a loyal supporter.

Rousseau, with Le Vasseur and her infirm mother, moved to
the dwelling Mme d'Épinay had renovated for him, the Hermitage, a short distance from her château – though only after a
sharp exchange with his hostess in which he obdurately asserted his financial self-sufficiency. In the Hermitage, he enjoyed, in

Mme d'Épinay's words, 'five rooms, a kitchen, a cellar, an acre and a quarter of kitchen garden, a spring of running water, and the forest for a garden.' She had even ingeniously reconstructed the fireplaces so that one fire heated several rooms.

By this time, the German-born Friedrich Grimm, a hard-up aristocrat who was editor of the cultural newsletter, *Correspondance littéraire*, had become Mme d'Épinay's latest *amour*, and he was a fixture at the chateau, as was Mme d'Épinay's sister-in-law, Countess Sophie d'Houdetot, with whom Rousseau would fall unbearably in love.

In Paris, Rousseau's departure from the capital was derided and there were confident predictions of his speedy return. But for Rousseau the adjustment from town to country signalled a self-conscious sloughing off of his Parisian skin, a bid for independence and authenticity, and a denial of the *philosophes'* approach to life that privileged reason above feeling. He was convinced that the seething immorality of the big city had dripped poison into his spirit. Following this escape, 'I recovered my own true nature.'

His own true nature was ready to embrace Nature itself. The atmosphere in Paris had become abhorrent to him. The triumph of his opera, he mused in the *Confessions*, 'sowed the seed of those secret jealousies which did not break out till long afterwards.' Even by 1756, he observed in literary men, including Grimm and Diderot, a distinct absence of their previous cordiality. When he was invited to the soirées given by the richest member of the *philosophe* circle, Baron Thiry d'Holbach, the other guests, regular members of the baron's coterie, whispered in one another's ears while Rousseau was ignored. Later, in 1757, when Diderot composed a play, *The Natural Son*, he included a line that Rousseau *knew* was aimed at him: 'The good man lives in society; only a wicked man lives alone.' He was deeply hurt.

Rousseau had entered a period of psychological transformation that he recorded in exalted terms. In the *Confessions*, he portrayed himself as having become intoxicated with virtue: an intoxication that started in his head but flowed to his heart. It 'was the origin of my sudden eloquence, and of the truly celestial fire that burned in me and spread to my early books.' He also experienced a surge in confidence in his dealings with others. The effect of these changes on Rousseau can be seen in his 1758 *Letter to d'Alembert on the Theatre* – a clash with Jean-Báptiste le Rond d'Alembert that involved both Diderot and Voltaire. D'Alembert, Diderot's co-editor on the *Encylopédie*, was a pioneering mathematician and theoretical astronomer, a sparkling conversationalist and talented mimic. He was generally held to have a lovable character, free of extreme passions – except for his invincible ambition.

Following an excursion to Geneva, in the course of which he visited Voltaire, d'Alembert wrote an article on the city for the *Encyclopédie*. Among other darts aimed at the Calvinist structure, and incited by Voltaire, he advocated the establishment of a theatre in Geneva, belittling the fears of the city fathers that it would corrupt morals. The resulting uproar threw the future of the *Encyclopédie* itself into doubt.

Calm was just returning when Rousseau published a defence of Geneva, including a condemnation of the theatre and all forms of drama. A theatre, Rousseau fulminated, would be a vehicle for degeneration, immorality and fake passion. He strongly objected to the theatre's artificiality, believing people should generate their own entertainment.

The essay was not directed solely at d'Alembert. Obviously, Voltaire was a target; at that time he was known primarily as a dramatist, and his plays had been produced privately at his Genevan home. But Diderot was also hoping to make his name as a playwright. Later, he noted, '[Rousseau] is a monster . . .

He said he hated all those he had reason to be grateful to and he has proved it.'

Diderot and d'Alembert were not the only victims of Rousseau's belligerence. Between 1756 and 1758 Rousseau became possessed with suspicion of 'a vast and diabolical conspiracy' against him. One altercation – so tangled that it is impossible to discern where the truth lies – led to a complete break with both Mme d'Épinay and Grimm.

According to Rousseau, Diderot and Grimm plotted to besmirch Rousseau's reputation. Mme d'Épinay was going to Geneva for treatment by the eminent Dr Théodore Tronchin. A jowly, broad-faced, broad-shouldered man, pompous and long-winded, if well-meaning, Tronchin was a pioneer of vaccination and a medical innovator. (Rousseau should have approved of him as a medical man, for Tronchin prescribed fresh air and a country life.) Rousseau was asked to escort his benefactress – and refused. Whether she was ill or simply pregnant by Grimm is debatable, though illness seems more likely. However, Rousseau, who was himself unwell, concluded the conspirators intended him to be seen parading in Geneva as her lover, responsible for her.

Grimm pressed him to do his duty towards his patron. Rousseau replied in blunt, ungracious terms that he owed her nothing. 'If Mme d'Épinay has shown friendship to me, I have shown more to her . . . As for benefits, first of all I do not like them, and I owe no thanks for any that people might burden me with by force . . . After making one sacrifice to friendship [keeping her company], I must now make another to gratitude.' Grimm boiled over: 'If I could pardon you, I should think myself unworthy of having a single friend. I will never see you again while I live, and I shall think myself happy if I can banish the recollection of your conduct from my mind.'

Inevitably, Rousseau moved out of the Hermitage. When

Diderot came to see him just before he left, the reunion ended in tears. The encyclopedist wrote that he had parted from a madman, and that Rousseau had given him a glimpse across the abyss to the devil and hell. In the twentieth century, Lytton Strachey would depict the breach between these two comrades in more abstract terms – between the old rationalist world and the new world 'of self-consciousness and doubt, of infinite introspections amid the solitudes of the heart.'

Once again, prosperous benefactors came to Rousseau's aid. In accepting largesse, Jean-Jacques Rousseau, the evangelist of equality and simplicity, had progressed from the provincial Mme de Warens, to the patronage of wealthy tax farmers' wives, to the pinnacle of French society – in the form of Charles-François-Frédéric de Montmorency-Luxembourg, Duc de Luxembourg and Maréchal of France, a distinguished soldier, and his wife Madeleine-Angélique.

Happily, Rousseau sensed an affinity with the maréchale. When young, she had led a strikingly debauched life, but at this period it was said by one of her former lovers that she provided 'a rare example of a pretty woman's victory over time, of an immoral woman's victory over opinion, and that of a friendless woman over friendship.' Horace Walpole's appreciation was just as double-edged, 'She has been very handsome, very abandoned, and very mischievous. Her beauty is gone, her lovers are gone, and she thinks the devil is coming.' She presided over an eminent salon, was an arbiter of manners and taste – and was a staunch backer of Rousseau. For his part, when he set eyes on her in 1759, according to the *Confessions,* he immediately became her 'slave'.

Rousseau had relocated from the Hermitage to a friend's rickety house at Mont-Louis, on de Luxembourg's estate. The maréchal called on him there and, on seeing the dilapidated conditions Rousseau was enduring, urged him to accept a suite in the 'enchanting abode' of the Little Château at Montmorency while the Mont-Louis dwelling was renovated. The Little Château was the perfect setting. Rousseau worked in 'deep and delightful solitude, amongst the woods and the waters, to the sounds of birds of every kind, and amidst the perfume of orange blossom, in a continuous ecstasy.'

Rousseau's relationship with his latest hosts casts light on his Platonic ideal of a pure, untainted friendship in which there was space for neither condescension nor any imbalance of power. In spite of their wealth and status, he approved of the maréchal and maréchale because they treated him as an equal; they never compromised the freedom he demanded for himself, nor fussed over his income or means of survival. But although he revered his hosts, he divined that there was a strict limit to how familiar he could be with them, anguishing over this incompleteness of intimacy. He wrote to Mme de Luxembourg in October 1760, 'Friendship, Madame! Ah, there lies my misfortune. It is good of you and the maréchal to use such a term, but I am a fool to take you at your word. You are amusing yourselves and I am becoming attached to you, and there will be fresh sorrows for me at the end of the game.'

Meanwhile, relations between Rousseau, the citizen of Geneva, and Voltaire, who had been forced out of the city and now lived at Ferney near the border with France, were fracturing. Voltaire had no patience for Rousseau's assaults on property or the theatre. He would later dismiss as abject hypocrisy Rousseau's instructions on how to raise children. On his side, the proud citizen of Geneva resented Voltaire's cultural influence in the place of his birth. In June 1760, he dispatched one of his rudest-ever letters to the dramatist:

> I do not like you Sir . . . You have ruined Geneva, in return for the asylum you have been given there . . . It is you who have

made living in my own city impossible for me; it is you who force me to perish on foreign soil, deprived of all the consolations of the dying, cast unceremoniously like a dog on the wayside . . . I despise you. You wanted me to. But my hatred is that of a heart fitted to have loved you if you had wanted it.

Voltaire did not answer. To Mme d'Épinay he said, 'Jean-Jacques has gone off his head.'

Rousseau could feel quite at ease with one creature: the dog given to him when the animal 'was quite young, soon after my arrival at the Hermitage, and which I had called Duke . . . a title he certainly merited much more than most of the persons by whom it was taken.' Rousseau changed its name to 'Turc' to avoid giving offence to the maréchal, who was a duke.

In 1761, an accident befell Turc and he had to be put down. Rousseau was inconsolable: 'Although poor Turc was only a dog he possessed sensibility, disinterestedness and good nature. Alas! As you observe, how many pretended friends fall short of him in worth!' Several of Rousseau's correspondents expressed their sympathy and talked of finding a substitute. The maréchal said the one possibility he had seen so far was 'too pretty' for Rousseau's taste. A grief-stricken Rousseau asked them to desist: 'It is not another dog I must have, but another Turc, and my Turc is unique. Losses of that kind are not replaceable. I have sworn that my present attachments of every kind shall henceforth be my last.'

The years 1761 and 1762 were Rousseau's *anni mirabiles*. Settled in Montmorency, he produced a sweep of works that in their imaginative force, power of expression and acute analysis broke free of the prevailing culture and confronted readers with the shock of the modern. First came his romantic epistolary novel, *La Nouvelle Héloïse ou Lettres de Deux Amans*, also entitled *Julie*, which he had begun in 1757. The seminal political tract, *On the Social Contract*, fired the fuse of revolt. Its opening phrase has resonated in the ears of revolutionaries down the centuries: 'Man is born free; and everywhere he is in chains.' Then Rousseau overturned the established wisdom on the nature of childhood and education with a radical discourse on the training of the young, *Émile*. This last, in particular, was to bring the wrath of Church and State down upon him. Together, these books mounted a sustained, fundamental challenge to religion and the established order. They also made Rousseau by far the highest-paid author in Europe.

Héloïse, especially, was a phenomenon. Set against a background of pastoral bliss, it is a romantic tragedy that can be read both as an homage to nature and community and as a heartbreaking tug-of-war between virtue and passion. Illustrated by the finest engravers, the work was an instant and international success, its brew of natural love and natural beauty influencing a generation. Appreciative and tear-stained letters to the author streamed in from across Europe. In Paris, demand so outstripped supply that booksellers saw a market in renting out the book by the hour (sixty minutes for twelve sous). Into the book Rousseau had poured his passion for Sophie d'Houdetot, an ardour that had left him sighing, weeping, taking to his bed, and experiencing attacks of palsy. She remained loyal to her absent soldier lover, though with misunderstandings aplenty on Rousseau's side. 'I was drunk with love without an object,' moaned the distraught author.

But *Héloïse* was not the problem. Until *Émile* and *On the Social Contract*, Rousseau's political writings had been indulged. Although the chief censor, the director of the book trade, Lamoignon de Malesherbes, had approved *Émile*, official tolerance of the author now abruptly came to an end. The fourth part of the book, entitled 'The Profession of Faith of the

Savoyard Vicar', caused the work to be condemned and burned for contesting the authority of the Church and the rule of dogma. To the question, 'What role should the clergy play in a child's training?', Rousseau's answer was simple: none at all.

By 1762, Rousseau had become one of the most controversial figures in Europe. In the *Confessions* he looked back at 'the cry of execration that went up against me across Europe, a cry of unparalleled fury . . . I was an infidel, an atheist, a lunatic, a madman, a wild beast, a wolf . . .'

Living under the wing of de Luxembourg, Rousseau was conscious of the commotion over *Émile*. He observed how congratulatory letters from such as d'Alembert were unsigned. 'Everything that was said, was said with the strangest precautions, as if there had been some reason for keeping any admiration for me secret.' But he could not believe he was personally endangered. His patrons were more apprehensive. In the *Confessions*, he recalled that Mme de Boufflers, a friend of Mme de Luxembourg's, 'went about with a perturbed air, displaying a great deal of activity and assuring me that [her lover] the Prince de Conti was also taking active measures to ward off the blow that was being prepared for me . . .' None the less, she asked Rousseau to return her note praising *Émile*.

Mme de Boufflers sought to persuade Rousseau to go to England where she could introduce him to several acquaintances including the 'celebrated Hume', whom she had known for a long while. She pointed out that if he were arrested and interrogated, he might incriminate his current patron, Mme de Luxembourg. (Rousseau agreed he might, as he always told the truth.) She also floated the notion of arranging a spell for him in the Bastille – presumably in comfort – as prisoners of the State there were immune from the Paris *parlement*'s power of arrest. The prospect did not appeal.

The events of the night of 9 June 1762 in Mont-Louis make the most dramatic episode in the *Confessions*. They signalled that yet again the Genevan would have to move on – this time as the fugitive he would be for the next eight years.

It was two in the morning. Rousseau was awake; he had just closed his Bible on the story of the Levite of Ephraim. Voices echoed, torches flared and footsteps sounded in the stillness of the dark countryside. Mme de Luxembourg's confidential servant, La Roche, burst in with a note from Mme de Luxembourg. It contained a letter from the Prince de Conti saying the Paris courts were determined to proceed against Rousseau with all severity: 'The excitement is very high. Nothing can avert the blow.' Rousseau must go to Mme de Luxembourg, La Roche declared. She would not rest until she had seen him.

Rousseau found her upset; he had never known her in such a state. But at this critical moment, he could rely on such influential friends to stave off his arrest. The *maréchal* arrived, trailed by Mme de Boufflers with the latest news from Paris. A writ of *prise de corps* had been issued against Rousseau by the *parlement*. *Émile* was ordered to be burned by the public executioner. However, Conti had secured a concession: if Rousseau escaped, he would not be pursued. He could even take a few days to think over his plans.

Rousseau declined the breathing space. At four that afternoon he departed for Switzerland, riding in plain view in an open cabriolet belonging to the *maréchal*. His route took him through Paris, where he passed the officers of the law: 'four men in black in a hired coach who saluted me with smiles'.

He left Thérèse to follow him with his papers. It was the first time they had been separated for sixteen years.

5
Exile with the 'Friendly Ones'

On the Social Contract: burned by the authorities, it still fanned
the flames of revolution

Here begins the work of darkness in which I found myself engulfed.

Jean-Jacques Rousseau, *Confessions*, writing of summer 1762

From 1762 to late 1765, Rousseau's fate was to be shunted along the northern shore of Lake Neuchâtel, in a futile quest for a secure refuge.

The proud citizen of Geneva deliberately avoided his home city. He believed it was too susceptible to French influence, a judgement that was vindicated almost immediately. On 18 June 1762, Geneva's ruling body, the *Petit Conseil*, assembled to discuss his case, voting the next day that if he ever stepped inside the city he would be arrested. They ordered the burning of *On the Social Contract,* as well as of *Émile.* Helping to orchestrate the campaign against him was another member of the powerful Tronchin clan, Jean-Robert Tronchin, the prosecutor general in Geneva who had presented the case for suppressing the two books.

Rousseau came to rest first in Yverdon, a spa town under the jurisdiction of Bern at the southern tip of the lake, on the edge of the triangle formed by Geneva, Zürich and Basel. But the Council of Bern promptly followed Geneva's lead. On 1 July 1762, a session of the Bernese Senate resolved both to forbid the sale of *Émile* and to expel the author from the republic. He was given fifteen days to leave. Behind this decree lay the hand of the Paris *parlement*. The *parlement* had exercised its influence before: at its behest, in 1758 the government of Bern ordered all the impressions of Helvétius's *Of the Spirit* and of Voltaire's *Maiden* to be seized for burning. The Bernese were capable of ironic resistance. On this occasion, the officer of justice came into the Council to report, 'Your magnificences, after all possible searches, throughout the town we have been able to find only a little spirit and not one maiden.'

On 10 July 1762, Rousseau moved north to the village of Môtiers. The village sits above the lake at the bottom of the Val de Travers, a wide valley between the gorges of the Jura and Lake Neuchâtel, and midway between Yverdon and the fortress city from which the lake takes its name. Home was to be a run-down dwelling owned by the niece of an old friend. Ever sensitive to his independence, Rousseau insisted on paying rent. Le Vasseur soon joined him.

Understandably, Rousseau remained on his guard. At the end of July, he wrote to Mme de Boufflers about the turbulent local priests. 'They behold me with horror; it is with great reluctance that they suffer me to enter their temples.' He accused 'the poet Voltaire' and 'the juggler' (trickster) Tronchin of rousing the priests. He was waiting to hear from the King of Prussia about asylum in Môtiers, he added.

By a quirk of dynastic fate, the territory of Neuchâtel was under the jurisdiction of Prussia, whose ruler, Frederick the Great, was the highest ranking of Rousseau's supporters. In addition to being a brilliant military strategist, Frederick was a connoisseur of the arts and a patron of the Enlightenment, his application of Enlightenment principles to government earning him the accolade of 'philosopher king' and the censure of 'enlightened despot'. (Like Rousseau, he was also a pet-lover: when his favourite dog was ill, he summoned ten doctors.) He had appointed a Jacobite exile as Neuchâtel governor, the hereditary Earl-Marshal of Scotland, George Keith, Earl Marischal. Portraits of the Earl show a thin, long, drawn face, and an aquiline nose.

The Earl had fled Scotland as a youth after joining the Jacobite uprising of 1715; he then took part in the Jacobite–Spanish landing on the west coast of Scotland in 1719. Following that fiasco, in which he was badly wounded, he was tried *in absentia* and outlawed. He entered Frederick's service, becoming ambassador to France and to Spain. The King also bestowed on him the Neuchâtel governorship, which became a none-too-arduous retirement post. Marischal was pardoned by George II in 1759, but though he visited Scotland and bought back one of his former estates, he could not feel at home. The septuagenarian earl – 'his opinions were as tolerant as his nature was kind' – became a father-figure for Rousseau, who was a regular guest at his château, calling the governor '*mon père*', and being addressed back as '*mon fils*', or 'my son the savage'.

In requesting asylum, Rousseau showed both confidence in his standing and trust in the graciousness of despots. Earlier, he had been critical of Frederick the Great, but, according to Marischal, Frederick thought it wrong 'that a man of an irreproachable life is to be persecuted because his sentiments are singular'. The King proffered wine, corn and firewood, believing Rousseau would accept gifts in kind more readily than money. He also wanted to build him a hermitage with a little garden. Rousseau said no: he would rather eat grass and grub up roots than accept a morsel of bread that he had not earned.

Earl Marischal had another useful contact: he was a staunch friend and admirer of David Hume. He cautioned Hume that Rousseau was vulnerable in Neuchâtel because of 'the power of the people'. Britain was a better bet.

The Earl was not alone in thinking of Britain. Rousseau recorded that Mme de Boufflers strongly disapproved of his going to Switzerland, 'and made fresh endeavours to persuade me to go to England. I remained unshaken. I have never liked England or the English; and all Mme de Boufflers's eloquence, far from overcoming my repugnance, served for some reason to increase it.'

Mme de Boufflers had initiated a correspondence with Hume not long before, sending him a note about how utterly 'sublime' she considered his books. Like Earl Marischal, she sought to engage Hume in the quest to secure Rousseau asylum. She wrote to the Scottish historian in mid-June 1762 to say that she had advised Rousseau to go to England, adding a character study. There was praise for the Genevan's 'eccentric, upright heart [and his] noble and disinterested soul'. Dependency he dreaded: he would rather make his living copying music than receive benefits from his best friends. Only in solitude could he be happy. 'I do not believe you will find anywhere a man more gentle, more humane, more compassionate to the sorrows of others, and more patient under his own. In short, his virtue appears so pure, so contented, so equal, that until now, those who hated him could find only in their hearts reasons for suspecting him.'

Hume cast aside his customary moderation to live up to her enthusiasm for a man with whom he had no previous connection. He had, Hume gushed,

> . . . esteem, I had almost said veneration, for [Rousseau's] virtue and genius. I assure your ladyship there is no man in Europe of whom I have entertained a higher idea and would be prouder to serve . . . I revere his greatness of mind, which makes him fly obligations and dependence; and I have the vanity to think, that through the course of my life I have endeavoured to resemble him in those maxims.

Hume, who was in Edinburgh, added that he had connections with men of rank in London and would make 'them sensible of the honour M Rousseau has done us in choosing an asylum in England. We are happy at present in a king, who has a taste for literature; and I hope M Rousseau will find the advantage of it, and that he will not disdain to receive benefits from a great monarch who is sensible of his merit.' However, the hero wor-ship was qualified. Hume disparaged *Émile*, in which, inter-mingled with genius, there was 'some degree of extravagance . . . one would be apt to suspect that he chooses his topics less from persuasion, than from the pleasure of showing his invention, and surprising the reader by his paradoxes.'

The Scotsman offered the Genevan the use of his house in Edinburgh for as long as he liked. Later Hume explained, 'No other motive was wanting to incite me to this act of humanity than the account given me of M. Rousseau's personal character by the friend who had recommended him.' Hume also made overtures about a royal pension for Rousseau: he believed that assisting Rousseau would yield a propaganda triumph over the French worth a hundred victories in battle.

In return, Rousseau, a being of intuition, imagination and feeling, rhapsodized to Mme de Boufflers about the detach-ment of David Hume:

> Mr Hume is the most genuine philosopher I know of, and the only historian who has ever written with impartiality . . . I have frequently mingled passion with my researches; whereas his are enhanced by his enlightened conceptions and his beautiful genius . . . He has contemplated, in every point of view, what passion has not permitted me to contemplate but from one side.

However, Rousseau went on, he was deterred by the distance and expense of the journey to England. Nor did he relish inhal-ing the 'black vapours' of London streets. 'Habit has so attached me to a country life, that I die with spleen the moment I am no longer in the immediate vicinity of trees and bushes.'

As the November chill gripped Môtiers, Earl Marischal resigned himself to the exile's remaining there. He notified Mme de Boufflers that Rousseau had even turned down a proposal of accommodation at Colombiers, a medieval town on the lake, a stone's throw from Neuchâtel, where the weather was milder and there were ample fruit and vegetables that would otherwise rot. 'He is much more savage than any savage of America,' he said, adding that while a hungry savage would accept fish offered by another savage who had caught too much, Rousseau would refuse. 'I no longer talk to our friend about quitting his mountain.' In this letter, Marischal described his plan ('a mere castle in the air') for himself, Rousseau and Hume to live in scholarly retreat in his newly recovered Scottish property, and added the paradox, 'One of the principal reasons, which would induce Jean-Jacques to realize this project is, that *he is not conversant in the language of the country*. This, on his part, is a reason perfectly in character; and perhaps, after all, it is a good one.'

Meanwhile, the long-distance paper relationship between Rousseau and Hume was evolving and deepening. In early 1763, Rousseau confided to Hume that he regretted trusting his own countrymen, who had treated him with insult and outrage, rather than going to England. Earl Marischal had

> made you so often bear a part in our conversation; he has brought me so well acquainted with your virtues, while I before was only with your talents; he has inspired me with the most tender friendship for you, and the most ardent desire of obtaining yours, before I knew you were disposed to grant it. Judge then of the pleasure I feel, at finding this inclination reciprocal . . . Your great views, your astonishing impartiality, your genius, would lift you far above the rest of mankind, if you were less attached to them by the goodness of your heart . . . I can hope only to see you united with [the Earl] one day in the country you have in common, which will become mine . . . With what transports of joy will I cry

out on touching the happy soil where Hume and the Marshal of Scotland were born. '*Salve, fatis mihi debita tellus!/Hic domus, haec patria est.*' ['Hail land destined as my fate, here is my home, here is my country' – Virgil, *Aeneid*.]

Of course, Rousseau had not the slightest intention of exchanging his Swiss for a Scots hearth. His objective was solely to communicate his amity, respect and courtesy, and he did it with his customary rhetorical flair: he went on to explain that ill-health prevented him from making so extended a journey.

This was merely an excuse. Rousseau was no Anglophile and was unimpressed by the liberties that the English so prided themselves on. Representative democracy delivered only illusory freedom. 'The English people think they are free,' states *On the Social Contract*. 'They are badly mistaken. They are free when they elect members of Parliament; as soon as those are elected, the electorate is enslaved; it is nothing.' He worried that the English would remember a remark he made about them in a note in the second book of *Émile*: 'I know that the English congratulate themselves on their humanity and the good nature of the nation, describing themselves as "good-natured people", but much as they might proclaim this, nobody else repeats it after them.'

Outwardly, Rousseau was settling in at Môtiers. He would sit on his porch weaving silk ribbons, chatting with passers-by. The ribbons were presented to young women about to marry, on condition they breast-fed their babies rather than put them out to wet-nurses. This, he said, was nature's way. He had taken to dressing in an Armenian costume (made by an Armenian tailor who passed through Montmorency), and cut a striking figure – jacket, caftan, fur cap with a gold tassel and a silk belt. The loose caftan made it easier for him to cope with his ever more taxing bladder condition. He consulted the local pastor about the garb: he said Rousseau could wear it, even to church. When Earl Marischal first saw Rousseau in Armenian robes, 'he greeted me quite simply with *Salamaleki* [peace be with you]. This ended the matter and I never afterwards wore any other dress.' He must have been an incongruous vision amidst the crags, meadows and vineyards of the valley.

When opinion eventually turned against him, some locals convinced themselves he was possessed by a devil. 'I was treated like a mad wolf as I walked in my caftan and fur hat amid the insults of the *canaille* and sometimes their stones. Sometimes as I passed their cottages I heard a cottager exclaim, "Bring me my gun and I'll shoot him."' In the winter of 1764, in need of more company, Rousseau acquired a dog and a cat; although the dog was of a nondescript breed, he named him regally, 'Sultan'.

Visitors beat a constant path to his door from all parts of Europe; hundreds of letters arrived, some seeking his views, some insulting. From this period dates Rousseau's friendship with the rich financier Pierre-Alexandre Du Peyrou, who suffered from gout but who was none the less persuaded by Rousseau to go on botanical expeditions, and then pursued his new recreation with the fanaticism of the convert. French by origin, but one of Neuchâtel's great benefactors, Du Peyrou became a lifelong supporter of Rousseau's, keeping his manuscripts and publishing the first collected edition of his works in 1782.

Rousseau's reputation was such that he was asked to approach young Edward Gibbon (the future author of *History of the Decline and Fall of the Roman Empire*) over Gibbon's broken-off love affair in Lausanne with Mlle Suzanne Curchod, known to history as the wife of Louis XV's banker and minister of finance, Jacques Necker, and the mother of Mme de

Staël, the illustrious hostess and woman of letters. Rousseau replied, 'I hope Mr Gibbon will not come; his coldness makes me think ill of him. I have been looking over his book again [*Essay on the Study of Literature*]; he runs after brilliance too much, and is strained and stilted. Mr Gibbon is not the man for me, and I do not think he is the man for Mademoiselle Curchod either.'

However, a bright, irrepressible Scot was more successful at winning Rousseau's approval, and from him we have an engaging glimpse of his home life in Môtiers.

On Monday, 3 December 1764, the twenty-four-year-old James Boswell pulled up at the *Maison de village* and cast a glance towards a white house with green window-boards similar to that in *Émile*, which he had read together with *Héloïse*. Before calling on Rousseau, he wrote a letter he described as 'really a masterpiece. I shall ever preserve it as a proof my soul can be sublime.' The contents are comically Rousseauesque: 'I present myself, Sir, as a man of singular merit, as a man with a feeling heart, a lively but melancholy spirit. Ah, if all that I have suffered does not give me a singular merit in the eyes of M. Rousseau, why was I made as I am? Why did he write as he has written?'

Boswell was not too overcome to play his trump card – his acquaintance with his compatriot Marischal. Alerted by the Earl, Rousseau granted Boswell an audience – on condition he did not stay long.

To collect himself before the appointment, Boswell went for a stroll:

. . . pensive, in a beautiful wild valley surrounded by immense mountains, some covered with frowning rocks, others with clustering pines, and others with glittering snow . . . I recalled all my former ideas of J.J. Rousseau, the admi-

ration with which he is regarded over all Europe, his
Héloïse, his *Émile*: in short, a crowd of great thoughts. This
half hour was one of the most remarkable that I ever passed.

Despite Boswell's trepidation, Rousseau received him warmly.
On first acquaintance, Boswell observed 'a genteel black man
in the dress of an Armenian'. He was to visit the household
another four times, dining well *chez* Rousseau. One meal
included:

1. A dish of excellent soup. 2. A *boulli* of beef and veal.
3. Cabbage, turnip and carrot. 4. Cold pork. 5. Pickled trout
which he jestingly called tongue. 6. Some little dish which I
forget. The dessert consisted of stoned pears and of chest-
nuts. We had red and white wines.

Boswell's note of his host's conversation conveys the directness
that French society had found so unpalatable. Here is
Rousseau on the French: 'The French are a contemptible
nation.' On the Scots: 'Sir, your country is formed for liberty.'
On mankind: 'Mankind disgusts me. And my housekeeper tells
me that I am in far better humour on the days when I have been
alone than on those when I have been in company.' On his critics: 'They do not understand me.' On his temperament: 'I was
born placid. I have no natural disposition to melancholy. My
misfortunes have infected me with it.'

Rousseau showed off Sultan. As Boswell recorded, 'He put
some victuals on a trencher, and made his dog dance round it
. . . I think the dog's name was Sultan. He stroked him and fed
him, and with an arch air said, "He is not much respected, but
he gets well looked after."'

The evenings were infused with a lively charm. Boswell
remembers his host singing a song from scene five of *Le Devin
du village*, and amusing a lady from Neuchâtel with a little

ditty: 'We live in a house/where goodies rain in abundance/Sugared sweets, dainty dishes/charming verses/inviting girls/And the mistress with one word/has the best of what's on offer.'

The beguiling visitor had gone out of his way to ingratiate himself with Thérèse, who acted as Rousseau's gatekeeper. She had been waiting for him when he arrived still in a state of anxiety for that first encounter with Rousseau. He later jotted down, 'She was a little, lively, neat French girl and did not increase my fear.' She was in fact two decades his senior. She told him, 'I have seen strangers enough in the twenty-two years that I have been with Monsieur Rousseau, and I assure you that I have sent many of them packing because I did not fancy their way of talking.'

Some spark might have passed between Mlle Le Vasseur and the priapic Boswell. Departing, he told her he wished to present her with a gift. What would she like? A garnet necklace, she said. The ardent young man proved as good as his word. It arrived from Geneva, 'a modest token from a worthy Scot'. Boswell went on, 'I shall never forget your accomplishments. You weave. You cook. You sit at the table. You make jokes. You get up; you clear the table; the dishes are washed; all is tidy and Mlle Le Vasseur is with us again. Only a conjurer could perform such feats.' On the same day, Boswell also felt the (guilty?) need to explain himself to Rousseau. He hoped his host would not mind if he corresponded with Le Vasseur from time to time: 'I swear I have not formed a design to abduct your housekeeper. I often form plans that are romantic but never plans that are impossible.'

If, on one level, Rousseau was leading a quiet, gentle, rustic existence, on another, his opinions were being challenged from a phalanx of powerful figures – in Paris, Geneva, Neuchâtel, Môtiers, Bern. Never before had Rousseau experienced such all-round hostility, and he had to fight back from the fragility and insecurity of exile.

The opposition was hydra-headed. Not long after his flight, the Sorbonne condemned *Émile* and censured Rousseau. Next, Christophe de Beaumont, archbishop of Paris, condemned *Émile* for the views expressed in the fourth part of the book, 'The Profession of Faith of the Savoyard Vicar'; this affected Rousseau the more because he had always respected de Beaumont. He hit back with *Letter to Christophe de Beaumont*, a trenchant forty-thousand-word defence of his religious views. When, under pressure from the French, the twenty-five-member Genevan ruling *Petit Conseil* prohibited the letter from being published, the formerly 'Proud Citizen' of Geneva resigned his citizenship in disgust.

Rousseau now became caught up in the bitter political conflict that had riven the city-state for over thirty years, between its traditional ruling oligarchy that controlled the *Petit Conseil* (and was supported by France) and the disenfranchised bourgeoisie, the Party of Liberty, as Rousseau calls it in the *Confessions*. The Party of Liberty had added Rousseau's treatment by the *Petit Conseil*, to its campaigning grievances. The prosecutor general, Jean-Robert Tronchin (whom Rousseau loathed but whose intellect he never underestimated), entered the fray as the council's champion. With *Letters from the Country*, published anonymously in the autumn of 1763, Tronchin defended Geneva's customary mode of government and alleged that Rousseau posed a deadly danger to both church and state. The adherents of the Party of Liberty were left reeling.

Initially, Rousseau himself stood apart from the political battle. But the Party of Liberty pressed him to intervene, and with some hesitation he took on Tronchin with *Letters Written from the Mountain*. This polemical rejoinder, printed in 1764, robustly condemned the censorship of his work and charged the executive body in Geneva with despotism: they had trampled on the city's traditions and destabilized its delicate balance of powers.

Rousseau's original hesitation over intervening was justified: all prospect of a quiet life vanished. In the *Confessions,* he remarks wryly, 'There seemed to be general astonishment in Geneva and Paris that such a monster as I could be permitted to breathe.'

This exchange with Tronchin also caused a final and irreversible break with Voltaire. In late 1764, *Sentiments des citoyens sur les lettres écrites de la montagne* [*Views of the Citizens on Letters Written from the Mountain*] hit at Rousseau with a viciously personal attack that he saw on the last day of the year. It was anonymous, but, in the literary culture of the day, that was no surprise. Authors used anonymity to shield themselves from assault or a challenge to a duel, and, in France, the omnipresence of a hundred royal censors stimulated evasive tactics. Anonymity, pseudonyms, printing in Holland and smuggling over the border, disguising works of philosophy or pornographic fiction as history or letters – these were all commonplaces of publishing.

Although Rousseau immediately accused a Genevan pastor (and old acquaintance) of being the author, on grounds of the pamphlet's Calvinist style, *Sentiments* is now generally accepted as being from Voltaire's pen. It painted Rousseau as heartless, ungrateful and hypocritical. Some of the 'secrets' it exposed about him, such as the abandonment of his children, were true; others were disingenuous or downright falsehoods.

The pamphlet asked whether this 'writer is a scholar who debates with scholars? No. He is the author of an opera and two unsuccessful plays.' It also claimed Rousseau was syphilitic and charged him with responsibility for the recent death of his mother-in-law. Rousseau was described as a man 'who still bears the deadly marks of his debauchery and who in the costume of a mountebank drags with him from village to village and from mountain to mountain the wretched woman whose mother he killed and whose children he exposed at the gates of an orphanage . . . abjuring all natural feelings even as he strips himself of honour and religion.'

The butt of these calumnies remained profoundly shaken by their tone and content, but posterity can be grateful to Voltaire. To clear his name, Rousseau finally decided to publish a fully open account of his life, feelings and motives, and so conceived the *Confessions*. (He had been procrastinating over an autobiography since his publisher suggested it in 1761.)

In Môtiers, the local priest, who believed he had obtained a prior pledge from Rousseau that he would not publish anything contentious, now banned Rousseau from the next communion, and went on in his sermons to whip up opinion against him as a heretic. He even (unsuccessfully) attempted to have Rousseau excommunicated. The villagers were turning against him; the atmosphere became increasingly threatening. Rousseau was abused in the street. In King Frederick's name, Marischal issued an order to protect him: it was ignored.

On 1 September 1765, Rousseau's house was stoned, though no windows were broken. The next night there was an attempt to break down the front door. The following week, on Friday, 6 September, Môtiers held a fair with much drinking and rowdy merry-making. Late at night, the house was attacked again, more violently than before: a terrifying experience as Rousseau recollected in the *Confessions*.

A shower of stones was thrown against the window and the door which opens on to the gallery and they fell on to it with so much force that my dog, who usually slept there and had started to bark, fell silent with fright and escaped to a corner, gnawing and scratching at the floorboards in an effort to escape.

A rock 'as big as a head' nearly landed on Rousseau's bed, and he and Thérèse huddled together by a far wall. So many stones were hurled at the house that when the local steward finally arrived, he declared, 'My God. It's a quarry.'

All the local notables wanted him to go. 'I gave in, and I took very little persuading; for the spectacle of the people's hatred caused me such anguish that it was more than I could bear.' He and Sultan fled Môtiers, leaving Thérèse behind, and after one night with Du Peyrou in Neuchâtel, the philosopher and the dog arrived on Isle St Pierre, in Lake Bienne, just beyond the city. The territory was under the jurisdiction of Bern.

In Rousseau's posthumously published *Rêveries*, these five weeks on Isle St Pierre are portrayed as blissful, passed amid an Eden of orchards, meadows, vineyards and woods, with a solitary dwelling. His chief balm was walking and botanizing – his ambition was to compile a list of all the island's plant life. Rousseau and Sultan would ramble through a nearby island that was uninhabited, though Sultan disliked water and the boat journey made him nervous.

Isle St Pierre proved a short-lived sanctuary. Thérèse joined him in late September, but on 18 October, 'when I was least expecting it', he received notice from the Bern authorities that he must leave their territory within two weeks. His plea to remain imprisoned on the island until his death, in return for being left in peace, was ignored. He told one correspondent that he was being 'violently' expelled.

Within three years, Rousseau had been driven from France, banned from Geneva, and forced out of Yverdon, Môtiers and Isle St Pierre. The King of Prussia's protection had been to no avail. His enemies were triumphant. Europe's foremost radical was on the run again.

6

The Lion and le Coq

The politician and the ambassador: General Conway and his brother
the Earl of Hertford. Hume depended on their influence

The newspapers have given the rage of going to Paris a good name; they call it 'the French disease.'
Horace Walpole, October 1763

His features were covered with mask within mask. When the outer disguise of obvious affectation was removed, you were still as far as ever from seeing the real man.
T. B. Macaulay on Walpole, *Critical and Historical Essays*

In April 1763, Francis Seymour Conway, Earl of Hertford, was invited to be British ambassador to France, the first since the Treaty of Paris put an end to the Seven Years War. Historians have dismissed Hertford as a mediocrity, though Hume described him as 'the most amiable nobleman of the Court of England'. Quite why Hertford then asked the Scottish philosopher to accompany him to the Paris embassy remains obscure. Hume was Hertford's second choice, and the most likely explanation is that his name originally came up among mutual Scottish friends in London, supported by an under-secretary of state and classical scholar, Robert Wood, whom Hume had met in 1758. Wood had studied at Glasgow University.

Why Hume said yes is clearer, for the call afforded an escape from his frustrations in Britain. His own account, in the *Life*, carries little conviction: 'This offer, however inviting, I at first declined, both because I was reluctant to begin connections with the great, and because I was afraid that the civilities and gay company of Paris would prove disagreeable to a person of my age and humour; but on his Lordship's repeating the invitation, I accepted it.'

As so often before in his life, the prize was flawed. The invitation was to be Hertford's secretary, a position with £1000 a year and the prospect of still higher office. However, officially the position was already filled – by Charles Bunbury, later Sir Charles, twenty-three years old and married to the beautiful, wild Lady Sarah Lennox. To some a 'somewhat vain and ignorant' rake, to others Bunbury was an affable devotee of horse-racing. (His horse won the first Derby in 1780.) The upright Hertford thought him distasteful and proposed that Hume would be his under-secretary with the promise of his taking over when Bunbury could be enticed away from the post. How the sceptical philosopher might accommodate to the pious Earl was the subject of some amused speculation. In Paris, another English diplomat observed that Hertford's choice of secretary 'has occasioned much laughing here. Questions are being asked whether Mr Hume as part of the family will be obliged to attend prayers twice a day.'

A web of family and social ties connected many of those who were now setting the course of Hume's life. Thus, on the British side, there was Hertford's brother, General Henry Seymour Conway, and their cousin, Horace Walpole. Lady Hertford should not be forgotten: she was a granddaughter of Charles II, and cousin of the Duke of Grafton, a future prime minister. Their various roles also demonstrate how Hume had now mortgaged his career to London politicians and to the Court.

Conway, in particular, was a leading figure on the national stage, central to this politically messy, pre-party period of cabals, nepotism, patronage and royal influence. A staple of three contemporary governments, all weak and shaky, he nonetheless preserved a reputation as a conscientious monument to integrity and honour – so much so that he was always on the verge of resignation, with Walpole in the background urgently counselling him to stand his ground.

A member of the House of Commons from 1741 to 1784, Conway started his career in the military and rose to lieutenant-general. He was handsome, with a mellifluous voice and a gracious manner, thoughtful and well read. He was also courageous, and ready to suffer for his beliefs. When he voted against George Grenville's government in February 1764 on the issue of general warrants, under which people could be arrested and property seized without prior evidence of their guilt or any personal identification (for example, the warrant could be for the arrest of 'the authors of a seditious paper'), he was dismissed from his post as Gentleman of the Bedchamber *and* as the Colonel of his Regiment. It was seen as foul play that he should be deprived of both.

Soon after, in July 1765, when Grenville fell and the Marquess of Rockingham (known to his peers for his laziness and to the public for his zeal for horse-racing) became prime minister, Conway received one of the two key offices outside the Treasury, secretary of state for the Southern Department, though his irresolution made him unsuitable for office and the dark skills of managing the Commons. He served under a series of fragile administrations, switching to the Northern Department in 1766. The King had come to depend on him. Walpole recorded that George III told Conway, 'he hoped never to have an administration of which he should not be one'.

Conway's elder brother, the Earl of Hertford, was also a confidant of George III. Religious and good-natured, he was, thought Horace Walpole, a man of 'unblemished morals'. But others disparaged him as self-interested, avaricious and ambitious. A contemporary described him in 1767 as having a 'constant appetite for all preferments for himself and family, with the quickest digestion and the shortest memory of past favours of any of the present noblemen.' He was swift to distance himself from his brother's stand on general warrants; shortly after, he supplicated the King (unsuccessfully) for elevation from earl to marquess.

To their cousin, Horace Walpole, youngest son, and fierce defender of Sir Robert Walpole, we could apply the phrase used by Walter Bagehot of Charles Dickens: 'a special correspondent for posterity'. His letters and journals provide an invaluable insider's commentary on the period – busy, well informed, unsentimental. He was a man of many parts: dilettante, wit and gossip, place-holder and MP, a consummate expert in corridor intrigues. His father left him well provided with sinecures – to the tune of £3,400 a year – and a parliamentary seat: he is said to have visited his constituency and spoken in the House only once.

His interests and accomplishments were multifarious. He invented the Gothic novel with *The Castle of Otranto*, published in 1764; he was a diarist and scholar, and a printer. He had an acute, though narrow, taste for the arts and was a jackdaw collector – everything from the country's finest collection of miniatures to a vulcanized date from Herculaneum to Cardinal Wolsey's red hat. And, of course, he created his lasting monument as the decorator and gardener of his true love, his 'little Gothick castle', Strawberry Hill, the small box of a house in Twickenham, south west of London, that he bought in 1747, adding Gothic features over the years.

Walpole was warm, lively, generous and humane, and constantly fascinated by the ways of the world. He was patriotic, though he opined that 'a good patriot is a bad citizen'. 'Paris revived in me that natural passion, the love of my country's glory. I must put it out: it is a wicked passion and breathes war.' He was also a man of causes. He spoke out against the execution of Admiral Byng in 1757 for 'losing' Minorca to the French (or *'pour encourager les autres'*, as Voltaire quipped), he was a critic of general warrants, supported a free press, was for the American colonists, and rejected slavery – 'that horrid trade . . . it chills the blood'.

Despite these attributes, the picture that emerges of him from Parisian soirées in the freezing winter of 1765–66 is not altogether flattering. He comes across as gossipy and malicious, treating society, particularly when involving intellectuals, as a source of sour amusement. None the less, aged forty-eight, Walpole became the passion of the most formidable of Paris hostesses, his 'blind, old, *débauchée* of wit', seventy-year-old Mme du Deffand, with whom he had a correspondence of over 800 letters. She bequeathed him her dog, Tonton (who was not house-trained). She had an apt description of Walpole as '*le fou moqueur*' ('madcap jester'). Walpole quoted this with relish.

Reflecting the cosmopolitan nature of Anglo-French elite society, there was little hostility in France towards the embassy or visitors such as Walpole, although Britain had just fought, and won, the Seven Years War, the latest in a bloody series that punctuated relations between these two global competitors.

The Seven Years War culminated triumphantly for Britain in the Treaty of Paris in 1763. This was Britain's hour. The British navy had carried all before it. In Canada, India and the West Indies, French possessions fell to British arms. So did Havana, the key to Spain's West Indian empire. It seemed that Britain could out-sail, out-fight and out-trade any of its European rivals.

For British merchants, alive with patriotic fervour, there were commercial spoils of victory: the colonies would supply raw materials and buy British goods. But, as traders rejoiced, for the nation as a whole there were also costs. Freed from fear of a French invasion, the American colonists began to assert themselves. The expense of warfare required post-war economies, including in the navy, and forced the government to look for new sources of taxation that in turn stirred discontent in America. Inflation at home, the escalating cost of corn and the fear of famine provoked bouts of disorder.

The Treaty of Paris, negotiated by Bute and signed on 10 February 1763, was politically contentious. The British retained most of their gains, though Bute handed back some conquests to France and Spain on the principle that such a gesture would lay the basis for future peace. It was still a major blow to French power, but George III called it a 'noble treaty'. Bute's enemies, meanwhile, denounced it as 'having saved England from the ruin of certain success'. Hopes that it would lead to some kind of détente took no account of the hostility embedded in the DNA of relations between France and Britain (though some Scots felt the ties of the 'auld alliance' and were more comfortable in the French capital than in London). As Hume settled into Paris, the agonistic brew of fright, contempt and admiration that permeated cross-Channel attitudes would be familiar today.

In fact, that far-sighted politician and subtle diplomat, the Duc de Choiseul, then responsible for the fleet and shortly to be minister of war, was already pushing ahead with rebuilding French military power with the aim of recouping French losses. Walpole was one of those sounding the alarm. 'At my return from France, where I had perceived how much it behoved us to be on our guard against the designed hostilities of that Court, as soon as their finances should enable them to renew the war, I laboured to infuse attention to our situation.'

None of this held the English nobility back from visiting Paris. Walpole went for a six-month stay in the French capital in September 1765 and, in a letter to a friend in England, he commented on the throng of his fellow citizens keeping him company:

If there is no talk in England of politics and parliaments, I can send your ladyship as much as you please from hence – or if you want English themselves, I can send you about fifty head; and I can assure you we will still be well stocked. There were three card-tables full of lords, ladies, gentlemen, and gentlewomen, the other night at Lady Berkeley's, who keeps Tuesdays.

It was just as well that Walpole had a slice of the London *beau monde* to entertain him. He found Parisian society humourless, though he appreciated French manners: 'It may not be more sincere (and why should it?) than our cold and bare civility; but it is better dressed, and looks natural; one asks no more.' In a letter of 19 October 1765 to his intimate friend Sir Thomas Brand, he complained about his boredom. He had been confined to bed with gout in both legs, and declared that he had not laughed since Lady Hertford went away. 'Good folks, they have no time to laugh. There is God and the King to be pulled down first; and men and women, one and all are devoutly employed in the demolition. They think me quite profane for having any belief left.'

Traffic was not all in one direction. The French, too, flocked to England. And, notwithstanding their cherished differences, both sides peered at each other across the Channel to spot the latest trends in fashion. What was *à la mode* in Paris immediately became *le dernier cri* in London – and vice versa.

Grimm listed the objects of mutual desire:

We in France now set as high a value upon English postillions as the English ever placed upon our poor Huguenot waiting maids; we have the same taste for their horses, their punch, and their philosophers, as they have for our wines, our liqueurs, and our opera dancers . . . we are mad for their steel, they are eager for our silver; we can no longer support anything but English carriages, gardens, and swords, they cannot admire anything but our workmen, particularly our cabinet-makers and our cooks. We send them our fashions and in return bring back theirs . . . In short we seem reciprocally to have imposed upon ourselves the tasks of copying each other, so as to efface entirely all vestiges of our ancient hatred.

In that, at least, Grimm was an optimist.

Grimm also noted the French partiality for English translations, which appeared with great rapidity, evidence of the impressive degree of cultural exchange. They included Hume's philosophical papers. There had been a cult following for Samuel Richardson ever since the publication of his *Clarissa* (1747). French pilgrims sought out English locations described in *Clarissa*. Rousseau's opinion was that 'in no other language is there a novel equal to *Clarisse*, or even approaching it.'

Hertford had taken the monumental Hôtel de Lassay for his personal use; a visitor said she had never seen a house as beautiful, but the rooms were inconvenient and dirty. There, according to a British visitor, Hume made 'a good honest droll good-natured sort of figure at their table, and really puts you in mind of the mastiff-dog at the fire side.'

Away from the piety of the Hertfords' somewhat spare table, Hume's embassy position and his association with Lord Hertford assured his entrée to the luxurious divertissements of the Court and the drawing rooms of the aristocratic elite. However, many of Hume's tasks must have seemed insufferably mundane. The neophyte assistant secretary had among his official duties the issuing of embassy news to the London press. On 6 June 1765, he sent a report to the *London Chronicle* on the King's birthday celebrations in Paris:

Paris. On Tuesday the fourth of June, being the anniversary of his Majesty's birthday, the Earl of Hertford, Ambassador from England, invited all the English of rank and condition in the place, to the number of seventy persons, who dined with him and celebrated that solemnity. The company appeared very splendid, being almost all dressed in new and rich cloaths on this occasion; the entertainment was magnificent, and the usual healths were drunk with great loyalty and alacrity by all present.

Then, between 21 July 1765, when Hertford left Paris having given up his appointment, and 17 November 1765, when the Duke of Richmond took his place, Hume was chargé d'affaires and his responsibilities became more serious. In these four months he handled negotiations on various detailed problems left over from the Treaty of Paris, such as the demolition of the fortifications of Dunkirk.

Hume solved none of these issues, Conway praised his negotiating skills.

Hume should have been cheerier than ever before. He had a challenging job and sufficient remuneration. Yet, beneath the jocund surface, anger was curdling. One reason for this was the politically inspired delay in his confirmation as embassy secretary. Since his arrival, his fate had been in the hands of the prime minister, George Grenville. And, throughout 1764 and the first half of 1765, Grenville was content for Bunbury to stay away from Paris (leaving Hume to do all his work), though he plainly had no intention of confirming the Scottish historian in his embassy post if Sir Charles took another.

Hume was no self-seeker but, in March 1764, Hertford persuaded him to contact his friends who might have influence. Hume portrayed himself as insouciant when the attempt failed. 'The King has promised it; all the Ministers have promised it: Lord Hertford earnestly solicits it: Yet have I been in this condition about six months: and I never trouble my head about the matter.'

According to Walpole, Hertford was not liked either by the Earl of Bute or by the Grenville government, and it was indicative of the poor relations between Hertford and the administration that when he had put in for the expenses of his going to Paris, these were turned down though normally paid. Hertford suspected that his brother's opposition in parliament had caused the denial. If so, the same bad blood might have been behind the refusal to confirm Hume. However, the Grenville correspondence also shows that the prime minister and his close allies were contemptuous of Hertford's dealings with the French and wished he would come home. Discussing how to replace the ambassador, they were not likely to promote his assistant.

By the summer of 1764, nettled by French insinuations of his impotence in London, Hertford dispatched a querulous letter to Grenville, pointing out, first, that in the absence of a secretary he trusted, he could not leave his post or be ill and, second, that Hume was very well suited to act as his deputy if he was confirmed: 'I am desirous, in friendship to Mr Hume and for His Majesty's future service, to see so able a man invested in [the post].' Grenville ignored the letter. In February 1765, his diary records him upbraiding the King for appointing a secretary to the embassy in Spain, 'apprehending that Lord Hertford might require the same appointment for Mr Hume in Paris'.

Finally, the political wheel of fortune rotated in Hume's favour, if only briefly.

Exasperated by Grenville, the King sought and failed to find a successor, leaving Grenville stronger than before. As Walpole put it, 'The King is reduced to the mortification, and it is extreme, of taking his old ministers again . . . Grenville has treated his master in the most impertinent manner, and they are now actually digesting the terms that they mean to impose on their captive . . .'

Their captive and master, the King, was in no position to resist concessions, chief among them the complete exclusion of Bute. In the subsequent shuffling of posts, Bunbury was appointed secretary to the new lord lieutenant of Ireland. Hertford predicted that Bunbury's departure for Dublin would finally result in Hume's confirmation. Hume fancied it would not happen, that 'I, a philosopher, a man of letters, no wise a courtier, of the most independent spirit, who has given offence to every sect and every party, that I, I say, such as I have described myself, should obtain an employment of dignity and a thousand a year.'

But, at last, he did. Politically, Grenville might have won a short-term political battle but his relations with the King, vital to matters of patronage, were irrevocably breaking down and the monarch was scheming to topple him for good. Possibly because it was politically convenient, the prime minister gave way on Hume. Hertford's confidence was justified.

On 3 June, hearing of his appointment, Hume wrote happily to Sir Gilbert Elliot: 'In spite of atheism and deism, of Whiggism and Toryism, of Scotticism and Philosophy, I am now possessed of an office of credit and of £1,200 a year.' He also had £300 for his equipage and an allowance for furnishing his table as appropriate to his new title. On 13 July, Hume's commission under the Great Seal as secretary to the embassy was delivered into his hands.

But London politics would ensure that his pleasure in the job would be temporary. Grenville had been dismissed on 13 July 1765 and Charles Watson-Wentworth, Marquess of Rockingham, formed a patched-up administration. Conway became one of the two secretaries of state and through his office, his brother, Hertford, was offered the lord lieutenancy of Ireland.

Hertford's reluctant successor in Paris would be the Duke of Richmond, brother-in-law of Sir Charles Bunbury. In the event, the undiplomatic Richmond went to Paris for only four months – November 1765 to February 1766 – making himself universally unpopular.

For Hume, Richmond's appointment signalled the end of Paris, raising the question whether he could or would follow Hertford to Ireland as secretary there. The job paid £3,000 a year. While he claimed that all he wanted was a book and a fireside, his letters show his ambition, his relish at being well thought of by the King. In late July, Hume wrote to Blair, 'You see what a splendid fortune awaits me; yet you cannot imagine with what regret I leave this country. It is like stepping out of light into darkness, to exchange Paris for Dublin.' He told Adam Smith that the Dublin post was one of 'great dignity, as the Secretary is in a manner prime minister of that kingdom'.

His aspirations seem naive. After all, he was scarcely qualified for Dublin, having no capacity for hard drinking or low politicking. Nor did the political elite take such a prospect seriously. The Rockingham ministry was determined to show its anti-Bute – in other words, anti-Scottish – credentials, pandering to widespread English prejudice. Lord Hertford did what he could for his protégé, but as Hume himself commented, 'The cry is loud against the Scots, and the present Ministry are unwilling to support any of our countrymen, lest they hear a reproach of being connected with Lord Bute.'

Hertford's son went to Dublin instead, in keeping with Hertford's reputation for looking after his family. However,

Hertford secured Hume a pension of £400 p.a. as compensation – and had an apartment prepared for him in Dublin Castle. Yet even a visit to Dublin proved impossible. Lady Hertford encouraged Hume to stay away because of the popular prejudice against him in Ireland as both a sectarian and a freethinker. (The Hertfords themselves remained in Ireland for barely a year: the Earl returned to London and went on to the preferment he had long coveted, Lord Chamberlain, at the heart of the Court.)

Once again, the stout philosopher's career had been blocked by his nationality, his beliefs and perhaps his social standing. Even his pleasure at finally having his commission as secretary had a worm chewing at it. At the end of 1765, Walpole recorded Hume's suspicion that Walpole had been sent to Paris by London to advise the new ambassador behind Hume's back.

However, Hume had been living a double life in Paris. If, for Hume the secretary, it felt the worst of times, for Hume the philosopher and historian, it was unquestionably the best.

7

He Would Always Have Paris

In the Salon of Four Mirrors, Mme de Boufflers serves tea in moderation

During those twenty-six months in Paris, Hume was subject to
the pull of two contrasting societies: political England was his
paymaster; cultural France was his home away from home.
While he was dished up thin gruel from the governments of
King George, he feasted on the lavish applause of the Republic
of Letters.

The date 18 October 1763 was the day of David Hume's
epiphany. In Paris, French society greeted his arrival as under-
secretary with what can only be described as rapture. In England
or Scotland, such unreserved public acclaim had never – could
never have – been his.

Hume's friends, travelling in France, had already told him
about his incomparable standing. 'They would go to the Indies
to serve you,' gushed the wine merchant John Stewart in 1759.
'You're the man in the world they hold in the highest esteem.'
A year later, one of Hume's Edinburgh chums agreed: 'No
author ever yet attained to that degree of reputation in his own
lifetime that you are now in possession of at Paris.' It was
taken as a measure of Hume's towering stature in Paris that he
displaced Samuel Richardson and Laurence Sterne as the hal-
lowed figures of English literature. A claim of acquaintance
with Hume opened doors to the most exclusive salons. The
French longed for him to appear among them.

And there he was, that first evening, still in his travelling
clothes, whisked from one noble drawing room to another. At

the final engagement of the night, the compliments of the Dauphin were relayed to him.

It was only the opening round of a heady two years of being all the rage. On 26 October, Hume wrote to Adam Smith that he had 'everywhere been met with the most extraordinary honours, which the most exorbitant vanity could wish or desire.' He was introduced to Mme de Pompadour, the mistress of Louis XV, who spoke to him at unusual length, and to the Dauphin's children – the future Louis XVI, Louis XVIII and Charles X – who assured him that he had many friends and admirers in France. Walpole's Journal entry for 24 December 1765 makes reference to the Dauphin's terminal illness: 'Physicians had ordered the Dauphin 460 medicines. The Dauphin said to [the] Duc de Nivernois, that he was "glad to have such a book behind me as Mr Hume's *Essays*".'

There were dinner invitations from an array of French dukes and princes. In his best English, Prince Louis de Rohan's secretary, Abbé Georgel, wrote to Hume, '*M. L'Abbé Georgel fait un million de complimens à M. Hume.* He makes great account of his vorks, admires her wit, and loves her person.'

In the brief, dry autobiography Hume penned four months before his death in August 1776, he recollected, modestly, 'The more I resiled from their excessive civilities, the more I was loaded with them.' On 1 December 1763, he adopted more poetic language when describing his situation for his fellow Scottish historian William Robertson. 'I can only say that I eat nothing but ambrosia, drink nothing but nectar, breathe nothing but incense, and tread on nothing but flowers. Every man I meet, and still more every lady, would think they were wanting in the most indispensable duty, if they did not make to me a long and elaborate harangue in my praise.' Hume had his own explanation for the plaudits lavished on him: 'What gave me chief pleasure was to find that most of the elogiums bestowed on me, turned on my personal character; my naivety & simplicity of manners, the candour & mildness of my disposition &c.'

As for his intellectual accomplishments, the culture of the Republic of Letters was infinitely more congenial and welcoming than London. To begin with, in Paris, he was not viewed through the distorting prism of anti-Scottish feeling, nor belittled because of his scepticism or assumed politics. And more, the profession of letters was taken seriously. In April 1765, Hume wrote to Hugh Blair:

> In London, if a man have the misfortune to attach himself to letters, even if he succeeds, I know not with whom he is to live, nor how he is to pass his time in suitable society. The little company there that is worth conversing with are cold and unsociable; or are warmed only by faction and cabal; so that a man who plays no part in public life becomes altogether insignificant; and if he is not rich he becomes even contemptible. Hence that nation are relapsing into the deepest stupidity and ignorance. But in Paris a man that distinguishes himself in letters meets immediately with regard and attention.

And in Paris, quite unlike England – or Scotland, for that matter – many of those who paid this obese, jowly philosopher the warmest regard and attention were women. He had never experienced anything like it. Charlemont observed how, 'no lady's toilette was complete without Hume's attendance. At the opera, his broad unmeaning face was usually seen *entre deux jolis minois* [between two pretty faces].' And not just *jolis minois*. In *The Present State of Polite Learning* (1759), Oliver Goldsmith (who would dine with both Hume and Rousseau in London) was impressed by the intellectual attributes of French women: 'A man of fashion in Paris, however contemptible we may think him here, must be acquainted with the reigning modes of philosophy as well as of dress to be able to entertain his mistress agreeably.'

Hume was not a man *of* fashion, he was *the* fashion. Hume's presence in Paris, so reported an observer, was 'regarded as one of the most beautiful fruits of the peace . . . The great and pretty ladies play up to him for all they are worth.' The introduction to the 1820 publication of his *Private Correspondence* observes that 'all the pretty women of France were fond of Hume, and the stout Scotch philosopher appeared highly delighted with their society . . . It is not, indeed, surprising that a temper, serene and tranquil like his, should have preferred the witty conversation of accomplished Parisian ladies, in their elegant saloons [*sic*], to the boisterous political discussions of English gentlemen, over their bottles at taverns and coffee houses.'

In other words, Hume's reputation had secured him entry to the Republic of Letters, that unique territory governed by outstanding women.

The deadening boredom and hierarchy of the French Court were prime reasons for the existence of the Republic of Letters. In its salons, private amusement co-existed with intellectual sharp-shooting, and once invited into a salon, public figures were treated equally, irrespective of their social rank.

An abundance of excellent food and wine sustained dancing and parlour games, music and singing, brilliant sallies and earnest debate, information and learning. Crucially, the salons supplied informal networks of communication that supported an ease of expression and critical inquiry impossible at Court. Together with the constant correspondence this engendered, the salons became the transmission system of the French Enlightenment, creating, focusing and broadcasting radical opinion. However, it would be wrong to see the salon system simply as a progressive network. That was only a part of its social influence. Mme Suzanne Necker (née Curchod) saw that the salon 'formed the invisible power which, without finances, without troops, without an army, imposes its laws upon the town, on the Court, and even on the King himself.'

These 'brilliant schools of reason', as the salons have been described, also expressed the manners of the age. Hume found Parisian decorum most agreeable compared with that on the barbarian banks of the Thames. Crafted epigrams and *l'air galant* were indispensable, as was urbanity. Essential for men was the deft demonstration of adulation; for women, holding their 'lovers' captive through charm and intelligence rather than favours.

Women hosts were the constant factor. They served the Republic of Letters as firm but delightful regulators of tact and etiquette: hosts who wanted the guests to shine but could set the tone of the discussions and insist on clarity of language. Their art was the creation and maintenance of civilized conversation. In the 1760s, the *philosophes* might attend a salon two or three times a week.

It is not hard to imagine Hume's sense of well-being as he settled into this enriching landscape. He did the round of the salons, starting with the 'empress', Mme Geoffrin, who took immediately to her 'fat wag', her 'fat rascal'. Foreign ambassadors and visiting monarchs were among the guests. To her Monday dinners, she invited artists and art-lovers. Mozart first dazzled Paris in her drawing room. Her literary dinners took place on Wednesdays and buoyed up the *Encylopédiste* movement – which, in its darkest days, she kept afloat with a private gift of 100,000 *écus*.

Mme Geoffrin's bitter rival was the blind Mme du Deffand. Any one of *her* regulars who visited Mme Geoffrin's circle was viewed as a traitor in the du Deffand apartment above a convent in the rue Saint-Dominique. (Walpole was the exception: he saw both women, and yet seems to have survived intact.)

Unlike Mme Geoffrin, the Marquise du Deffand belonged to the so-called *noblesse de l'épée* – the high nobility who (or whose ancestors) had served on the field of battle with the king. She separated from the marquis in 1722, having been for a brief, if notorious, interlude – a fortnight – mistress of the regent, Phillipe, Duc d'Orléans. That liaison, together with her much longer membership of his scandalous circle, brought her a royal pension. Her salon was celebrated for what Walpole called 'the prodigious quickness' of her wit. Her reputation was founded on the *bon mot* about the martyred St Denis, who walked several miles after his execution, carrying his head under his arm: 'It is only the first step that counts.' She attracted a who's who of scientists, writers, and leading figures in the world of letters and society. She was a free-thinker, ridiculing religion: 'What is faith? It is to believe firmly in what one does not understand.' For forty-three years she corresponded with Voltaire; they were amicable foes.

Although Hume had joined her salon early in his stay, his tenure did not last. Partly his break was a consequence of his choice to frequent the salon of Julie de L'Espinasse, something not forgotten by Mme du Deffand when later he sought her support. The illegitimate offspring of Mme du Deffand's eldest brother, in 1754 the twenty-two-year-old Mlle de L'Espinasse had been invited by Mme du Deffand to assist at her salon. The great hostess had recognized her warmth, her wit and intelligence; with her niece's presence, Mme du Deffand's salon achieved a decade of pre-eminence.

However, it became apparent that some, particularly the *philosophes*, preferred the company of the younger woman; she developed her own informal reception when habitués called on her in the afternoons while her aunt was in repose.

D'Alembert fell in love with this embodiment of passionate and romantic sensibility. In 1764, Mme du Deffand expelled her. It was a misjudgement. D'Alembert set her up with a house and a pension. He moved in when seriously ill and she nursed him back to health, though his love for her was unrequited.

Many of du Deffand's regulars departed with her niece, who then established her own formal salon in the same street, frequented by a galaxy of stars of the French Enlightenment. Besides Diderot, they included a leading mathematician, an apostle of science and logic in government, and the sparkling journalist who became editor of the *Gazette de France* – in other words, Jean-Báptiste Le Rond d'Alembert, Anne-Robert-Jacques Turgot and Jean-Báptiste Suard.

According to Hume's biographer, Ernest Campbell Mossner, it was at de L'Espinasse's salon that Hume joyfully discovered a 'feast of reason' and 'the quiet appreciation of his own talents'. D'Alembert's presence guaranteed real intellectual weight. Hume and d'Alembert achieved an almost instant rapport.

At this point, Hume also came across the multi-talented Diderot, Hume's equal in profound conversation. A big man himself, Diderot was amazed at Hume's bulk – like 'a portly, well-fed Bernadine monk'. Even two centuries later, Bernadine monks were notorious for luxurious living: '*Les Gros Bernadins*', in the words of a 1930s French popular song.

Hume basked in the unconditional adulation of Paris. It was social death not to be acquainted with him or, worse, not even to recognize him in the flesh. In his *Journal*, Walpole records an anecdote told by a former French ambassador to London. 'A French lady asking him who Mr Hume was, and being told, begged him not to mention it, as it would make her look very ill-bred not to know him. It is incredible the homage they pay him.'

Hume made less of an impression on his, possibly envious, compatriots. George Selwyn, wit and politician, wrote to Lord Holland, 'In common society he seems a man of the most clumsy capacity I ever saw, and to speak the truth, the fuss which the people of this country have made with a man on account of perfections of which I am confident they are no judge, and whose manners are so unlike their own, has lessened them not a little in my opinion.'

Hume was treated, said Walpole, with 'perfect veneration'. He added tartly that Hume was 'the only thing in the world that [the French] believe implicitly; which they must do, for I defy them to understand any language that he speaks.' Whether Walpole was mocking Hume's French accent or his distinctive Scottish brogue – or both – is unclear.

The Scotsman was certainly not all elegant phrases and flashing epigrams in the entertainments staged at home. An anecdote of Mme d'Épinay has him in a 'café', dressed as a sultan and seated between two beautiful 'slaves' whom he was supposed to seduce. All he finds to say, slapping his knees and stomach, is: 'Well, my young ladies. Well. Here you are then. Ah well . . . *Eh bien! Mes demoiselles. Eh bien! Vous voilà donc; eh bien! vous voilà, vous voilà ici?*' His performance was not a success. The 'slaves' said he was good only at eating veal.

Hume was also a regular at the dinners at one of the few all-male salons – held by the massively wealthy Paul-Henri Thiry Baron d'Holbach, who was at the very hub of the French Enlightenment. Holbach, German-born, was both a major financial supporter of and a contributor to the *Encyclopédie*, writing and translating articles on subjects as diverse as mineralogy and chemistry, politics and economics. Before Hume came to Paris, he had written to the Scotsman of his desire to meet 'one of the greatest philosophers of any age'.

He presided over what Rousseau in his rage called '*la coterie holbachique*', a group that included Diderot, Grimm and d'Alembert. None the less, Rousseau is thought to have taken d'Holbach as the model for Wolmar, an upright atheist of Christian virtues, in *Héloïse*.

The baron's luxurious residence offered a salon with a difference: governed by *philosophes* for *philosophes*, it was a cockpit of their Enlightenment. Meetings of the Encyclopedists occurred there twice a week. No hostess imposed her rules of conversation and propriety of subject. After d'Alembert, Hume judged d'Holbach the man most worthy of trust.

At d'Holbach's, Hume encountered Friedrich Grimm. Hume's name had first surfaced in Grimm's *Correspondance littéraire* in 1754 with a French translation of the *Political Discourses*, though a little later Grimm gave the Scotsman only a qualified vote of approval: 'In spite of the fame that he has acquired in his country, and the reputation that he is beginning to have in France, he does not appear to be a man of the first power.' But by 1759, he was praising Hume as 'one of the best intellects of England; and as philosophers belong less to their native country than to the universe which they enlighten, this man can be included in the small number of those who by their wisdom and by their works have benefited mankind'. As for his personality, after being exposed to Hume in Paris, the shrewd, clear-sighted Grimm reached an ambivalent verdict:

M. Hume should like France; he has received there the most distinguished and flattering welcome . . . What is still more pleasing is that all the pretty women have latched on to him, and the fat Scottish philosopher is so delighted to be in their company. This David Hume is an excellent man; he is naturally serene, he listens sensitively, he speaks sometimes with

wit although he says little; but he is heavy, he has neither
warmth, nor grace, nor anything suited to joining in the war-
bling of those charming little machines we call pretty women.

Whatever their reservations, the *philosophes* sought Hume
out. Next to d'Alembert, Turgot, then an enlightened royal
administrator of the Limoges district in central France, was
his closest friend. Their band included Suard (who later
translated a crucial document for Hume) and the magistrate
and chief censor for the French book trade, Lamoignon de
Malesherbes. Early on in his stay, Hume told Hugh Blair that
the men of letters there were really very agreeable: all of them
men of the world, living in entire, or almost entire, harmony
among themselves, and quite irreproachable in their morals.

Ironically, the only cultural gap that Hume had difficulty in
bridging was over religion. His problem was not that the
philosophes were overly religious – quite the reverse. Hume
squirmed at the disdain directed at believers. Once, dining
with d'Holbach, Hume claimed he had never seen an atheist
and questioned whether they really existed. But there were
seventeen at that very table, replied d'Holbach. (Diderot,
who recounted this anecdote, feared it would scandalize the
English, who still believed a little in God, whereas, in his
judgement, the French scarcely did at all.) It seems Hume was
fated to be damned on one side of the Channel for having too
little religion and on the other side for having too much.

Mossner hazards that this – and the fact that his metaphysi-
cal scepticism was never fully embraced in Paris – contributed
to an intellectual loneliness and might have been one reason
why *le bon David* never returned to France. We might hazard
another – that he wanted to avoid Mme de Boufflers.

Even at a distance of 250 years, it is impossible to resist the
appeal of Marie-Charlotte-Hippolyte de Campet de Saujon,

Comtesse de Boufflers-Rouverel. Hume's odd relationship with her reveals the constraints on his capacity for sentiment. She also acted as an essential link between him and Rousseau.

Mme de Boufflers exemplified the adage that in England marriage took place to end a young woman's indiscretions, while in France it began them. In 1746, she had been married to Edouard, Comte de Boufflers-Rouverel, but for over twenty years was the mistress of a prince of the blood royal, Louis-François de Bourbon, Prince de Conti. In Paris, he resided at the magnificent Temple – originally a fortified monastery of the Knights Templar. Hence Mme du Deffand's dismissive reference to Mme de Boufflers as '*l'Idole du Temple*'.

When in the capital, Mme de Boufflers lived in rue Notre Dame de Nazareth in the Temple precincts. There she held her illustrious salon, serving tea *à l'anglaise* in the glittering Room of the Four Mirrors. One such *séance* can be seen at Versailles in Michel-Barthelémy Ollivier's painting, commissioned by Conti in 1766, 'English Tea, in the Room of Four Mirrors, at the Temple, with all the Court of the Prince de Conti.' Chaperoned by his father on his second European tour, the young Mozart is giving a recital. Her salon was in the grand style, an eclectic mix of high nobility, writers and thinkers, including Hume, Gustave III of Sweden, Grimm and d'Alembert. On Fridays, she entertained a chosen few – again including Hume – in her own house.

Beautiful, clever, she was the *adulée* of many and the jealous target of some. Her taste for letters gave her another nickname, 'learned Minerva'. Walpole had reservations:

> She is two women, the upper and the lower. I need not tell you that the lower is gallant, and still has pretensions. The upper is very sensible, too, and has a measured eloquence that is just and pleasing – but all is spoiled by an unrelaxed

attention to applause. You would think she was always sitting for her picture to her biographer.

Mme du Deffand pronounced her '*drôle*', having damned her with faint praise:

> Her good qualities, for she has several, result from the emptiness of her character and from the slight impression that everything around her makes on her . . . she is occupied solely with herself and not with others. She is like a flute that pronounces laws and delivers oracles, in a voice so pretty and a manner so sweet.

Mme de Boufflers did indeed devise moral maxims. She hung a copy of her 'Rule of Life' on her bedroom wall. It was a litany of eighteenth-century manners and included:

> In conduct, simplicity and reason; in appearance, propriety and decency; in manners, propriety and decorum; in actions, justice and generosity; in the use of wealth, economy and liberality; in conversation, clearness, truth, precision; in adversity, courage and pride; in prosperity, modesty and moderation; in society, charm, ease, courteousness; in domestic life, integrity and kindness without familiarity; to sacrifice everything for tranquillity of soul; to permit oneself only innocent railleries, which cannot wound . . .

She did not expect her friends to flout these standards.

Mme de Boufflers opened contact with Rousseau in 1758. She was staying with Mme de Luxembourg at Montmorency and asked Rousseau if she could see him. In the *Confessions*, he records, 'I sent the conventional reply, but I did not stir.' He then relishes his developing romantic attachment to her:

> If I did not commit the foolishness of becoming [Conti's] rival, I narrowly escaped doing so . . . She was beautiful and

still young . . . I was nearly caught. I think that she saw it . . . But for this once, I was sensible . . . Having perceived the emotion she caused me, Mme de Boufflers could also see that I had triumphed over it.

Her dealings with Hume went back to March 1761, when she had taken the initiative in writing to him: 'I dare only add that in all the products of your pen, you show yourself a perfect philosopher, a statesman, an historian of genius, an enlightened political scientist, a true patriot.' Thus began a correspondence that lasted until his death. In a letter eighteen months after starting opening communication, she offered a description of herself approaching forty:

A great part of my youth is over. Some delicacy in features, mildness and decency in countenance, are the only exterior advantages, I can boast of. And as for interior, common sense, improved a little, by early good reading, are all I possess. [My English is confined but] if I am intitled [*sic*] to some elegancy I owe it to the repeated readings of your admirable works.

Their correspondence took on a passionate note, though it is possible that Hume misread its significance for her. An editor of Walpole's letters points out that in pre-revolutionary Paris, a woman of fashion passed through well delineated states:

When young she was *galante*; on becoming more mature, she became a *bel esprit*. These were as strictly defined and observed as changes of dress on a particular day of the different seasons. A woman endeavouring to attract lovers after she had ceased to be a *galante* would have been not less ridiculous than her wearing velvet when all the rest of the world were in *demi-saison*.

So, lively and romantic language, expressions of attachment, could be used in the epoch of *bel esprit* without any fear of misunderstanding by society or the 'loving' partner. Did Hume recognize this where Mme de Boufflers was concerned? Did he imagine that there was more to her sentiments than the regard of an ardent spirit? Walpole appears to have been aware of the convention: in a letter of 11 July 1766, he describes her as 'a *savante, philosophe,* author, *bel esprit*'. As for Hume's own response, there is the curious episode of the encounter that did not take place during their burgeoning attachment.

In the spring of 1763, Hume had the opportunity to see his correspondent for the first time, when she came to England on what became a celebrity tour. She travelled to London on 17 April, confiding to her cousin and escort Lord Elibank that the true purpose of her journey was to meet Hume.

In London, 'Madame Blewflower' (as the mob called her) was the sensation of the moment, with the pick of the *beau monde* vying to entertain her. She visited Horace Walpole at Strawberry Hill. She stayed with several dukes, and a play was put on in her honour. When she visited Dr Johnson, the sage hurried to show her to her coach, which was considered a remarkable tribute.

Elibank did his best to get Hume to London. 'You cannot in decency neglect the opportunity of gratifying this flattering curiosity, perhaps passion, of the most amiable of God's creation.' However, Hume did neglect it. Mme de Boufflers had intended only a two-month sojourn, but lingered on in hope of the absent Hume emerging. He had gone visiting in Yorkshire, and it was not until 3 July that he sent his rather feeble and evasive excuses for not seeking her out:

I am only afraid that, to a person acquainted with the sociable and conversible parties of France, the showy and dazzling crowds of London assemblies would afford but an indifferent entertainment, and that the love of retreat and solitude, with which the English are reproached, never appears more conspicuously, than when they draw together a multitude of 500 people.

Frustrated, she eventually returned to Paris on 23 July.

The philosopher and *l'Idole* still did not come face to face until several months after his transfer to Paris. She was away in the country suffering from measles and then depression, occasioning from Rousseau a pretty sympathy: 'Ah! How could melancholy dare take up her abode in so beautiful a soul, adorned with a garment which so admirably becomes its wearer.'

However, once they did get together, some of Hume's letters suggest they grew so close that he felt the need to assure her of his rectitude. He probably again misinterpreted her *bel esprit*. The role she had for him was fond courtier, always subordinate to her governing relationship with the Prince. (A recognized term had been coined for the constant but chivalrous attendant, *cicisbeo*, also used to mean a hanger-on.) While formally rejoicing in the role, Hume lacked commitment to the time it implied, as well as the willingness (and ability?) to make the needed emotional investment.

The death of Mme de Boufflers's husband in October 1764 shook her world to its foundations. Without the cover provided by marriage, her remaining with Conti risked being seen as improper: she was desperate to marry him. He was equally determined not to wed her.

Hume's part now evolved from fond courtier to compassionate adviser. Seemingly with some relief, he stepped back, became objective, supportive and shrewd. In a series of letters, he advised that, without a husband in the background, she could no longer properly be at Conti's side; she should set up on her own and build a new social life.

It was not what she wanted to hear. Still fixed on marriage to Conti, and feeling ill and wretched, she then sought relief in England. In a letter to the Duchesse de Barbantane, Hume remarked on her leaving in such a miserable state, and added,

> I can hope for no event that will restore her peace of mind, except one, which is not likely to happen; and she herself is sensible of it. I have wrote in the terms, *which the Prince desired* [authors' italics]; though I wonder he should expect a great effect from anything that can be wrote or said by anybody on that head. If he does not choose to apply the proper remedy, he need expect no cure.

In other words, when he counselled his unhappy friend so sympathetically, he seems to have been acting as the Prince's agent.

No doubt this was a well-intentioned deceit by *le bon David* with the aim of helping the *Minerve savante* face up to unwelcome facts. Happily, she never knew of his deception. But later she was put out to discover another. He had promised to return to Paris, and she had arranged and lovingly furnished rooms for him. What he had not told her was that before leaving the capital he had tried to rent other houses there with the assistance of other friends, no admirers of *l'Idole*.

With the arrival of the Duke of Richmond at the embassy on 9 November, the end of Hume's rapturous posting had come into sight. There were rumours in London, of which Hume was unaware, that he might be appointed embassy secretary in Lisbon. The man himself was vacillating. Home to Edinburgh? Rent a house in Paris? Take an Italian trip with d'Alembert? Of one thing he was certain. There was no question of London.

But thither he went on 4 January 1766. He bade farewell to

'the best place in the world', its salons, its conversation, and its adoration. Bound for London, Rousseau at his side, Rousseau's dog Sultan running ahead of the carriage.

8

Stormy Passage

Safe in Conti's Temple sanctuary, Rousseau flaunted his
immunity from arrest

I was born for friendship.
Jean-Jacques Rousseau

His soul is made for yours.
Mme de Verdelin to Rousseau

Hume had been kept abreast of Rousseau's predicament. In March 1765, a brilliant young mathematician, Alexis-Claude Clairaut (working from Newtonian principles, he had predicted the return of Halley's comet in 1759), had shown Hume a 'pathetic letter' from Rousseau, depicting the beleaguered exile as subsisting in abject misery and penury. Hume responded with a plan he circulated among friends of Clairaut's and Rousseau's in Paris. Aware of Rousseau's reluctance to accept anything that smacked of charity, they intended a degree of subterfuge. The idea was to arrange for the London publication of his *Dictionary of Music*, and to slip the publisher additional money to pass off to the author as 'royalties'.

Urging Hume to assist Rousseau was yet another noble-woman, the Marquise de Verdelin. (She was close to Rousseau's would-be *amour*, Sophie d'Houdetot.) He first encountered the marquise during his stay at the Hermitage in 1757. She was twenty-nine, and had a pale face and a strikingly long neck. Rousseau must have given an ill-mannered impression, stalking off when she turned up with Mme d'Houdetot. She then came to see him at Mont-Louis but did not catch him at home. When he failed to return her visits, she sent him pots of flowers for his terrace, forcing his acknowledgement.

Rousseau thought Mme de Verdelin distinctly unappealing. 'Spiteful remarks and witticisms rise so simply to her lips that one needs to be perpetually on the watch – a very tiring thing for me

– to see when one is being laughed at.' The strictures in the *Confessions* run on, 'I rarely heard her say anything good of her absent friends without slipping in some damaging word. What she did not construe in some bad sense, she turned to ridicule.' Her incessant notes and messages were a nuisance, 'unendurable'.

Mme de Verdelin's father was an impecunious nobleman who had married her off at the age of twenty-two to a rich marquis more than four decades her senior. Her persistence and her many kind letters to Rousseau at Môtiers eventually won him over. She even became a soul mate. In times of trouble they consoled one another, and this need for each other's company, Rousseau conceded, made him overlook her flaws: 'Nothing draws two hearts together so much as the pleasure of weeping together.' He records the satisfaction it gave him when she visited him at Môtiers with her daughter, where they witnessed how he was persecuted. Mme de Verdelin implored him to flee to England.

Clairaut's untimely death on 17 May had put an end to the original project for rescuing Rousseau. It was at the express desire of Mme de Verdelin, after her return to Paris from Môtiers in October, that Hume began to collaborate on the scheme for Rousseau's escape to England. (Curiously, de Verdelin was one of the few French noblewomen immune to Hume's charms: 'Mr Hume is the darling of all the pretty women here; that is probably why he is not one with me.') Hume's representative in London was to be John Stewart, who travelled from Paris with his instructions. Gilbert Elliot would lend a helping hand. The new idea was for Rousseau and his *gouvernante* to be provided with rooms and board in the country at £50–£60 a year, for which he would pay only £20–£25. Hume would privately make up the difference.

Meanwhile, Rousseau had been driven on. Yverdon, Môtiers, Isle St Pierre. Now his flight took him on 27 October 1765 to the small lakeside city of Bienne. He had received so warm a welcome, he told Du Peyrou that same day, that he hoped to winter there and go to England in the spring – 'where I ought to have gone in the first place'. Mme de Verdelin received the same message. She had promised to arrange a *laissez-passer* for him to cross French territory on his way into exile. Rousseau seemed to have made a volte-face: he told her that England was 'the only country where some liberty remains'. But in fact, he had still not finally made up his mind. Invitations had arrived from Vienna and Corsica; Prussia and Silesia were also canvassed. The main contender was Berlin where Earl Marischal had promised asylum, though he worried the climate was too cold. However, Rousseau was mistaken about Bienne hospitality. On 28 October, he told Du Peyrou he was leaving on the morrow – before he was chased out. Forty-eight hours later he was in Basel, writing to Le Vasseur. He would head for Strasbourg; after that he did not know what he would do. He added that during the journey Sultan had done ten leagues at a gallop.

He left Switzerland, 'that murderous land', never to set foot in it again, and headed north, back into France.

On the second day of November, Rousseau entered Strasbourg (French territory since 1697) and put up at La Fleur inn. There he received a fateful letter from Hume. It had been dispatched from Fontainebleau on 22 October, the address written by Mme de Verdelin: '*à Monsieur Rousseau à Isle Saint Pierre au Canton de Berne en Suisse*'.

Not expecting to assume personal charge of Rousseau's welfare or even to be in England if Rousseau sought refuge there, Hume trod carefully in his approach to the exile. He was 'afraid of being in the number of those troublesome people, who, on the pretence of being your admirers, never cease persecuting you with their letters'. However, he continued, if

Rousseau still wished to go to London, he had arranged for Gilbert Elliot to take care of him:

> If you let him know of your arrival, he will immediately wait on you, and will conduct you to your retreat . . . As the English booksellers can afford higher prices to authors than those of Paris, you will have no difficulty to live frugally in that country on the fruits of your own industry. I mention this circumstance, because I am well acquainted with your resolution of laying mankind under obligations to you, without allowing them to make you any return.

In England, Rousseau would be free of persecution, 'not only [because of] the tolerating spirit of our laws, but from the respect, which everyone there bears to your character.'

Rousseau responded from Strasbourg, on 4 December, to 'the most illustrious of my contemporaries, a man whose goodness surpasses his fame', and put himself under Hume's wing, apparently without qualms:

> Your goodness affects me as much as it does me honour. The best reply I can make to your offers is to accept them, which I do. I shall set out in five or six days to throw myself into your arms. It is the advice of my Lord Marischal, my protector, friend and father: it is the advice also of [Mme de Verdelin], whose good sense and benevolence serve equally for my direction and consolation; in fine, I may say it is the advice of my own heart, which takes pleasure in being indebted to the most illustrious of my contemporaries, to a man whose goodness surpasses his glory. I sigh for a solitary and free retirement, where I may finish my days in peace.

He was already thinking ahead to how he could best organize his passage. In a letter to Mme de Verdelin, he wrote, 'P.S. I forgot to tell you, Madame, that I will find at Paris a companion for the journey to London. He is a business man, and these people have, and procure, great facilities for travel.' Jean-Jacques de Luze was a prominent citizen of Neuchâtel, and President of the Corn Exchange. Thérèse was still in Isle St Pierre – Rousseau would have to send for her later. 'I really cannot drag her with me . . . until I have found a refuge.'

However, exhausted by nervous stress and the constant journeying, Rousseau was in no hurry. Initially, he took meals alone at the inn with only Sultan for company, but when word spread that he was in town, local people queued to pay their respects, and he became caught up in a social whirl. The director of the theatre even put on a packed and rapturously received production of *Le Devin du village*, and then offered to stage Rousseau's plays. But on 9 December at seven in the morning, Rousseau left for Paris. His post-chaise rolled through Porte Saint-Antoine exactly one week later.

At last the Swiss fugitive would come face-to-face with his Scottish patron.

How the opening encounter between saved and saviour went appears not to have been recorded by either. Indeed, there is a mysterious lacuna in Rousseau's letters from this period as a whole: missing are any details of his time together with Hume. One would be hard put to know they had even met. However, to Mme de Verdelin, on 18 December, Rousseau made apparent his gratitude. He was, he said, 'even more touched than proud because of the interest this sublime genius deigns to take in me.'

At the end of December, Hume wrote an unreserved panegyric to Blair, comparing Rousseau to Socrates – only with more genius – and, like a starry-eyed lover, seeing beauty in his adored one's blemishes:

I find him mild, and gentle and modest and good humoured

. . . M. Rousseau is of small stature; and would rather be ugly, had he not the finest physiognomy in the world, I mean, the most expressive countenance. His modesty seems not to be good manners but ignorance of his own excellence. As he writes and speaks and acts from the impulse of genius, more than from the use of his ordinary faculties, it is very likely that he forgets its force, whenever it is laid asleep.

Hume also reported that he had been assured (not saying by whom) that 'at times he believes he has inspirations from an immediate communication with the Divinity: he falls sometimes into ecstasies which retain him in the same posture for hours together.'

Rousseau's appearance in Paris coincided with a prolonged spell of dreadful weather. Walpole complained that there had not been two good days together since October: he had not anticipated living in Siberia. Happily for Rousseau, his lodgings offered every protection.

He was initially housed with the widow of his recently deceased Paris publisher Nicolas-Bonaventure Duchesne, but after three days Conti moved him to the Hôtel Saint-Simon in the Temple, which afforded him both luxury and security, though Hume reported to Blair that the magnificence of the apartment made the Swiss uneasy.

It would have been natural for a wanted man given such sanctuary to remain out of sight and to stay within the Temple precincts, where he could welcome guests. Not Rousseau. Although he told his correspondents that he was resolved to remain unobtrusive, he paraded through the streets, his Armenian costume flapping, Sultan by his side. Perhaps he had been notified that the *parlement* had decided not to enforce its warrant while he was merely passing through.

In the *Correspondance littéraire*, Grimm recorded that Rousseau received a multitude of visitors in the hotel and that the day after his entrance into Paris, '[he] walked in the Luxembourg in Armenian garb; but as no one knew in advance, no one profited by the spectacle. He also walked in the boulevard nearest his lodging at a certain time every day. His reappearance created great excitement: crowds gathered wherever he went.'

An observer said that 'If you asked one half of the people what they were doing, they replied they wanted to see Jean-Jacques; and if asked who he was, they replied that they did not know anything about that, but that they were waiting to see him pass.' In a belated report about the buzz from Paris, the *St. James's Chronicle* of 21 January informed its readers that the 'celebrated Rousseau' was 'perpetually besieged by crowds that thronged to see him.' One of those paying homage was the fugitive radical John Wilkes, who might well have had some sympathy with his fellow exile.

In letters to Edinburgh, Hume left a sketch of their first conversations in the Temple. Rousseau spoke about his treatment in Switzerland: the stone bench laid above his door, the woman who objected to his theology and who said she would have liked to blow out his brains, his being banned by the canton of Berne. As related to Hume, all this was the consequence more of his democratic than of his religious principles. (That was certainly Dr Tronchin's view. The citizens of Geneva, he complained, had been inspired to campaign for political reform by *On the Social Contract*.)

Hume acted as Rousseau's Temple gatekeeper, waving away those visitors he considered undesirable or unwelcome to his charge. Mme de Boufflers, his supporter and fellow resident of the Temple, was present when Rousseau remarked how odd it was that he should be so beloved by French women whose morals he had decried and so hated by Swiss women whom he had so much extolled. She resolved the paradox gracefully. 'We are fond of you because we know that, however much you might rail, you are at bottom fond of us to distraction. But the Swiss women hate you, because they are conscious that they have not merit to deserve your attention.'

Indeed, according to Hume, ladies beseeched him to introduce them to Rousseau: 'Were I to open a subscription with his consent, I should receive £50,000 in a fortnight . . . Voltaire and everybody else are quite eclipsed by him.' 'Even his maid La [sic] Vasseur who is very homely and very awkward, is more talked of than the Princess of Morocco or the Countess of Egmont, on account of her fidelity and attachment toward him.' As Mlle Le Vasseur was still in Switzerland, it is not clear how Hume actually knew what she looked like, but he was plainly the recipient of Rousseau gossip from his *philosophe* friends. He went on, 'His very dog, who is no better than a coly [sic], has a name and reputation in the world.' (Hume might not have been so dismissive had Sultan been a socially acceptable spaniel.) De Luze remarked that the *gouvernante* was the chief cause of his leaving Neuchâtel: 'She passes as wicked and quarrelsome, and tattling.'

Robert Liston (a tutor to the sons of one of Hume's friends), who suffered badly from Rousseau fever, did gain access. On the morning of Rousseau's departure for London, Liston was introduced to him at the Hôtel Saint-Simon. This involved an encounter with Mme de Boufflers, ingenuously described by Liston as 'a very famous woman and a great protectress of men of learning' who 'made me some compliments'. Rousseau received him 'very well':

I was about an hour there, saw him dine, and had the honour to help him into the chaise. He said he would be glad to crack [converse] with me when I came to England &c. His person is very thin & delicate looking, his face, and especially his sharp black eyes, promise everything he has shown himself possessed of. His manners simple and affable.

Rousseau had initially seemed in no rush to leave Paris, but the mobs he attracted had begun to make him uneasy and he was becoming impatient to be alone. He wrote to de Luze, 'I do not know how much longer I can endure this public scene. Could you for pity's sake hasten our departure?'

In the absence of any agreeable alternative, Hume had at last resigned himself to going back to London and was also anxious for them to move on. The Duc de Choiseul, then in charge of the Admiralty but just about to become minister of war, had notified the Prince de Conti and the British Embassy that there was a limit to how much longer the authorities could ignore Rousseau's open defiance of the warrant and the authority of the *parlement*.

Grimm passed the news on to his readers: 'The police told him to leave without delay if he did not want to be arrested; in consequence, he left on 4 January, accompanied by Mr David Hume who was returning to England but proposed to come back to spend a lot of time in Paris.' To give them a breathing space from sightseers and well-wishers, Hume publicly announced their departure for 2 January while always planning it for the fourth.

Some of Hume's friends fretted that he had no idea what he was undertaking. After all, Diderot, d'Alembert and Grimm had previous experience of Rousseau. The Scotsman was duly warned about Rousseau's suspicious mind and persecution mania.

Hume sought out Mme de Verdelin, cross-examining her in his quest for reassurance. She wrote to Rousseau that Hume had said, 'I do not want to serve a man merely because he is celebrated. If he is virtuous and persecuted, I would devote myself to him. Are these stories true?' She managed to stiffen Hume's resolve, so she claimed to Rousseau. 'I commended him to your welfare. He is worthy of the trust . . . His soul is made for yours.'

Then, on the threshold of their journey, at about nine in the evening, Hume went straight from visiting Mme de Boufflers and Rousseau to see d'Holbach, presumably to make his final farewells. Their conversation took an unexpected turn. Apologizing for puncturing Hume's illusions, the baron warned him in chilling tones that he would soon be sadly disabused: 'You don't know your man. I will tell you plainly, you're warming a viper in your bosom.' Hume expostulated, but according to Mossner's colourful account, as Hume left, d'Holbach's words rang in his ears: 'You don't know your man, David, you don't know your man.'

D'Holbach was not the only observer filled with foreboding on Hume's behalf. On 2 January Walpole wrote to Lady Hervey:

> Mr Hume carries this letter and Rousseau to England. I wish the former may not repent having engaged with the latter, who contradicts and quarrels with all mankind, in order to obtain their admiration. I think both his means and his end below such a genius. If I had talents like his, I should despise any suffrage below my own standard, and should blush to owe any part of my fame to singularities and affectations.

On 4 January, in a letter to Lady Mary Coke, Walpole returned to the subject but in frivolous vein: 'Rousseau set out this morning for England. As he loves to contradict a whole nation, I suppose he will write for the present opposition. Pray tell me if he becomes the fashion.'

The little party, Hume, de Luze, Rousseau and Sultan, departed Paris in two post-chaises. As Mossner tells it, Rousseau had instructed de Luze, 'You will take your post chaise and Mr Hume will take his, and we shall change from time to time.' Presumably, Sultan insisted on running ahead for part of the way, and perched with Rousseau for the rest.

They passed four nights on the road, putting up successively at Senlis, Roye, Arras and Aine, before reaching Calais on 8 January. In either Senlis or Roye (accounts disagree), the three men had to share a room. During the night, Rousseau had an unnerving experience that preyed on his mind. He heard Hume muttering, repeatedly, '*Je tiens Jean-Jacques Rousseau.*' ['I hold Jean-Jacques Rousseau.'] Rousseau broke out in a cold sweat as he lay there, wakeful and listening.

In Calais, while they waited for the wind to come round in their favour, Hume mentioned the possibility of Rousseau's being given a pension from George III. Rousseau queried how he could accept one from George III when he had refused one from Frederick the Great. Hume maintained that the cases were quite different, though it is unclear where he thought the distinction lay. Rousseau said he would consult Earl Marischal. Hume also, in his words, 'exhorted' Rousseau to start on his memoirs. Rousseau said he had already started, and went on, 'I shall describe myself in such plain colours, that henceforth everyone may boast that he knows himself and Jean-Jacques Rousseau.' 'I believe', said Hume, 'that he intends seriously to draw his own picture in its true colours: but I believe at the same time that nobody knows himself less.'

After twelve storm-tossed hours, they finally made Dover on 11 January. Hume, now released from his seasickness, was struck by the apparent inconsistency between his guest's chronic complaints of illness and his staying in the open during the crossing. To Mme de Boufflers he remarked that though

Rousseau claimed to be infirm, he is 'one of the most robust men I know', and that he had passed the night in the voyage on deck, when the seamen were frozen to death, and he came to no harm.

They set out for London, breaking their journey at Canterbury and Dartford, and reached the capital on 13 January.

Rousseau's presence was news, immediately announced to their readers by the London papers. And, for once, Hume was in demand in the English capital: society was agog to see his prize.

9

A London Sensation

David Garrick in a favourite role, the asinine Lord Chalkstone

The English are such a mobbish people . . .
David Hume

Rousseau was all the rage. The papers trumpeted both his docking in Dover and his appearance in London. The *Gazetteer and New Daily Advertiser* revealed that, 'The ingenious Mr. R arrived in town last Monday in company with David Hume esq.' Intriguingly, the *London Chronicle* gave details of Rousseau's and Hume's itinerary on separate pages, as if they were in no way connected – possibly at Hume's request.

Crowds came on to the streets. Lionized in Paris, Hume now found himself, in the words of a Scottish friend, 'the show-er of the lion'. London society esteemed Rousseau's work, sympathized with his predicament, and congratulated itself on welcoming him. In Britain, the Swiss author enjoyed an unrivalled reputation – higher than in any other part of Europe. Almost all his works had received favourable reviews, especially *Héloïse* and *Émile*, and the British press had closely followed his persecution. Long extracts from *Héloïse* had been reproduced in the *London Chronicle*, where he was compared to Samuel Richardson. The *London Chronicle* had also published passages from *Émile* and urged mothers to breast-feed their children, though it warned readers that Rousseau mistook 'novelty of opinion for justness of thinking'.

Booksellers cashed in on the publicity, advertising Rousseau's books in the newspapers. Hume benefited; his *History* was also heavily promoted. Two papers that initially reported Hume's securing a place for Rousseau in Richmond, published a correction, identifying his proper address as Buckingham Street, just below the Strand on the north bank of the Thames.

The British were inordinately proud of their country as the land of tolerance and free speech. In *The Comedian* in 1732, Fielding wrote that free speech was 'that pure and perfect state of liberty which we enjoy in a degree superior to every foreign nation.' The Swiss exile reflected this self-image back to them. The *Public Advertiser* notified its readers that Rousseau had been

> brought into much trouble and vexation, both in Switzerland and in France, for having ventured to publish, in many works, his sentiments with a spirit and a freedom which cannot be done with impunity in any Kingdom or state except this blessed island. And 'tis with pleasure we find he has chosen an asylum amongst a people, who know how to respect one of his distinguished talents.

The significance of the papers at this period is difficult to exaggerate. The effective end of press licensing at the beginning of the century, improvements in technology, a reduction in costs and an explosion in literacy had created an unprecedented interest in books, magazines and papers. There was a boom in sales of both novels and works of non-fiction.

The British public's deepening love affair with newspapers – in the provinces as well as the capital – fundamentally altered the flow of information through society. In the capital, sixty newspapers were published. Readers could glut themselves on political news and comment, foreign news, Court news, crime news, news of births, marriages and deaths. There were campaigns for technological developments and agricultural developments – in 1766 the Society for the Encouragement of Arts,

Machines and Commerce offered twenty pounds for the best machine invented for slicing turnips. There were appointments, advertisements (given the over-abundance of prostitutes, an unsurprising number promoted cures or palliatives for venereal disease), theatre reviews, financial reports, shipping news, opinion and, naturally, gossip about notables. The recognized use of coded references protected the purveyors of scandal and vituperative personal attacks on public figures. Hume worried about the growing power of the fourth estate and its lack of deference – in a private letter he railed against 'the abuse of liberty'.

In the literally rambling novel *Humphrey Clinker*, which Hume's compatriot Tobias Smollett started in 1768, the focal character, well-to-do Squire Bramble says:

> I have observed, for some time, that the public papers are become the infamous vehicles of the most cruel and perfidious defamation; every rancorous knave – every desperate incendiary, that can afford to spend half-a-crown or three shillings, may skulk behind the press of a newsmonger, and have a stab at the first character in the kingdom, without running the least hazard of detection or punishment.

And the real-life Horace Walpole, in the postscript to his *Memoirs*, complained that the daily and evening newspapers 'printed every outrageous libel that was sent to them'.

However, the number of press outlets, the freedom of comment and the avid readership meant that London was the celebrity capital of Europe, leading the way in the culture and practice of instant fame.

For the moment at least, Rousseau was a figure of intense fascination. He was a literary giant, the subject of prurient rumours, the source of idle chatter in the coffee houses. On

Monday, 13 January, the day of his arrival in the capital, the *Public Advertiser* reported, 'All the world are eager to see this man, who by his singularity, has drawn himself into much trouble; he appears abroad but seldom, and dresses like an Armenian, probably on account of an infirmity which has remained with him since the operation he underwent for a retention.'

Knocking on his door at Buckingham Street was a string of admirers. They included General Conway, the Duke of York (Rousseau was out), and the Prince of Wales. George Harcourt, Viscount Nuneham, a fervid follower of Rousseau, called on him, as did George III's brother-in-law (the Hereditary Prince of Brunswick), and the Reverend Richard Penneck, keeper of the Reading Room of the British Library. There were dinners to go to, for instance an invitation to the British Museum with the under-librarian Dr Matthew Maty, who was instrumental in establishing the Library's collection of portraits. (Rousseau's cousin came to London and also paid him a visit.)

Hume was struck by the extent of the attention. 'It is incredible the enthusiasm for him in Paris and the curiosity in London,' he wrote to his brother in February, 'I should desire no better fortune than to have the privilege of showing him to all I please.' 'Showing him' echoes Hume's appraisal of his guest as 'the most singular man surely in the world', but the distinction – in Paris, enthusiasm; in London, curiosity – has a spiteful quality. Hume, meanwhile, must have been missing the warm embrace of Paris. Rockingham's *Memoirs* record, '[Hume] went to France a plain, unaffected Scotchman. He came back with the airs and feeling of a Frenchman.' He had a habit of launching into encomiums about the French, the *Memoirs* complain, comparing their loyalty and 'their peaceable demeanour with the turbulence of his own countrymen.'

In the same letter to his brother, Hume described the public tumult when, on 23 January, he accompanied Rousseau to the royal performance at Drury Lane Theatre.

The British monarch and the king of thespians – George III and David Garrick – both wanted a glimpse of the city's most distinguished newcomer. Garrick sent an invitation to Rousseau via Hume. It was so spontaneous that Mrs Garrick was obliged to clear her husband's private box by putting off earlier guests.

That night the theatre was packed. Garrick was a playwright and impresario as well as an actor. He had taken over the management of the Drury Lane company in 1747, rebuilding the theatre and restoring its theatrical and commercial fortunes. The pre-show atmosphere was boisterous: many theatregoers had to wait a couple of hours for tickets, and there would be a surge when the doors finally opened. In years gone by, people had died in the crush.

Milling around the theatre, the social gamut of London life was on display. Drury Lane was a bottleneck for coaches and chairs; attempts to reduce the anarchy by instituting some kind of one-way system had so far come to nothing. Outside the building, prostitutes plied their trade – inside too, and not just in the foyer. Several years after Rousseau's West End experience, *The Times* declared that the boxes at Drury Lane Theatre were 'licensed stews for the abandoned and profligate to meet and pair off from'. Could not theatre management at least bar such action from 'a less glaring spot'? asked the paper. Pickpockets, normally boys about twelve years old, worked the crowds, and were guaranteed rich pickings from the nightly gathering of the well-to-do, dressed-up and preening.

Rousseau almost did not make it. At the very last minute, he flew into a sudden panic: what if Sultan escaped into the streets and lost his bearings while Rousseau was out? There was no Le Vasseur to keep the dog company. Hume, exasperated but ever the rationalist, proposed a solution. Why not lock Sultan up in the bedroom? This they did, though the dog's howling was almost too much for his master to bear. In a letter to one of his Parisian connections, Hume wrote,

> I caught him [Rousseau] in my arms, and told him, that Mrs Garrick had dismissed another company in order to make room for him; that the King and Queen were expecting to see him; and without a better reason than Sultan's impatience, it would be ridiculous to disappoint them. Partly by these reasons and partly by force, I engaged him to proceed.

There was much to look forward to. This season (1765–66) had been boosted by Garrick's return from two years abroad on the grand tour, complete with prints of himself to hand out to admirers. The actor's mobile features famously enabled him to shift in an instant from emotion to emotion, and he was equally at ease in all dramatic genres – though Reynolds's 1761 painting *Garrick Between Tragedy and Comedy* shows him torn between those two. Garrick himself thought comedy required more skill.

In 1740, a year before his first role, as Richard III, established him as an acting prodigy, Garrick had won a reputation as a playwright with his comedy *Lethe*. Initially, he performed three of its twelve parts – a poet, a drunk, and a Frenchman. But it was a play he constantly reworked, adding topical material, and in 1756 a new character – Lord Chalkstone (colloquial for kidney stone), a wealthy, amoral and ludicrous nobleman whom Garrick was to play forty-eight times in his career and was to play again. The comedy was designed to leave the audience with a warm glow, and it culminated in a jolly musical chorus.

However, it was only ever intended as the frothy, light dessert of a double-bill, what was known as the afterpiece. On

23 January, the moralistic main course was *The Tragedy of Zara*, written three decades earlier by Aaron Hill, whom Pope had satirized in his paean to dullness, *The Dunciad*. Garrick, wearing a long white wig, played an old man, Luzignan, a captured crusader. It was one of his cherished parts. For years he had appeared in the role at least once a season. Zara was played by the well-known actress Mrs Yates.

Ironically, in the light of Rousseau's attendance, *Zara* was an adaptation of a play, *Zaïre*, by his arch-enemy Voltaire. And in his preface to the play, Hill begged Voltaire's indulgence for his alterations, the motives for which 'are to be found in the turn of our national difference'. In fact, Voltaire had approved the translation. Garrick further amended it to avoid offence to Christians.

The drama is set in thirteenth-century Jerusalem; the background is the Crusades. Zara is a young woman who was captured as a child and brought up in the seraglio of the Sultan, who subsequently falls in love with her. She persuades him to release Luzignan who is, it transpires, Zara's natural father. The tragedy lies in Zara's eventual murder by an incensed Sultan, under the mistaken impression that she is guilty of infidelity.

Despite the presence of Garrick on stage and the King in the royal box, it was Rousseau who attracted all the attention. He was in his robe, and sporting his distinctive fur bonnet and gold braid. The *London Evening Post* reported:

> Thursday, just as their Majesties came into Drury Lane theatre to see *The Tragedy of Zara*, the celebrated John James Rousseau made his appearance in the upper box, over the stage box, fronting their Majesties. He was dressed in a foreign dress and accompanied Mr Hume. The crowd was so great at getting into the theatre that a great number of Gen-

tlemen lost their hats and wigs, and Ladies their cloaks, &c. There was a great disturbance in the Upper Gallery at the above theatre, which prevented Mrs Yates and Miss Plym from going on, just as they had opened the piece.

What the commotion was about is unclear. Another notice reported that it began as soon as Garrick emerged to deliver the prologue, whereupon there was 'a general clap and a loud huzza, – and there was such a noise from the house being so crowded, very few heard anything of the prologue. – As soon as the play began there was a great disturbance in the gallery, and some called out, Guards Guards!' It was standard practice for two grenadiers carrying muskets to be stationed by the stage door.

Rousseau must have marvelled at such rowdiness. Social class dictated who sat where. The boxes went to the rich; the gentlemen were in the pit; the tradesmen took seats in the middle gallery, while the cheap upper gallery was for hoi polloi, who would take in oranges for refreshment and use the dusted, bewigged heads below as targets for the peel. (Sometimes they would throw more dangerous missiles: in 1755, a young lady suffered a serious injury from a sturdy piece of cheese.) Fashionable ladies wore hats, and this season there was an animated debate in the newspapers about their size, with bitter complaints that they obscured vision. Fights and riots frequently erupted among all sections of the audience. Garrick had himself caused two violent mutinies: once on the eve of the Seven Years War when he put on a production with French players, and again in 1763, when he stopped half-price seats for late-comers. Boswell always took a cudgel with him to the middle of the pit.

That night, the actors would have had to fight for the audience's concentration. While Rousseau watched the stage, the King and Queen scrutinized Rousseau, and Hume scrutinized the King and Queen: 'I observed their majestys to look at him more than at the players.' According to *Lloyd's Evening Post*, Rousseau was so absorbed in the production that he hung over the front of the box while Mrs Garrick, anxious that he might go the way of the orange peel, clung to his clothes.

For Drury Lane, the night of 23 January was a triumph, and for Garrick personally the double-bill brought critical acclaim. 'It is impossible to express how finely he played both characters,' enthused one paper. After the performance, 'the celebrated Mr Rousseau', as he was invariably tagged in the press, went the short distance to Garrick's town house overlooking the Thames at 5 Adelphi Terrace, where the Garricks hosted a supper. Oliver Goldsmith was among the guests, though no unrestrained admirer of Rousseau: 'Rousseau of Geneva: A professed man-hater, or more properly speaking, a philosopher enraged with one half of mankind, because they unavoidably make the other half unhappy.'

The thespian had once affirmed that with his performance as Luzignan he aimed to make people cry. He certainly succeeded that night. At supper, according to *Lloyd's Evening Post*, Rousseau was effusive: 'Sir, you have made me shed tears at your tragedy, and smile at your comedy, though I scarce understand a word of your language.'

His open enjoyment of the show might seem inconsistent with his philosophy. Theatre was a form of entertainment that he had condemned. Among his objections, perhaps the most trenchant was his conviction that the theatre drags us into an amoral mire. At the theatre we cry at the tragedy lived out on the stage, and our emotional response creates a warm glow of self-satisfaction. Then, when we leave, we dry our eyes and carry on as normal; perhaps we behave even worse than before. The stage, thought Rousseau, turns us from agents to witnesses, and the desire to fight inequality and injustice drains out, too, with our tears.

However, Rousseau would not have conceded that his enjoyment of *Zara* and *Lethe* was hypocritical, believing that he himself was beyond corruption, whether by theatre or by wealth. In any case, it was only in the ideal state, with its ideal citizens, that theatre would be superfluous and injurious. In the swarming cities of the world, where human life had already been soiled, pragmatism was the rule: 'When it is no longer a question of leading people to do good, one may at least distract them from doing evil.'

Whatever his display in Drury Lane, and although Paris had made plain his (short-term) love of public parade, Rousseau professed he had come to Britain in search of peace and anonymity. Even after the French capital, his first exposure to the dynamic, anarchic city that was London must have given him culture shock. He was never likely to feel at home amidst the noise, the bustle, the fervour, the surging life and the self-regard of the greatest, the richest, the fastest-growing city on earth.

A contemporary map of the capital announced itself as being 'A plan of London on the same scale as that of Paris', before boastfully concluding that London, at 5,455 acres, exceeded Paris by 1,427 acres. Indeed, London was the first trading centre of the age, and expanding pell-mell, its population increasing from 300,000 in 1700 to 750,000 when George III ascended the throne in 1760, and approaching a million in 1800.

The capital had become the lodestone for the talented and ambitious, foreign trade producing new wealth and shaking up the class order. In *Humphrey Clinker*, Squire Bramble paints a picture of ploughboys swarming down to the metropolis to enter liveried service, since every trader and attorney now kept servants. Commerce created bourgeois employment: finance, trade, bureaucracy.

A manic construction boom was under way, ushering in a townscape of grand and elegant squares. The demand for bricks was such that they were delivered hot from the kiln – in 1766, several carriages carrying them burst into flames. Green fields and orchards clung on north of Tyburn Road (now Oxford Street), but the potential for development possessed their ducal landowners. The government began to bring in the services the town needed. Every month, there appeared better drains, more pavements (the landmark Westminster Paving Act was passed in 1762), more street lights. Visitors from out of town as well as foreigners raised their eyes to the sky, struck dumb by the brightness.

Rousseau would have been quite unaccustomed to the din and the energy. Up from his country estate, Squire Bramble is assailed by clamour 'at all hours of day and night: watchmen calling the hour and thundering at every door'. London was a city on the go – and at all hours. Pierre Jean Grosley's *A Tour to London* in 1772, observed how 'the English walk very fast; their thoughts being entirely engrossed by business, they are very punctual to their appointments, and those, who happen to be in their way, are sure to be sufferers by it.' Speed's cousin was discourtesy: there was no time for patience or politeness.

Of course, there was a degree of silence in the squares and the lawyers' inns of court, and in side streets such as the one off the Strand running down to the river, noted by an eighteenth-century traveller, where there was 'so pleasing a calm' that it struck the senses. This could be Buckingham Street. And it would not have been surprising if, for much of the time, Rousseau had closeted himself in his lodgings there.

His was one of four smart streets, each named after a different part of the landowner's name: George Villiers, Duke of Buckingham. ('Of' was an alley.) Hume had procured lodgings for them through Hume's wine-merchant friend John Stewart, who lived in the same street. Less than a minute's walk away were the steps leading down to the Thames. A century before the construction of the Victoria embankment, the river was much wider and shallower, and the primary route for the nation's foreign trade: tea, coffee, sugar, cocoa, rum, rice, tobacco, hemp, and tallow, china, iron and linen – all flowed in a constant stream of ship-borne commerce.

In the other direction, also a minute away, was the Strand, which, eastwards, merged into Fleet Street. Among its myriad shops were drapers, haberdashers, hatters and hosiers, jostling for space with tailors, wine merchants, cabinet-makers, pawnbrokers and booksellers. Rousseau would have seen at least two booksellers stocking his own works, especially *Émile* and *Héloïse*. Printing and journalism were already clustering around Fleet Street, as were workshops making precision instruments, such as those used in navigation and astronomy.

It was not a pleasant stroll down the Strand, deep in mud and filth. And there was an ever present threat of violence. When Rousseau came to London, the capital was still in the grip of a crime epidemic linked to the return of soldiers from the Seven Years War. The voice of working people with political, religious or economic grievances was heard through endemic rioting. The night Rousseau and Hume reached town, there was an altercation on the Strand, close to Rousseau's temporary home. Imports of French silk had undercut homemade British produce, sparking riots among the silk-weavers who worked at home around Spitalfields. Many weavers were emigrating to Boston, New York and Philadelphia. A march on Parliament in 1765 had won a ban on foreign silk imports. The newspaper recorded the altercation:

A gentleman detected a fellow in throwing *aqua fortis* upon a gentlewoman's gown, as she passed along the Strand, and a crowd soon gathering, he pleaded in excuse, that he was a poor journeyman weaver, who, with a wife and four children, in this severe season, were almost starving to death, for want of employment, and that the lady's gown on which he had thrown the *aqua fortis* was French wrought silk, the wearing of which was contrary to law, he was thereupon suffered to depart without molestation.

But however genteel Buckingham Street or enticing the nearby shops and coffee houses, however alluring the 'see-and-be-seen' parade of the fashionable in nearby St James's Park, for Rousseau the pressing issue was, yet again, where to settle. He liked neither London nor being the focus of attention, and he became preoccupied with moving to somewhere quieter, and as quickly as possible. Hume's frustrating search for a haven acceptable to Rousseau contributed to his growing disenchantment with the guest he swore he would love all his days.

Together, they scouted out various options. In Paris, it had been reported that Rousseau would live with a French market-gardener in Fulham, just a couple of miles to the west of London, but the place proved too small and dirty, with an invalid occupying one of the two spare beds. An agreement was then reached for an ancient farmhouse in Wales. Rousseau liked the sound of its remoteness and the savagery of the countryside. However, the farm had a sitting tenant and could not be made ready in time.

A more likely prospect was residence with a wealthy devotee of Rousseau's, a Mr Townshend – 'a man of four or five thousand a year', according to Hume. Rousseau could state his own terms. This plan foundered over Mlle Le Vasseur. Rousseau insisted that his *gouvernante* be permitted to dine at Mrs Townshend's table. That was not to Mrs Townshend's taste. Hume had still not met Le Vasseur, but he grumbled to Mme de

Boufflers about the havoc she was causing, even at a distance of hundreds of miles. 'This woman forms the chief encumbrance to his settlement . . . she governs him absolutely as a nurse does a child. In her absence his dog has obtained that ascendant. His affection for that creature is above all expression or conception.'

Rousseau then rejected the offer of a house on the Isle of Wight: the island was too expensive, with too many people and too few trees. The exile was aware that his finicky approach to choosing somewhere to lay his head must have been wearying to Hume: 'You see I am grown difficult with respect to my host,' he confided to Mme de Boufflers.

Rousseau was right about Hume's feelings. Those who knew Hume well also sensed his growing impatience. A member of his Scottish network, William Rouet, recorded that 'David Hume is busy to get Rousseau disposed of. Till then he is a kind of prisoner.' Rouet was writing only three days after Rousseau's arrival. Hume was 'confoundedly weary of his pupil, as he calls him; he is full of oddities and even absurdities.'

Among those oddities was Rousseau's attitude to a young Swiss who was staying in Hume's regular London quarters in Lisle Street: Louis-François Tronchin, the son of the detested 'trickster' of Geneva, Dr Théodore Tronchin. This Scottish-run boarding house might have been a recommendation of Adam Smith's: he had taught Louis-François at Glasgow University. According to Rouet, Rousseau 'looks upon Tronchin's being here as a spy set by Geneva on him; and his accidentally being lodged where Hume always used to lodge (and where he is to come as soon as Rousseau is fixed in the country) confirms him in this foolish conceit.' To Adam Smith Hume disparaged Rousseau as 'a little variable and fanciful'.

In other circles, regard for Rousseau was also waning. On 5 February, Lady Sarah Bunbury took up her pen to write to

Lady Susan O'Brian: 'By way of news Mr Rousseau is all the talk: all I can hear of him is that he wears a pelisse and fur cap . . . His dressing particularly I think is very silly . . . he sees few people, and is to go and live at a farm in Wales, where he shall see nothing but mountains and wild goats.'

Indeed, Rousseau had had enough of London. On 31 January, he went to lodge in the village of Chiswick, west of London. Hume returned, one imagines with relief, to his rooms in Lisle Street and its familiar faces and accents.

Rousseau could hope not only for a measure of tranquillity but the longed for arrival of his life-time companion.

What are we to make of Thérèse Le Vasseur, and her relationship with Rousseau? Among his biographers, Maurice Cranston was no fan: 'an extraordinarily ignorant woman'. Another biographer, J. Churton Collins, terms her 'that wretched woman'. She has been called poisonous, coarse and degraded, a harridan, a shrew, even a Lady Macbeth figure. She is held responsible for aggravating her lover's rows and inflaming his paranoia. She 'had just enough intellect to assist the cunning of her depraved heart', according to David Hume.

Whether her detractors, all of them male, were justified is debatable. Some French noblewomen, Mme de Luxembourg for one, treated her with sympathy and kindness. But the obvious challenge to these depictions is to ask why Rousseau then stuck by her. And the obvious answer is that she had many virtues. Foremost among them was her loyalty. Living with Rousseau cannot have been easy. He was often short of money, he was stubborn, he was irritable and morose, and he made no secret of his lust for other women. He was also, by political necessity, a wanderer. Yet, throughout, Thérèse stayed at his side, forgiving this man of sensibility his infidelities, his idiosyncrasies and his often crass selfishness. In his later life,

Rousseau had abruptly to uproot and flee, travelling in haste and alone, and then sending for her only after establishing himself in alien territory – alien for her, above all, a Parisian scullery maid, away not just from the comforts of the familiar streets of Paris, but its easy banter, its patois and gossip. Still, James Boswell reported that despite the hardships and deprivations of such a life, Mlle Le Vasseur told him, 'I would not give up my place to be Queen of France.'

The first forced parting was at Montmorency. In the *Confessions*, he describes this farewell in affecting terms. Rousseau was with the Luxembourgs when the marshal sent for

> my poor 'aunt', who was consumed with cruel anxiety as to my fate, and as to what would become of her, and was momentarily expecting the officers of the law, without any idea of how to behave or how she should answer them . . . When she saw me she gave a piercing cry, and threw herself into my arms. Oh friendship, union of hearts and habits, dearest intimacy! In this sweet and cruel moment were concentrated so many days of happiness, tenderness, and peace spent together, and it was with deep pain that I felt the wrench of our first separation when we had scarcely been out of one another's sight for a single day in almost seventeen years . . . When I embraced her at the moment of parting, I felt the most extraordinary stirring within me, and said to her in a burst of emotion that was, alas, prophetic: 'My dear, you must arm yourself with courage. You have shared the good days of my prosperity. It now remains for you, since you wish it, to share my miseries.'

In some ways, Le Vasseur was the personification of Rousseau's idealized primitive being. As a domestic servant, she was close to the lowest rung in the social ladder (half a step above vagrants and prostitutes). That Rousseau felt tremendous affection for, and gratitude to, her is clear. And for good reason. She looked after him, nursing him during his bouts of illness, bringing him his chamber pot, cleaning his catheters, sewing, cooking (she was a first-rate cook of plain country fare, thick soups, veal, rabbit, pâté). Rousseau acknowledged his debt to her. In early 1763, when his bladder complaint worsened, the agony was such that he feared he was dying. He drew up his will, bequeathing her everything and 'only regretting that I cannot better repay the twenty years of care and devotion that she has given me, during which she has received no wages.' When he fled Switzerland, and was still unsure where he was going to end up, he assured her, 'Of all the choices which are open to me I shall prefer that which will bring us together most quickly.' Rousseau knew her better than anybody. His descriptions of her character, 'amiable', with 'a gentle disposition', 'a beautiful soul', 'an excellent heart', are diametrically at odds with those of her critics. We can assume among those critics a degree of intellectual and class snobbery.

Was she attractive? Reports differ. Boswell certainly found her so, but in 1761 a Hungarian count, Joseph Teleki, who visited Rousseau, related, 'A girl, or rather a woman, dined with us . . . she was not beautiful, so no one would suspect that she was something else.' Unlike so many of Rousseau's female acquaintances, she had worked long days of relentless labour in kitchens and washhouses that would have left her with coarse skin and roughened hands.

Theirs was not a conventional love affair. Rousseau felt little passion for Le Vasseur – and she little for him. They both saved their ardour for others. Although they produced five offspring, by 1761 Rousseau confessed that because of the deterioration in his bladder, they had been living together for years as 'brother and sister'. His attachment had become one of affection and habit rather than love. The terms Rousseau deployed to describe their relationship excluded a sexual connection. As well as 'sister', he talked of her as his aunt and his *gouvernante* – housekeeper or steward, in charge of the household. Still, in the *Confessions* (written after a twenty-five-year relationship), he said she was emotionally so 'cool' that he had no need to fear other men.

But if there was no passion, their personalities meshed perfectly. They almost never argued, though Rousseau once became upset when he discovered that his *gouvernante* and her mother, whom he looked after for years despite finding her an intense irritant, had not told him that they had accepted an allowance from Grimm and Diderot. 'How could she, from whom I have never kept a secret, keep one from me? Can one conceal anything from a person one loves?' However, such complaints were rare.

Never wanting to be dependent upon any other person, Rousseau made a single exception: Le Vasseur. In his autobiography, when describing his becoming acquainted with her, he explained that his strongest 'most inextinguishable need' was for *intimacy*. And it was this he sought in the scullery maid; though this need was so deep that even 'the closest union of bodies could not be enough for it'.

Rousseau has been accused of relegating women in his writings to a secondary function in society. In *Émile*, Sophie is not educated to the same degree as the eponymous pupil – her skills of reading and writing will not be so useful – though Rousseau thought she should receive some education, not least so she could converse with her man. Julie in *Héloïse* embraces her destiny: 'I am a wife and mother; I know my place and I keep to it.' On the other hand, at the time many women found his idealized notion of lover and mother appealing, and his female literary creations (like Julie and Sophie) were often stronger than the men – if more subtle and cunning in how they enforced their will.

So, what intimate conversations would Rousseau and Le Vasseur have had? What conversations of any kind? Although Rousseau sent graceful letters to Le Vasseur, reporting on his condition and giving her domestic instructions, she could scarcely read and was constantly making elementary mistakes. When we are first introduced to her in the *Confessions*, there is a tone of perverse pride in the author's account of her abject ignorance. It is quite possible that he took delight in defying social conventions and scandalizing his well-educated, well-dressed and well-spoken friends.

> Thanks to [Thérèse], I lived happily, as far as the course of events permitted. At first I tried to improve her mind, but my efforts were useless. Her mind is what nature has made it; culture and training are without influence upon it. I am not ashamed to confess that she had never learnt how to read properly, although she can write fairly well . . . She has never been able to give the twelve months of the year in correct order, and does not know a single figure, in spite of all the trouble I have taken to teach her.

That he remained with this intellectually disadvantaged creature brought censure and bewilderment from friends and acquaintances. In public, he did not treat his *gouvernante* well. Occasionally he was eager to show her off, like a rich man defiantly displaying his conspicuously tattered clothes. More often than not, however, he treated her like a below-stairs servant. Indeed, many visitors to the Rousseau household assumed that that is what in fact she was. When Rousseau had guests, she was routinely dispatched to the kitchen or scullery. However, that was *his* choice. As we have seen over the Townshends' refusal to dine with her, it was quite impermissible for anybody else to humiliate her in the same way.

So far, wherever Le Vasseur had followed him, French had

been the local language. Now her constancy and his dependency would bring the Parisian scullery maid to Chiswick, and exposure to a totally foreign land, language and culture.

10

Down by the Riverside

James Boswell: he looked after Mlle Le Vasseur on her journey to England

Kindness is in our power even when fondness is not.
Samuel Johnson

*A young gentleman, very good-humoured, very agreeable,
and very mad.*
David Hume on James Boswell

The choice of Chiswick remains a mystery. Hume told Mme de
Barbentane, 'He would not stay in London above a fortnight. I
settled him in a village about six miles from it; he is impatient
to remove from thence, though the place and the house are
very agreeable to him . . .'

The simplest explanation is that Chiswick was the next village up-river from Fulham and Rousseau could afford it. But
Hume would have been familiar with the location because his
former pupil, the mad Lord Annandale, had a property there.
Chiswick also enjoyed an historic reputation as a refuge – principally from the plague. It was close enough to London to keep
in touch while detached from the stews of the capital: its air
clean, the atmosphere bucolic, the gardens shaded by tall trees.

For Rousseau, it was a staging post. He informed Du Peyrou
that he still intended to go to the farmhouse in Wales, but
would wait for Le Vasseur in Chiswick, where they would benefit from a few weeks of a serenity impossible in London
because of the overpowering throng. He complimented the
English on their manners. They knew how to show their
esteem without fawning – quite unlike the populace of
Neuchâtel.

Chiswick nestles snugly on an oxbow bend in the Thames. In
1766, it had a population of about 1,000, and was surrounded
by farms and market gardens. Two other small villages lay to

the north west, and the three constituted the local parish. Five miles from the capital, it could be reached by foot (the river path led through Chelsea and Fulham), by boat (about an hour and a half), or by post-chaise, along the main road to the west – a route notorious for highwaymen.

Running parallel to the riverbank was the main street, Chiswick Mall; joining it at a right-angle, Church Street was home to a row of small stores that precariously rubbed up against one another, like a set of dominoes on the verge of collapse. At the junction of the two roads was (and is) St Nicholas's Church, dating from the eleventh century. The less well off, the bargemen and domestic staff, occupied higgledy-piggledy cottages round the back of the church. But elsewhere in the village, several mansions and a number of other substantial dwellings, many dating from the seventeenth century, bespoke affluence and substance. One of the pre-eminent painters of the century, William Hogarth, had a country retreat in Chiswick and was buried there in 1765: his wife, sister and mother-in-law lived on in his redbrick house. (The garden still contains its original mulberry tree – bearing the scars of a World War II bomb.)

However, there was little grandeur about Rousseau's lodgings. Somehow he found rooms with, in Rousseau's phrase, an 'honest grocer, well regarded by his peers', James Pullein, his wife Elizabeth and their two children.

Pullein's will indicates he was either deeply devout or feared the consequences of his business dealings. He was certainly apprehensive about the salvation of his soul, which he hoped could be entrusted to his 'dearest Saviour and Redeemer Jesus Christ'. As a grocer he would have sold dry provisions, flour, coffee, tea, sugar. The family probably occupied premises near Church Street, among a cluster of stores; the archives suggest they lived over the business. The 1766 rate books point to this being no ordinary shop. Its rateable value (known as the Over-seers Rate) was £16 – a figure more than twice that of the majority of houses in Chiswick.

The indications are that the Pulleins, who had only recently been living in a larger house, were in financial straits, one pos-sible explanation for their taking in a lodger. Unusually, they had arranged to stagger one of the required taxes – the church-warden rate – over four quarters, rather than settle it in one payment as was the usual practice. Rates funded a variety of social services, such as the local workhouse for the destitute, and paid for the ongoing battle to exterminate vermin, which were destroying crops and other produce. At the time the prickly Genevan was in the village, Chiswick was also overrun by hedgehogs. Sparrows were a terrible nuisance, too. The problem was so bad that the parish authorities placed a boun-ty on the pests' heads: four pence for each hedgehog, a meagre two pence for a dozen sparrow heads.

Rousseau seems to have fitted quickly into the Pullein fami-ly. He sat in the shop, teaching the daughter French. When Pullein's son went to Paris to learn the language (for his future career), Rousseau asked his publisher, Pierre Guy, to help him locate a cheap *pension* – or *demi-pension* 'as the English never take supper'. The boy's mother, said Rousseau, had been very attentive and he wanted to be of service to her. He thought Elizabeth Pullein 'a wife of merit'. Guy should do what he could without burdening his time or purse, and he, Rousseau, 'would count it as done for me'.

However pleasing the Pullein family, the village itself was scarcely the haven of peace he sought. The shopping area near Church Street was the busiest and noisiest part. Within a three-minute walk there were at least four inns. There were two large breweries, from which arose a constant rumble of barrels being rolled and loaded on to carts. Next door was a slaughterhouse, where animals squealed their way to the butcher's knife.

Then there were the idlers and gawpers. Reports, perhaps apocryphal, had both locals and day-trippers from the metropolis coming to stare at the persecuted lion as he sat in the grocer's shop. At least for Pullein, it was said, this had a beneficial effect: the constant traffic brought an upturn in business.

Unlike in London, however, Rousseau could put the din behind him, going for long walks by the river and through the fields, and indulging his passion for botany. Apparently, he was taken botanizing by a professor at the request of George III's favourite, the Earl of Bute: the former prime minister was a keen botanist and laid the foundation for the Royal Botanical Garden at Kew, just across the river from Chiswick. According to Hume's biographer, John Hill Burton, the professor was

> just explaining something about marine plants being acrid, when a cockney picnic party of youths, dressed as sailors, landed. Rousseau instantly took to his heels! The professor, being responsible for his safe restoration, followed, and after a considerable chase, succeeded in running him down. Rousseau, seeing that there were no other pursuers, passed the matter off by the observation that marine men were acrid.

In Chiswick, he was also away from Hume's fellow lodger in Lisle Street, Louis-François Tronchin. The young man (who was not unsympathetic to Rousseau) was well aware of his fellow Genevan's feelings: he told a friend that the Tronchin name was odious to Rousseau, and that Rousseau believed he (Louis-François) might have come to spy on his conduct, to persecute him, and even to assassinate him. Tronchin must have informed his father, the physician Dr Théodore Tronchin, who replied at the beginning of March that he was not surprised.

[Rousseau's] pride and his mistrust torment him. These are two demons who pursue him and pursue him everywhere. He knows us little if he thinks we pursue him too. I pity him. I know of no one more ill-starred. He has lost his friends and disturbed his country. The remorse that tears his spirit pursues him and pursues him everywhere. He fears me as God's rage. Because he knows I understand him.

Rousseau had been Dr Tronchin's patient and friend until July 1759. Their breach came when Tronchin was urging Rousseau to return to Geneva from his solitary life in France and asked Rousseau how it was 'that the proclaimed friend of mankind is no more the friend of men?'

But if distance from the young Tronchin promoted Rousseau's peace of mind, Chiswick brought still greater relief: for there at his side, at last, was his *gouvernante*. It had been four months since he had seen her in Isle St Pierre, by far the longest period they had been apart in over two decades. He had missed her and entreated her to join him. She had reached her home, Paris, but, not unnaturally, was frightened of journeying across the Channel to Britain.

A solution presented itself. However, withheld from Rousseau – for ever – were the exact details of her journey to England. And for good reason.

The solution had materialized in the shape of lusty, young James Boswell.

He was then at the end of his European tour and was passing through Paris some three weeks after Hume and Rousseau had left it. Visiting John Wilkes on Monday, 27 January, he picked up a copy of the *St. James's Chronicle* and saw that his mother had died. That evening he sought solace in a brothel. A letter arrived from his father the next day, confirming the bad news and asking his son to come home. Boswell was 'quite stupefied'. On Wednesday, having discovered Le Vasseur was in town, he went in search of her at the Hôtel de Luxembourg in the rue St Marc, where she was staying with the first lady in waiting to the Duchesse de Luxembourg. Le Vasseur shared her fears about her trip to London. 'If only we could travel together,' she said. That was exactly what he had come to propose, Boswell replied. She and Rousseau had been in regular contact. She showed Boswell a couple of letters from him. Apparently she could read well enough to follow his instructions on how to wash his new shirts, and to heed a warning about the future. 'Resign yourself to suffering a great deal.' 'Quackery,' commented Boswell.

In a depressed state of mind, preoccupied with thoughts of his mother, Boswell set out with his companion on Friday, 31 January.

There is no direct record of what followed *en route* to London. Boswell's *Journal* entries for the first eleven days of February 1766 vanished. A slip of paper took their place with the laconic comment, 'Reprehensible Passage', written by one of Boswell's literary executors. They were reconstructed by Colonel Ralph Isham, who had conserved the Scotsman's papers and must have read the appropriate passages: according to Frank Brady and Frederick Pottle, editors of Boswell's papers, the story is 'gleaned from his notes'.

Boswell had not planned a seduction. But on their second night on the road they slept together.

His initial attempt was 'a fiasco', and it was only after Le Vasseur comforted him that he regained some strength. He expected her plaudits – was he not youthful and ardent compared with Rousseau? Nevertheless, the next morning, he received a damning verdict on his performance: 'I allow that you are a hardy and vigorous lover, but you have no art.' Seeing his crestfallen face, she offered to give him lessons. That night he had to fortify himself with a bottle of red wine. Her advice was to be ardent but gentle, and not to hurry. Also, he should make better use of his hands. He wrote that she rode him 'agitated, like a bad rider galloping downhill'. When he grew fed up with the technical instruction, he tried to turn the conversation back to Rousseau – to hear some of his *dicta philosophi* – but this only bored her. It was a mistake, he reflected, to get entangled with an old man's mistress.

Rousseau, meanwhile, was worried. On 6 February he wrote to Mme de Boufflers – surely they should have arrived in England by now?

Le Vasseur and Boswell sailed into Dover on Tuesday, 11 February, and went straight to bed. His final entry of the voyage summed up the outcome, and perhaps restored his pride: 'Wednesday, 12 February. Yesterday morning had gone to bed early, and had done it once: thirteen in all. Was really affectionate to her.' As they were together for ten days, that is an impressive but not exceptional statistic.

They ate their first meal of the day – beefsteaks – late in the afternoon in Rochester. The night of 12 February, Le Vasseur probably stayed at Hume's. On 13 February, Boswell 'went to Mlle Le Vasseur, with whom was David Hume', breakfasted, then escorted her to Chiswick. On that journey Boswell gave his word that he would keep their affair a secret, until either Rousseau or Le Vasseur had passed away.

Boswell had not set eyes on Rousseau for a year and a half, and though they enthusiastically embraced, the younger man was disappointed and shocked by how aged and weak the exile looked. They had a perfunctory discussion: Rousseau talked of moving to Wales, and Boswell enquired whether Scotland had any claim over him, to which Rousseau replied, 'I shall act like the kings; I shall put my body in one place, and my heart in another.'

Leaving Le Vasseur in Chiswick, Boswell kept his widowed father waiting a little longer and scurried straight to the Mitre tavern off Fleet Street to renew his ties with Dr Johnson. Johnson promptly rebuked him for spending time with Wilkes and Rousseau. Did Johnson really see Rousseau as a bad man? asked Boswell. 'Sir,' the doctor rejoined, 'Rousseau is a very bad man. I would sooner sign a sentence for his transportation than that of any felon who has gone from the Old Bailey these many years. Yes, I should like to have him work in the plantations.'

A month later Earl Marischal, having heard about his reunion with Le Vasseur, wrote to Rousseau, 'I rejoice with you on the arrival of Mlle Le Vasseur, and with Mr Boswell on the pleasure he has received in being able to do you a service; he is a truly honourable man, a perfect gentleman.'

Not long after Rousseau and Le Vasseur were reunited, Rousseau went up to London for a sitting with Allan Ramsay in the painter's studio at 67 Harley Street. The next year, Ramsay would become the Principal Portrait Painter to George III and cease painting private sitters. He was a firm friend of David Hume: the year they formed their Edinburgh debating club, the Select Society of Edinburgh, 1754, was also the year Ramsay first painted Hume – portraying him in a scholar's cap and patterned white waistcoat.

Ramsay's 1766 depictions of Rousseau and Hume are considered among his finest accomplishments. He had never before encountered Rousseau, but was no fan of his works. He later wrote to Diderot, describing in derogatory terms Rousseau's championing of nature. 'Those who indulge in intellectual pursuits find little charm in the bare necessities of life. Reduced to bare necessity, one must bid farewell to poetry, painting and all the agreeable branches of philosophy, and embrace instead Rousseau's Nature – Nature on all fours.'

Although he sketched Rousseau and Hume at roughly the same time the portraits are striking for their differences. Hume is bewigged, and in diplomatic uniform of gold and crimson with a lace-cuffed shirt. His mien is calm and serious. He is looking straight ahead, his eyes wide and full, though he appears not to be seeing us while he pursues some thought, an impression reinforced by one side of his face being in partial shadow. (Light and shadow were significant means of displaying character for British portraitists of this period.) He lives partly in a hidden world. While his forehead is broad, and his neck dewlapped, he is not so porcine as the descriptions of 'fat David Hume' might lead us to expect. In a visual cliché, Hume's left arm rests on two thick leather-bound volumes, telling us we are in the presence of a man of learning. But, beyond that, the image is of a man of mature powers, of reason, deep thought and sceptical judgement.

In a study of the two paintings, the philosopher Nigel Warburton points out that Hume rarely wore such fancy clothes. On examining the portrait, even King George was moved to mention this, to which Ramsay riposted, 'I wished posterity should see that one philosopher during your Majesty's reign had a good coat upon his back.' Although, of course, Hume had been a diplomat, Warburton surmises that the dress was really an amusing and knowing nod to Hume's self-description as the 'ambassador from the dominions of learning to those of conversation'. However, there is evidence that Hume had in the past taken some delight in dressing up – in Turin his love of his elaborate lace-edged uniforms tickled a rear admiral who warned Hume that sea air might tarnish his 'lace locks'.

Ramsay's reading of Rousseau is more compelling still. Rousseau is seated sharply away from the artist, his face turned in semi-profile. Because of the angle of the body, he is forced to look at us from the corner of his eyes, giving an apprehensive quality to his glance, wary, even distrustful. The effect is multiplied by the lighting: only the face and shoulder are illuminated. He appears thin and tired and drawn. He is dressed in his habitual Armenian clothing, including his fur hat. He holds the edges of his cape together with his right hand: 'protectively', says Warburton. But Rousseau does not escape the cliché: the man of *sensibilité* has his finger pointing straight to his heart.

Initially, Rousseau seemed pleased with the outcome. To Du Peyrou he recounted that 'a good painter' had portrayed him in oil for Hume. Not only had the King wanted to see the work but an engraving was to be made. Subsequently Hume sent six prints to Mme de Boufflers in May to distribute among 'enthusiasts for our friend'. He told her it was 'done from an admirable portrait which Ramsay drew for me.'

As Rousseau wended his way back from sitting for Ramsay, he suffered a nasty jolt: Sultan ran off. It was not the first time. The dog was giving Rousseau 'unbelievable trouble'. Hume had reported one escapade to Mme de Barbentane only a fortnight earlier, in mid-February, though he was illustrating his charge's celebrity, not Sultan's mischief. 'Every circumstance, the most minute, that concerns him, is put in the newspapers. Unfortunately, one day, he lost his dog; this incident was in the papers next morning. Soon after, I recovered Sultan very surprisingly: this intelligence was communicated to the public immediately, as a piece of good news.'

Now Sultan had disappeared again. A Rousseau devotee promised the distraught owner he would put an advertisement in the press and on 4 March 1766, the following appeared in the *Public Advertiser*:

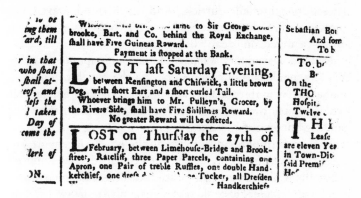

Whoever ... ... came to Sir George Colebrooke, Bart. and Co. behind the Royal Exchange, shall have Five Guineas Reward.
Payment is stopped at the Bank.

LOST last Saturday Evening, between Kensington and Chiswick, a little brown Dog, with short Ears and a short curled Tail. Whoever brings him to Mr. Pulleyn's, Grocer, by the River Side, shall have Five Shillings Reward.
No greater Reward will be offered.

LOST on Thursday the 27th of February, between Limehouse-Bridge and Brookstreet, Ratcliff, three Paper Parcels, containing one Apron, one Pair of treble Ruffles, one double Handkerchief, one dress ... ... Tucker, all Dresden Handkerchiefs

As it happened, there was no need for a reward. Sultan navigated his own way back to the Pulleins'.

The sitting for Ramsay was also memorable for another, more positive, reason. At the painter's, Rousseau finally solved his housing problem.

Throughout this period, Rousseau remained intent on moving to Wales. Hume, in his own words, was 'putting a hundred obstacles in the way', judging that Rousseau would be happier closer to civilization. In a letter to Mme de Barbentane, he remarked, 'Hundreds of persons have offered me their assistance to settle him; you would think that all the purses and all the houses of England were open to him.'

One of the hundreds offering assistance was the MP for Derbyshire and commissioner for commerce, William Fitzherbert, a member of Garrick's and Johnson's circle. Through Garrick, Fitzherbert suggested lodging Rousseau at his family seat, near Ashbourne in Derbyshire. Rousseau declined: Fitzherbert's sister would be in residence and, according to Hume, '[Rousseau] feared he would constrain her'. But a neighbour of Fitzherbert's then made a similar proposal, also passed on through Garrick. And so Richard Davenport, blessed with a character of uncommon compassion and generosity, entered Rousseau's life.

Richard Davenport was, in Hume's description to Hugh Blair, 'a gentleman of £5 or 6,000* in the North of England, and a man of great humanity and of a good understanding'. He had a remote house which 'pleases the wild imagination and solitary humour of Rousseau'.

Elderly, with one leg shorter than the other, Davenport was prone to agonizing gout. He had been educated at Westminster School and Cambridge University, and had read some law in the Inner Temple. He could trace his family to the twelfth century, and had recently bought back the family estate at Davenport in Cheshire. Rousseau's future place of asylum, Wootton Hall, was in the hills of Staffordshire (though so close to Derbyshire that its location has often been described as in that county).

Hume's sense of responsibility for the practicalities of the exile's well-being can be seen in his detailed interrogation of Fitzherbert about Wootton Hall:

> 1. Is there wood and hills about Mr Davenport's house? 2. Cannot Mr Rousseau, if he should afterwards think proper, find a means to boil a pot, and roast a piece of meat in Mr Davenport's house so as to be perfectly at home? 3. Will Mr Davenport be so good as to accept of a small rent, for this circumstance I find is necessary? 4. Can Mr Rousseau set out presently and take possession of his habitation?

Hume then told Fitzherbert that he had mentioned Davenport's offer to Rousseau, who had 'seemed to like it extremely' and would accept if Davenport would take payment. Hume

* Some £500,000 a year in today's value.

suggested £30 for 'board, firing and washing'. He met Davenport at the end of February, and then arranged for Rousseau to make his acquaintance at Ramsay's studio on Saturday, 1 March 1766.

However, Rousseau would not commit himself. He complained to Du Peyrou that as soon as he made up his mind where to go, everyone conspired to make him change it.

Hume pressed on, wearily and fruitlessly, with his searches, but on 10 March the exile finally decided on Richard Davenport's mansion, Wootton Hall, 'on the mountains of Derbyshire'. He would leave, he told Du Peyrou, on 19 March and 'finish his days there'.

Hume was sceptical that Rousseau would be content for long. 'Never was a man, who so well deserves happiness, so little calculated by nature to attain it.' To Hume, as to Diderot and Tronchin before him, the solitary life appeared unnatural. Their attachment to the discourse of reason was threatened by Rousseau's belief in the primacy of nature.

Hume proposed putting up Rousseau and Le Vasseur for one night in Lisle Street, on 18 March, before they took the chaise north.

11

Together – and Worlds Apart

SPECIMEN OF THE M.S. OF HUME'S HISTORY.
REIGN OF HENRY II. PUBLISHED IN 1762.

Hume scribbles his way into English history

Rousseau was pre-eminently the philosopher of human misery.
Professor Judith Shklar

He drew his pen and a system fell.
John Home on David Hume

To judge solely by his paeans of love and esteem for Rousseau, Hume must have been the happiest inhabitant of London during the first months of 1766. He lavished praise on his guest in letter after letter peppered with copious assurances of how well they got along.

Thus, on 19 January he described Rousseau to Mme de Boufflers as having an excellent warm heart, 'and in conversation kindles often to a degree of heat which looks like inspiration. I love him much, and hope that I have some share in his affections.'

On 2 February, he gave his brother a self-serving account of Rousseau's decision to choose London over Berlin, and Hume over Frederick the Great: '[Rousseau] . . . came to Strasbourg, with the intention of going to the King of Prussia, who pressed him earnestly to live with him. At Strasbourg my letter reached him, making him an offer of all my services; upon which he turned short, and having obtained the King of France's passport, came and joined me at Paris.' Hume was effusive about this 'very modest, mild, well-bred, gentle-spirited and warm-hearted man as ever I knew in my life. I never saw a man who seems better calculated for good company, nor who seems to take more pleasure in it.'

Exactly a fortnight later, he distanced himself from d'Holbach's grisly warning that he was nursing a viper in his bosom, telling Mme de Barbentane:

M. Rousseau's enemies have sometimes made you doubt of his sincerity, and you have been pleased to ask my opinion on this head. After having lived so long with him [less than two months in fact] and seen him in a variety of lights, I am now better enabled to judge; and I declare to you that I have never known a man more amiable and more virtuous than he appears to me; he is mild, gentle, modest, affectionate, disinterested; and above all, endowed with a sensibility of heart in a supreme degree. Were I to seek for his faults, I should say that they consisted in a little hasty impatience, which, as I am told, inclines him sometimes to say disobliging things to people that trouble him; . . . he is apt to entertain groundless suspicions of his best friends; and his lively imagination working upon them feigns chimeras, and pushes him to great extremes . . . but for my part, I think I could pass all my life in his company without any danger of our quarrelling . . .

D'Holbach received a similar note. The German baron replied (in English) that he was glad Hume had 'not occasion to repent of the kindness you have shown . . . I wish some friends, whom I value very much, had not more reasons to complain of his unfair proceedings, printed imputations, ungratefulness &c. For my part, I wish heartily [Rousseau] may find, in your country, that repose his imagination and the sourness of his temper have deprived him of hitherto.' The letter ends with an intriguing sentence: 'Mr Grimm pays his most sincere thanks for the piece of service you did about Rousseau's manuscript.' What did he mean by this? The eminent Rousseau scholar R. A. Leigh wondered if Rousseau had read to Hume the section of the *Confessions* that dealt with Grimm. If so, it would explain something of Hume's later panic and horror at the prospect of his also appearing in those pages.

While Hume was rhapsodizing about Rousseau, he was simultaneously pursuing the question of a royal pension for him, first broached on the boat to England. In late January, Hume informed Mme de Boufflers that a friend of his 'who possesses much of [the King's] confidence' had talked to His Majesty. The pension was agreed in principle, but Rousseau was seeking advice from his 'father' in Berlin – Earl Marischal – on whether to accept it. Since Rousseau was such a contentious figure, the pension would not be made public. 'You know that our sovereign is extremely prudent and decent, and careful not to give offence. For which reason, he requires that this act of generosity may be an entire secret.' A postscript says it will be £100 p.a., 'a mighty accession to our friend's slender revenue'.

For his access to George III, Hume was dependent on General Conway, who at the time had more pressing preoccupations. The Rockingham administration, and Conway in particular, was embroiled in the Stamp Act crisis. The Seven Years War had drained the Exchequer. In February 1765, under the previous Grenville ministry, stamp duties levied on paper used for all official documents (embracing everything from newspapers to marriage certificates to wills) had been applied to the American colonies, incensing the colonists, who were not represented in the British Parliament and who were never consulted. Faced with a wave of protest from across the Atlantic and at home from commercial interests, the new Rockingham government was seeking a way to repeal the detested Act while maintaining the right of Parliament to tax the Americans. In the British Isles, the idea that the free-riding colonists should contribute to the cost of campaigns that had lifted the French threat to North America was predictably popular.

In the *Memoirs of George III* Walpole records, 'The situation of the Ministers became every day more irksome and precarious.' Conway was under attack by Grenville for his handling of the emergency. Meanwhile, the King was fomenting opposition to his own ministers, worried that his right to tax his colonists was in jeopardy.

Perhaps it was the stress that dispatched Conway to his sickbed. According to Walpole, Conway had 'a scorbutic eruption, caught cold, neglected it, it turned to a high fever.' Recuperating on his country estate, the general nonetheless insisted on wandering the grounds despite the freezing temperatures, and suffered an inevitable relapse. The matter of the pension waited upon his recovery.

Thus, Hume's rejoicing over the pension was premature. And here we need to jump forward in time. Sure enough, Earl Marischal's seal of approval came from Berlin, but Conway could not speak to the King until 2 May. On that day, the general wrote in his formal way to Hume, 'His M: is pleased to consent to give him a pension of one hundred pounds per An: – desiring only it might be a secret one.' Conway did not have Rousseau's address and so asked Hume to pass on the King's offer:

> and that if it is agreeable to him, [George III] shall think himself extremely happy to have been an instrument in providing him any convenience or satisfaction, & in having contributed to procure for one of his distinguished genius and merit these marks of favour & protection which will do honour to this country & in a particular manner to the Royal hand from whom all bounty flows.

The next day, Hume forwarded Conway's letter, instructing Rousseau that it would be necessary to reply with his acceptance and thanks for Conway's good offices. The missive ends with some advice, designed to placate Rousseau, who had been mocked in the London press:

My dear friend, if you must fly from mankind, do not at once renounce the amusement and consolation of society, and feel all the pain which may result from the idle opinions of men and those misrepresented. The expressions contained in this letter of General Conway may convince you in what estimation you are held by all men of character in England. We only wish that you would like our company as well as we do yours.

In spite of Hume's stated confidence in his relationship with Rousseau, and his zeal in securing him a sanctuary and setting the pension in train, curiously, when Rousseau finally left London, he and Hume had agreed in the words of the *Monthly Review*, 'not to be troublesome to each other by a regular commerce of letters' and to communicate only about the pension so as 'not to have the restraint of a continued correspondence'.

'Restraint' rings oddly in this age of letter-writing, when every day people communicated with one another at length and post rarely went unanswered (a fact that makes this book possible). Would not saved and saviour have wanted to keep in touch?

The probability is that, whatever he might claim in his letters, Hume had rapidly grown tired of his charge and the weight of being responsible for him – 'the show-er of the lion' was 'weary of his pupil', as William Rouet had put it in mid-January. John Home, 'the Scottish Shakespeare', also noticed Hume's increasing frustrations 'with the philosopher who allowed himself to be ruled equally by his dog and his mistress'.

Lord Charlemont, who was able to compare Hume's current demeanour with his earlier impressions in Paris, picked up Hume's unease when he bumped into him in the park:

I wished him joy of his pleasing connection, and particularly hinted that I was convinced he must be perfectly happy in his

new friend, as their sentiments were, I believed, nearly similar – 'Why no, man,' said he, 'in that you are mistaken.
Rousseau is not what you think him. He is indeed a very sensible, and wonderfully ingenious man, but our opinions are by
no means the same. He has a hankering after the Bible, and is
indeed little better than a Christian in a way of his own.'

Hume's reservations about his guest reflected not just his
qualms about Rousseau's idiosyncratic views and personality,
but also nagging doubts about his rectitude. Was he quite what
he claimed? Their stormy passage had shown how hardy
Rousseau was, whatever his complaints of chronic illness.
What of his financial position? Was it, too, more robust than it
seemed? Hume's suspicion on that score arose in Paris. After
Rousseau had bemoaned his dire pecuniary state, Hume evidently primed some of his French coterie discreetly to investigate the exile's means. Possibly one of the *philosophes* had told
Hume that the Genevan was richer than his protestations of
poverty allowed. Indeed, when the successful author fled
France, he was not short of money. For *Héloïse*, *On the Social
Contract* and *Émile*, he was to be paid over 14,000 francs.

Back in London, Hume continued to probe. Mme de Boufflers was supposed to be making inquiries on his behalf with
Josué de Rougemont, a Parisian banker with whom Rousseau
had been associated since about 1762. The wording of Hume's
reminder to her is revealing. 'It is only a matter of mere curiosity. For, even if the fact should prove against him, which is very
improbable, I should only regard it as one weakness more, and
do not make my good opinion of him to depend on a single
incident.' Yet this pressing for something that might 'prove
against' the Genevan was plainly more than curiosity. And
while he might regard it as 'one weakness more', Hume's 'good
opinion' was potentially at stake.

Unknown to Mme de Boufflers, at Hume's request Mme de Barbentane was also pursuing the banker. On 16 February, Hume jogged her memory, too: 'I know not how your inquiries with M. Rougemont have turned out.' He enlisted the aid of d'Holbach in the same errand. The 'mere curiosity' begins to look like a fixation. Rousseau, of course, was ignorant of these letters flying between London and Paris, and of this attempted rummaging into his affairs.

Although it is not clear how, by early April Hume's sleuthing had borne fruit. Mme de Boufflers, Mme de Barbentane, and d'Holbach had not come up with anything. But on 3 April, in a long epistle to Mme de Boufflers, Hume wrote,

> . . . that in point of circumstance he is not to be pitied: for I have also discovered, that he has some little resources beyond what he mentioned [in Paris] . . . It is one of his weaknesses that he likes to complain. The truth is, that he is unhappy, and he is better pleased to throw the reason on his health, and circumstances, and misfortunes, than on his melancholy humour and disposition.

A note in French on 2 May 1766, probably to Jean-Charles Trudaine de Montigny (an enlightened economist who was Comptroller of Finances for bridges and embankments, and who had translated Hume's *Natural History of Religion*), spread the 'secret' of the royal pension, and added that Rousseau tried to make himself interesting by complaining of poverty and ill-health. But Hume had discovered 'by chance' that Rousseau had resources 'which he hid from us when he accounted to us for his assets'. 'By chance' is hardly an accurate rendering of Hume's persistent inquiries – and he was not finished yet.

As Hume became more and more wary of his famous dependent, so his dependent's state of mind became increasingly unsettled. He might now have been in the land of freedom, but a number of events were combining to perturb him.

First, as we have seen, early in Rousseau's stay in London, he heard that young Louis-François Tronchin was at Hume's lodgings in Lisle Street.

Then there was the circulation in Paris and London of a mocking letter, a spoof in the name of the King of Prussia satirizing Rousseau as wallowing in misery. The letter had appeared in the French capital before Rousseau left for England, and news of it pursued him across the Channel. On 18 January, Rousseau told Mme de Boufflers that Hume had just informed him about

> a pretended letter which the King of Prussia has written me. The King of Prussia has honoured me at every opportunity with his most decided protection and most obliging offers, but he has never written to me. As all such fabrications have no end, and probably will not cease very soon, I ardently wish that people would be kind enough to let me remain ignorant of them . . .

Hume mentioned the King of Prussia letter to Mme de Boufflers the following day: Rousseau's suspicion, he said, was that it had been made up by Voltaire.

Thirdly, there was Rousseau's problem in locating a permanent home far from the capital, its crowds, noise and bustle. Hume was not much more favourable to the wilds of Derbyshire than to Wales, as he explained to his old Edinburgh friend, the Presbyterian cleric Hugh Blair, in a peculiarly negative view of Rousseau and his prospects:

> He was desperately resolved to rush into this solitude, notwithstanding all my remonstrances; and I foresee, that he

will be unhappy in the situation, as he has always been in all situations. He will be entirely without occupation, without company, and almost without amusement of any kind. He has read very little during the course of his life, and has now totally renounced all reading: He has seen very little, and has no manner of curiosity to see or remark: He has reflected, properly speaking, and studied very little; and has not indeed much knowledge: He has only felt, during the whole course of his life; and in this respect, his sensibility rises to a pitch beyond what I have seen any example of: But it still gives him a more acute feeling of pain than of pleasure. He is like a man who were stripped not only of his cloaths but of his skin . . .

Hume's withering analysis revealed an absence of imaginative sympathy for his guest's state of mind, and was indicative that in both personality and creative style they were polar opposites. In terms of personality, while Hume's outlook was unadventurous and temperate, Rousseau was by instinct rebellious; Hume was an optimist, Rousseau a pessimist; Hume gregarious, Rousseau a loner. Hume was disposed to compromise, Rousseau to confrontation. In style, Rousseau revelled in paradox; Hume revered clarity. Rousseau's language was pyrotechnical and emotional, Hume's straightforward and dispassionate. Moreover, while they were both philosophers, two people with a hunger and capacity for abstract thought and with the power to express their ideas, they occupied separate philosophical universes. It was less that they disagreed than that they had no prospect of engagement.

Both were pivotal figures of the age, though each, in his way, stood apart from the era's stress on the primacy of reason in all aspects of human affairs. Their reasoning about reason showed that reason could get us only so far: they both used reason to demonstrate the limits of reason. Thus, for Rousseau, an appreciation of the world required not just reason but *sensibilité*; for Hume reason could never supply an underpinning to morality or religion. But, beyond that, they had in their sights two different targets. Rousseau took aim at common conceptions of man's link with society, and Enlightenment's proud boast of progress (that there had been progress in the human condition, and that with the systematic application of rationality and information, advances could be speeded up). Hume was concerned, much more fundamentally, with man's link with the world and man's claims to knowledge of that world.

The Scot's 'dead-born' *Treatise of Human Nature* is a seminal work in the history of philosophy, though these days its content tends to be absorbed by students through his later, less dense *Enquiries Concerning Human Understanding* and *Concerning the Principles of Morals*.

The overall impact of Hume's fusillade on common sense was, and still is, most unsettling. Applying the utmost intellectual rigour, he blows away the ground under our day-to-day assumptions: we are like the cartoon dog that runs in mid-air until he sees there is no ground under his paws. If that was where Hume's head led him, with his heart he was almost apologetic. He did not mean to disorientate. Even his demolition of religion, ruthless and unsparing in its analysis, caused him some agonized dissonance: to spare the feelings of friends and acquaintances, *le bon David* often downplayed the full extent of his scepticism.

Hume was what we now call an empiricist – that is, he believed that all our knowledge must originate in our experience, which we gain through our senses. Empiricism has a healthy image – in the Anglo-American world at least – of a plain-talking, feet-on-the-ground, no-nonsense philosophy. If it were a person, it would be the solid member of a jury – commonsensical, conscientious and moderate. But that was not Hume's empiricist.

Hume took empiricism to its logical conclusion: his empiricist was a destructive revolutionary. If knowledge cannot be detached from the internal state of the knower, if the world is what it seems to be to me, he argued, I cannot be sure that that is how the world objectively is. My senses are merely my senses; there is no guarantee that they are accurate, that they reflect the world beyond. The Scotsman showed that if we rely on experience, then we can have no complete confidence in the existence of the external world; we can have no complete confidence in our personal identity (that I am the same person today as I was yesterday); we can have no confidence in the 'laws of nature' that we take for granted, such as gravity or cause and effect.

Take the latter. Hume illustrated his problem with billiard balls. When one sees one billiard ball strike another, what reason does one have for believing that the impact of the first ball will bring movement in the second? Yes, we are convinced it will have this effect – but why? For, as Hume points out, when we see a relationship appearing to be one of cause and effect, all we experience in reality is one event followed by another. We cannot see, smell or touch the causation; we do not see, smell or touch any necessary connection. Each ball's movement is a distinct matter of fact; we observe the second movement following the movement of the first. And it is entirely conceivable that the second will not follow from the first. The second ball might stay rooted on its spot, or turn into a dove, the two balls might explode on impact, the first might just roll backwards. The problem of causation is related to that of induction – the inference of a future event on the grounds of past experience. We cannot logically infer that the sun will rise tomorrow just because it has risen on every previous day.

How then to explain our hitherto unquestioned assumptions about causality and induction? Well, says Hume, when events are constantly connected in time and space, we naturally make the mental leap from one to the other. Thus, we have experienced the temperature from a fire so often that when we place our hand near some flames, custom and habit lead us to anticipate heat. In place of a logical basis for our beliefs, Hume substitutes a psychological one.

His reflections on 'personal identity' were equally counterintuitive. You might have the idea that there is some enduring entity – the self – that constitutes the essential 'you', that makes the 'you' digesting these words now the same 'you' who absorbed the previous paragraph some moments ago, the same 'you' who went to kindergarten and who will eventually age and die. The Rousseau who fell on his knees before a blue periwinkle believed he was the same Rousseau who had picked a periwinkle three decades earlier when out walking with Mme de Warens. But, argues Hume, this notion of identity is illusory. Try to reflect on your 'self'. Try to locate this immutable thing that is supposed to make you, you. All you can detect is a disparate bundle of perceptions. In Hume's words: 'I always stumble on some particular perception or other, of heat or cold, light or shade, love or hatred, pain or pleasure, colour or sound, etc. I never catch my self, distinct from some such perception.' The various snapshots passing through one's mind are not linked by any invisible film.

In the face of Hume's sceptical juggernaut, we risk a psychological crushing. If all our deepest assumptions about the way the world works are shown to be illusory, to be derived neither from reason nor from the senses, how can we function, how can we force ourselves out of bed in the morning? Indeed, in the *Treatise* Hume confesses that his theoretical musings even have a debilitating impact on their creator, making him morose and lethargic. But he always finds a way to carry on. Fortunately, the human animal, even the Humean animal, can dwell on such reflections for only a short spell. Our instincts overpower our reason: we cannot help but assume the existence of causality and cannot help but rely and act on past experience. As Hume himself put it: 'I dine, I play a game of backgammon, I converse and am merry with my friends; and when after three or four hours' amusement I would return to these speculations, they appear so cold, and strained, and ridiculous that I cannot find in my heart to enter into them any further.' (And, indeed, his deliberations on economics and history take for granted personal identity, consistency in human conduct, and cause and effect in the material world.)

Philosophically, he subjected the idea of a rational foundation for morality to a parallel diagnosis. Hume knocks us down, and then lifts us up. First the overthrow: reason, said Hume, cannot tell us how we ought to act; it is 'perfectly inert'. That the world is a certain way furnishes no logical reason to act in a certain way. It is not inconsistent, or incoherent, or false both to recognize that there are starving children in the world and to deny that we have an obligation to feed them. Logic is an inappropriate tool for dissecting morality, like taking a carving knife to water. To quote another of his famous statements, ''Tis not contrary to reason to prefer the destruction of the whole world to the scratching of my finger.'

If reason does not prop up our moral values, what does sustain them? Hume derived his moral principles from an examination of human nature. According to Hume, our behaviour is dictated by sentiment. We are naturally a mixture of various passions, such as selfishness and altruism (his word for the latter was 'sympathy'). We are born neither utterly selfish nor wholly selfless. Sympathy awards us with a glow of warmth when we perform a virtuous act and instils a nagging sense of unease if we are responsible for a vicious one.

Although Hume, on occasion, hints at the beneficial spin-offs arising out of our innate sympathy, he maintains that it is futile to ask why we have this instinct. For Hume, it is simply a truth, and that is that. 'It is needless to push our researches so far as to ask, why we have humanity or a fellow feeling with others. It is sufficient, that this is experienced to be a principle of human nature.' All this was neatly encapsulated in Hume's aphorism, 'Reason is and ought to be the slave of the passions'.

These were revolutionary claims whose implications were revolutionary in another sense: Hume dragged man down towards his fellow animals. Human judgements about the world were really akin to instincts, and Hume pointed out how such instincts are to be found in 'brute beasts' as well as 'the most ignorant and stupid peasants'. 'The experimental reasoning itself, which we possess in common with beasts, and on which the whole conduct of life depends, is nothing but a species of instinct or mechanical power.' Dogs can be trained through a system of rewards and punishments, in which they act on the basis of past experience. It is clear that they are not engaging in any process of complex reasoning here, Hume argues. What happens is that animals behave instinctively and mechanistically, just as humans.

While Hume the historian is now studied principally for his philosophy, Rousseau the novelist is these days studied mainly for his political theory – for what he says about the relationship between government and citizens, for his radicalism, his egalitarianism, his understanding of liberty, for his (to some) notorious concept of the general will, and for his distinctive vision of the state of nature, linked to his posthumous reputation as a pre-Romantic.

Rousseau wrote a great deal about the state of nature: a primitive if unspecified period in which humans interacted with one another before the creation of political institutions (a notion deployed by political theorists for a multiplicity of purposes). Sometimes he seemed to use the phrase as though it were a depiction of an historical reality; at other times as though it were just a useful theoretical tool. But he gave the concept a unique twist. For unlike Thomas Hobbes's pessimistic vision of chaos and uncertainty, his was not a picture of violent anarchy. Quite the opposite, in fact: it was of a tranquil idyll in which man was free and self-sufficient, had an entirely fitting regard for his own well-being – *amour de soi* – but combined this with an instinctive sympathy for others.

What had happened to corrupt this primitive state? The rot set in with the invention of property. Property had bred inequality, conflict and war. Property had spawned an obsessive and invidious compulsion to compare oneself to others, leading to greed and jealousy, 'a black inclination to harm one another'. Property had transmuted the clean, simple and natural quality of *amour de soi* into an ugly self-satisfaction, an inflated self-conceit, *amour-propre*. Whereas, with *amour de soi*, we possessed an honest and direct self-knowledge and self-love, now our image of ourselves came back through the gaze of others; it was like staring into an ugly distorting mirror. 'Nature has made everything in the best way possible; but we want to do better still, and we spoil everything,' said Rousseau. Voltaire found the idea of a primitive world less alluring. After reading *The Origin of Inequality Among Men*, he playfully but bitingly told its author that he was 'seized with a desire to walk on all fours'.

In any case, by the time that Rousseau went into exile, he had relinquished the prelapsarian vision of man in a state of nature and had come to believe that this creature was stunted

and unfulfilled: maybe free, maybe happy, maybe self-sufficient, but not fully developed. In the state of nature, men were
not conscious of morality; only by becoming conscious could
they become virtuous. It was by participating in political society that man could live out his potential and be elevated to a
level above the rest of the animal kingdom, above the life of
creatures controlled by base instinct.

His image of the ideal political society in no sense resembled
the despotic governance of eighteenth-century France or the
enlightened despotism of his supporter, Frederick the Great of
Prussia. His task was to show how we could reclaim our freedom – and how freedom and the law could be compatible.

He sought to reconcile them through his concept of the general will: the general will is the will of the community, but it is
not calculated by any mathematical summation of individual
preferences. It is, rather, what is good for the community generally. The general will emerges through the coalescing of indi-
viduals into an organic whole. The niceties of how the general
will is to work in practice remain opaque in Rousseau's theory
but, since we are a part of the collective, the execution of the
general will is good for each of us.

That argument, later critics claimed, carries ominous over-
tones. In a phrase that has sent a chill down many spines,
Rousseau talks of us being 'forced to be free' – the origin of the
common charge that his ideas were a precursor of totalitarianism. If a person were compelled to obey the general will, he
would be forced into observing both the common good and
what was objectively best for him. Immanuel Kant and Karl
Marx would pick up on these themes. Kant, heavily influenced
by Rousseau, came to believe that autonomy rested in comply-
ing with the rules of reason; Marx employed the notion of false
consciousness (a state in which we are unaware of our real
interests).

Rousseau's theoretical writings were intertwined with his need for independence and yearning for innocent solitude. A leitmotiv in his work was the importance of men not being reliant on others. Dependence was the root of evil; not being dependent meant being free. It was modern man's downfall that to survive and thrive, he had come to rely on the contributions of others. Although Rousseau lived in a pre-industrialized world, the theme of man's alienation from property and from the fruits of his labour would be echoed a century later in Marx. Rousseau even fulminates against money in the *Confessions* – 'good for nothing in itself' – and claims he always regarded it with 'more horror than pleasure'.

Rousseau's bold prescription for how children should be nurtured and educated to lead their lives fully can be found in *Émile*. Initially, the infant is to be unconstricted. In this period of 'negative education', there is a recommendation that the child be deprived of all books, bar one: Daniel Defoe's *Robinson Crusoe* (1719), which provides a masterclass in survival and self-sufficiency. By bringing up the boy Émile outside the community, his tutor will enable the child to learn to know his own will, and not to be prey to popular opinion and the values of 'the conventional world'. (Among many passages acutely discomforting to a twenty-first-century Western outlook, Rousseau proclaimed that girls were not like boys, since 'dependence is a state natural to women'.)

Unlike Hume's, Rousseau's work and life were inextricably intermingled. For Rousseau, the state of happiness, as explained in the *Confessions,* was 'the absence of all that make me conscious of my dependent position'. And, in a letter to de Malesherbes in 1762, he describes the perfect day with friends as one in which 'no image of servitude and dependence troubled the good will' within the group.

Rousseau's unease about receiving presents and assistance

from others was a recurring theme in his life. He routinely rejected offerings of both money and goods – sometimes gracefully, more often tersely. In 1751, he threatened to break off one relationship unless the friend withdrew his present of coffee beans: 'Take back your coffee or never see me again.' And when Mme d'Épinay offered to supplement his income, Rousseau replied that her proposal struck a chill to his heart: she was degrading him – in his words, 'making a valet of a friend'. However, life was not theory: though the imaginary Émile is taught self-sufficiency, Rousseau's adherence to this ideal was somewhat less rigid. Thus, while irascibly spurning offers of free accommodation, he was willing to pay a nominal or below-market rent. By doing so, he could convince himself that his integrity remained intact.

Were there any scholarly topics Rousseau and Hume could settle down to discuss? Any shared cultural terrain where they could relish each other's company, even when disagreeing? Any prospect of intellectual consensus on that long post-chaise ride to Calais, or once settled in Buckingham Street, or at the grocer's shop in Chiswick?

Although the correspondence between Hume and Rousseau (some two dozen letters in all) is of interest in charting the rise and precipitous collapse in their relationship, what is absent from the letters is equally fascinating – these two giants praise each other effusively; they talk logistics; they pass information; they fall out. There is no dialogue or engagement about ideas. To some extent this may have been because they profoundly disagreed even where they dealt with the same issues.

Thus, in economics, Rousseau was a protectionist, Hume (like Adam Smith) a strong opponent of barriers to international trade.

In politics, Rousseau's theoretical political programme

would have required root-and-branch transformation. Hume's instincts were essentially conservative: he advocated careful, slow, piecemeal reform, and was concerned about violent interference with Britain's intricate pragmatism and delicate constitutional balance. (Of course, in freedom of expression and tolerance, British parliamentary government was far removed from the oppressive despotism of Louis XV or from Genevan oligarchy.) Hume even believed that the order and deference of a social hierarchy provided much needed stability.

As for human nature, Rousseau maintained it had altered over time, that man was born good but had fallen, while Hume regarded it as more or less constant. Indeed, that was precisely why the Scot believed it was possible to learn lessons from history – for example, from Europe's depressing catalogue of wars and revolutions. This belief is expressed most explicitly in *An Enquiry Concerning Human Understanding*: 'It is universally acknowledged that there is a great uniformity among the actions of men, in all nations and ages, and that human nature remains still the same, in its principles and operations.' Yet his conduct again parted company from his theory. As we know, he disregarded the cautions about Rousseau given by his friends, ignoring their evidence of Rousseau's past behaviour. His own work highlights how imprudent a policy this was:

> Were a man, whom I know to be honest and opulent and with whom I live in intimate friendship, to come into my house, where I am surrounded with my servants, I rest assured that he is not to stab me before he leaves it in order to rob me of my silver standish; and I no more suspect this event than the falling of the house itself, which is new, and solidly built and founded. – *But he may have been seized with a sudden and unknown frenzy.* – So may a sudden

earthquake arise, and shake and tumble my house about my ears.

However, it is their reflections about how and where man should live, and about the arts and luxury, that most sharply expose the fundamental contradictions of their brief union. Rousseau glorified nature. His state of nature was one of bliss. But, beyond the theory, his autobiographical writings are full of exaltations of nature itself. Of panoramic views, a walk in the country, open air, he writes in the *Confessions*: 'All this sets my soul free, gives me greater boldness of thought, throws me, so to speak, into the immensity of things.' The isolated rural life suited his ascetic self-image. Luxury made men soft. Frugality and the good life were inseparable. Hence his distress at what he believed was Diderot's deliberate stab in proclaiming that only the evil man lives alone. Rousseau associated the black vapours of the city with blackness in men's hearts.

While Rousseau's stance on the theatre and the organized arts was highly ambiguous, Hume unequivocally promoted the benefits of civilization. He was convivial, a city-lover (though preferably Edinburgh over London). His identification with the city was part of a wider urban cosmopolitanism. 'A perfect solitude', he regarded (in the *Treatise*) as 'perhaps, the greatest punishment we can suffer.' The Scot was an advocate of refined tastes, 'the study of beauties' such as poetry, music and art as well as science. These kept us off the streets, mentally challenged us and even made us more social and gregarious. Science and the arts elevated the human spirit. Thus enriched, he wrote in one essay, *Of Refinement in the Arts*, people would never be 'contented to remain in solitude, or live with their fellow citizens in that distant manner, which is peculiar to ignorant and barbarous nations.' That last phrase, had he been acquainted with it, would surely have angered Rousseau as much as had Diderot's.

City life, said Hume, was good for us. We humans were unusual beings, conspicuous among animals for our combination of physical vulnerability and exacting physical needs. Being puny creatures, he thought, and yet having to be clothed, kept warm, sheltered and fed, we have had to adapt and co-operate to survive. Only through organization and social activity have humans come to flourish. For humans, co-operation is natural. Hume concurred with his old friend Adam Smith's maxim about one of the distinguishing characteristics of the human race: 'Nobody ever saw a dog make a fair and deliberate exchange of one bone for another with another dog.' Of course, in Marischal's words, Rousseau's dismissive attitude to simple acts of generosity made him 'more savage than any savage of North America'.

At first glance, our two antagonists did at least share one basic position in common. Both assailed established religion in their homelands and both were hurt in consequence. Both railed against superstition; both shared a dislike of Catholicism.

Hume's assault on religion was the more intellectually rigorous and sustained, but barely rattled the foundations of the established churches in Scotland and England. In France and Switzerland, Rousseau's challenge was seen by the authorities as highly threatening. Hume's career suffered but Rousseau's life was endangered. The stones that smashed through Rousseau's windows in Môtiers were missiles that, in effect, had the blessing of the priesthood.

Yet even their critiques of religion were very different: different in argument, different in motivation. Rousseau's religious views had pleased nobody – neither Christians, nor the atheists and deists. (Deism held that knowledge of God was possible only through reason. Those who believe God set the universe off but then left it alone are also often called deists.) To the *philosophes*, split between a minority who were deists and the majority who were outright atheists, Rousseau's conviction that God existed, his professed love of God, his belief in God's goodness, his certainty that there was an afterlife and that the soul was immortal – all this was risible. Deeply suspect too was his attitude towards the beauty of nature. He saw God in mountains and valleys, in brooks and waterfalls, in thunder and sunshine, in flowers and trees. 'Atheists', he once said, 'do not like the country.'

There were also instrumental grounds that justified religion: it was useful, Rousseau believed, in promoting patriotic and civic values. But this was not the case for the institutions of religion. By teaching men that salvation lay in the next life rather than this one, these institutions actually undermined the state.

This was not the only point on which he criticized the Christian church (particularly the Catholic Church) as misguided. And when we read the 'Savoyard Vicar' section in *Émile*, it is obvious why its passages were regarded as so egregiously blasphemous. Thus, Rousseau thought the direct route to God was through introspection, through the examination of the heart, the pursuit of what he called the 'inner light', through reason. It was not through the clergy and their overblown rituals, nor through scripture. Priests should be excluded from a child's upbringing. They had no special claim to religious truth – if anything, they were obstacles to its discovery.

As for Hume, he did not intend to cause umbrage – 'I would not offend the Godly' – and he amended his *History* to make its relatively bland remarks on religion blander still, though his view was that the Church had played a corrupting role in British life. None the less, the comments he did make landed him in trouble, as we have seen, stalling his career. He wrote to

Blair to complain: 'Is a man to be called a drunkard, because he has been seen fuddled once in his lifetime?'

In fact, he was not seen fuddled once only. Try as he might, he could not conceal his contempt for religion and its superstitions. The religious fanatic was a peculiarly dangerous animal, thought Hume, and clerics were hypocrites. He admitted that 'the Church is my particular aversion'.

His deconstruction of religion followed a familiar strategy, the first stage of which was to examine whether there was any logical reason to believe in God. Take the claim that God reveals Himself through 'revelation': truths about the divine apparently shown in empirical/historical sources, such as miracles. In Section X of *An Enquiry Concerning Human Understanding*, Hume's painstakingly constructed case can be summed up in one sentence: we always have more reason to disbelieve a miracle than to believe in it. If a person claims to have witnessed an act which defied a law of nature – such as that Queen Elizabeth was seen walking and talking five days after her death – then we should ask ourselves whether there are other explanations. We should speculate about the person's motivation, enquire whether there were other witnesses and whether these witnesses were truly independent, and so on. In reality, there was never testimony that has met these stringent criteria. (He thought it no coincidence that sightings of miracles tended to occur 'among ignorant and barbarous nations'.) His chapter 'On Miracles' ends with a lacerating summary. 'So that upon the whole, we may conclude, that the *Christian Religion* not only was at first attended with miracles, but even at this day cannot be believed by any reasonable person without one. Mere reason is insufficient to convince us of its veracity.'

Hume's critique of natural religion, in which conclusions reached about God's existence are allegedly based on reasoning, is systematically laid out in *Dialogues Concerning Natural*

Religion. Composed as conversations between various characters, and published only posthumously, it is often said to be the
most important book on the philosophy of religion ever published. Hume scholars tend to concur that Philo, the sceptic, is
closest to the voice of the Scotsman.

Having shown – to his satisfaction at least – that received
arguments for believing in God were wretchedly inadequate,
Hume questioned why it was that so many people persisted in
their beliefs. Once more he located the explanation in the psychological rather than the rational. In particular, he believed
that religion was the crutch for our apprehensions and anxi-
eties. We have a fear of the unknown, Hume surmised, a fear
of those external events that derail our lives, a fear of the errat-
ic and unpredictable. The devastating Lisbon earthquake of
1755 had provoked much theological head-scratching. How
reassuring to believe that some Greater Being was making
sense of these events, imposing some (hidden) order on apparently random fortune or misfortune.

Host and guest could hardly have had outlooks less in sympathy.
The instant relationship between them inevitably had shallow
foundations: respect for each other's achievements, Hume's
compassion for the dispossessed, Rousseau's need for a haven,
some mutual friends, the courtesies of the age. There was little
else to create any affinity between these two cerebral beings.

In terms of a philosophical dialogue, they could not agree
about religion, human nature, the good life, politics or economics. However, what truly parted them, and held them apart,
was the profound disjunction in their intellectual characters.

Hume was all reason, doubt and scepticism. Rousseau was a
creature of feeling, alienation, imagination and certainty. In
Émile, the Savoyard Vicar states that his 'love of truth' is 'his
whole philosophy' whose method 'exempts me from the vain

subtlety of arguments'. He would 'accept as evident all knowledge to which in the sincerity of my heart I cannot refuse my
consent.' Observing the heart was not easy: it had to be perceived through opaque rather than clear glass. 'We see neither
the soul of the other, because it hides itself, nor our own,
because we have no mirror in the mind.' But introspection was
crucial. The most powerful validation for his beliefs came from
his heart.

Once the man of sensibility was settled, he and the man of
rational scepticism had no reason to keep in touch. In this context, Hume was the last person who might fulfil Rousseau's
dream of friendship, and the decision not to correspond
becomes comprehensible. Of course, Hume had never planned
to look after Rousseau from day to day, and we can sense the
relief when he later told Blair that Davenport had assumed
charge of him.

12

An Evening at Lisle Street

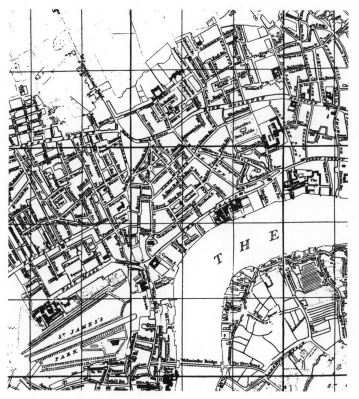

Hume's London retreat —≠Rousseau stayed for one memorable night

*I think I could live with him all my life in mutual friendship
and esteem. I am very sorry the matter is not likely to be put
to a trial! I believe that one great source of our concord is,
that neither he nor I are disputatious.*
David Hume to Hugh Blair, 11 March 1766

To tell a man that he lies, is of all affronts the most mortal.
Adam Smith

It was agreed with Davenport that Rousseau would leave for
Wootton on Wednesday, 19 March 1766, with the two beings
whose attachment to him was unconditional, Le Vasseur and
Sultan. Hume must have counted the days like a prisoner
whose release date comes in sight.

On the afternoon of 17 March, Hume passed on to
Rousseau and Le Vasseur an invitation from Conway and his
wife 'to do them the favour' of dining with them the next day.
Hume professed complete indifference to Rousseau's decision,
assuring him that, 'If you decline this invitation, from whatever reason, I shall endeavour to make your excuses. It is not
necessary, that you constrain yourself the least in this affair.'
Was he really so unconcerned – considering Conway's political
rank, his connection to the King, and his importance to
Rousseau's financial security?

On Monday evening Rousseau indeed asked Hume to make
his excuses: he was ill and not in a fit state to present himself;
as for Mlle Le Vasseur, she was 'a very good and estimable
person but not at all made to take her place amidst grand company.' (Yet, as we have seen, he had insisted on it with others
and she had joined him often enough with French nobility.)

On Tuesday, 18 March, Rousseau's little party came up from
Chiswick in Davenport's coach to sleep overnight at Hume's

lodgings before departing the next day for Wootton. Four or five days earlier, Hume had written to Rousseau to convey a piece of luck: Davenport had learned that a so-called 'retour' post-chaise was returning empty to Ashbourne, near Wootton, and so he had secured a bargain for the travellers. This was a white lie, designed to save Rousseau's purse. The kindly Davenport had hired the chaise and planned to pay the difference between the full and return fares.

That evening, as Hume and Rousseau sat together, their worlds collided. Rousseau had mused on the cut-price chaise and seen through the subterfuge, concluding it was too much of a coincidence – a retour chaise to so obscure a part of the country on the very day he was in need of one. At this point, we proffer only Hume's epistolary version of events, and a scene narrated a week later by Hume to Hugh Blair:

He communicated his doubts to me, complaining that he was treated like a child, that tho' he was poor he chose rather to conform himself to his circumstances than live like a beggar, on alms, and he was very unhappy at not speaking the language familiarly, so as to guard himself against these impositions. I told him that I was ignorant of the matter and knew no more of it than I was told by Davenport. *Never tell me that*, replied he, *if this be really a contrivance of Davenports, you are acquainted with it, and consenting to it; and you could not possibly have done me a greater displeasure.* Upon which he sat down very sullen and silent and all my attempts were in vain to revive the conversation and to turn it to other subjects: he still answered me dryly & coldly. After passing near an hour in this ill-humour, he rose up and took a turn about the room: but judge of my surprise when he sat down suddenly on my knee, threw his hands about my neck, kissed me with the greatest warmth, and bedewing all my face with tears exclaimed, *Is it possible you can ever forgive me my Dear Friend: After all the testaments of affection I have received from you, I reward you at last with this folly & ill behaviour: But I have notwithstanding a heart worthy of your friendship: I love you, I esteem you; and not an instance of your kindness is thrown away upon me.*

Hume was pleased with his sensitive reaction to this outpouring of feeling, aware of a reputation for being cold and detached: 'I hope you have not so bad an opinion of me as to think I was not melted on this occasion: I assure you I kissed him and embraced him twenty times, with a plentiful effusion of tears. I think no scene of my life was ever more affecting.'

Hume reprised the episode to Mme de Boufflers, desiring her to restrict the news of this altercation to the ladies in her circle, because 'I scarce know a male who would not think it childish'. But he asked her to transmit it on to Mme de Luxembourg, Mme de Barbentane 'and such of her female friends as you think worthy of it . . . Ask Mme de L'Espinasse whether she can venture to tell it to d'Alembert.' Short of his placing an advertisement in the *Brussels Gazette*, it is hard to think how he might have publicized the encounter more widely.

Hume acknowledged to Mme de Boufflers that he had not replied to a letter from Mlle de L'Espinasse in February. He did not add that he had failed to pass on to Rousseau her suggestion (in very complimentary terms) that he should write the late Dauphin's eulogy, as he would bring to it just the right sensibility. The Dauphin, shortly before his death, had praised Rousseau and regretted his persecution, she said. And a tribute from Rousseau 'would help to ease [his] return to France and to his friends.' It is unlikely that Rousseau would have responded positively to such an idea from someone so close to d'Alembert. But Hume's keeping to himself such superficially heart-warming news is distinctly odd.

Hume remained doubtful about Rousseau's sticking it out in Derbyshire, writing to Jean-Charles Trudaine de Montigny:

> If it be possible for a man to live without occupation, without books, without society, and without sleep, he will not quit this wild and solitary place, where all the circumstances which he ever required seem to concur for the purpose of rendering him happy. But I dread the weakness and inquietude natural to every man, and, above all, to a man of his character. I should not be surprised that he had soon quitted this retreat.

They had known each other for only four months and would not meet again.

13
The Fashionable Mr Walpole

Horace Walpole – alias the King of Prussia

In Borgia's age they stabbed with daggers, in ours with the pen.
Horace Walpole

*He loved mischief, but he loved quiet; and he was constantly
on the watch for gratifying both his tastes at once.*
T. B. Macaulay on Walpole

On 22 March, the chaise bearing Rousseau, Le Vasseur and
Sultan trundled through a wooded valley and up the long,
steep, muddy drive that led to Wootton Hall and the seclusion
for which the exile yearned. Wootton Hall was set on a lonely
eminence – the village of Wootton a little above it, the village
of Ellaston a little below – in a wild, remote part of Staffordshire, just across the border from Derbyshire and nestling in
the Weaver hills. Its isolation accounts for the local saying:
'Wootton-under-Weaver, where God came neever'. (The Hall
was demolished in 1931; in the past few years a new mansion,
in classical style, has been constructed on the site.)

Rousseau's impressions of Wootton Hall were recorded in a
letter to Mme de Luze in Neuchâtel:

Imagine a solitary house, Madame, one not very large but
very suitable, built half-way up the side of a valley whose
slope is broken enough to permit of walks on the level over
the loveliest lawn in the universe. The front of the house is
ruled by a great terrace whence the eye sweeps, in a semi-circle
of several leagues, a landscape composed of meadows, trees
and scattered farms, some houses more ornate, and the whole
bordered, like a basin, by rising land on each side which agreeably limits one's view when it cannot reach farther.

It is intriguing that Rousseau should have depicted Wootton
Hall as 'not very large' and, later, as 'small but very habitable

and well designed'. Either he was being disingenuous and eager to promote his image as a simple hermit, or else he had been spoiled by the ostentatious magnificence of the French aristocracy. In fact, Wootton Hall was a substantial home, its main castellated block three storeys high.

One of its features was a curving, expansive staircase with an elaborate oak balustrade leading to a projecting wing with a view on three sides. There, Rousseau claimed for himself 'only' two rooms, just above his host's apartments, where there was a drawing room and 'a kind of vestibule or antechamber which is very strange, lighted by a large glass lantern in the middle of the roof'. Above were the servants' quarters.

Although the calendar indicated spring, a bitterly cold spell was closing in. It snowed within a day of the exiles' arrival and the estate was entirely cut off from the outside world. After the bright lights of London and even the comparative bustle of rural Chiswick, what would have struck Rousseau was the utter stillness of the area – what he professed to want – and at night the darkness, which had always made him jumpy and afraid.

None the less, he had few regrets about his decision. The countryside was beautiful but sad, he wrote. Nature here was 'sluggish and lazy'. He missed the sound of nightingales. The trees, to his chagrin, had no leaves. He complained that the vegetables lacked flavour and the game had none at all. Ultimately, though, Wootton afforded 'a commodious, agreeable, and solitary habitation, where the master provides everything, and nothing is wanting: I am quiet and independent.' There was no one to disturb him.

He seemed genuinely content – even cheery. He turned down his landlord's offer of more reading material, though he requested from Du Peyrou that his botany books be forwarded, and his music books, too, for in Wootton he had the use of a spinet.

Contacting Hume was one of his first acts. 'As you can see

from the date of the letter, I have arrived,' Rousseau informed his *cher patron*. The letter was almost all gratitude. 'If I live in this agreeable asylum as happy as I hope to do,' he told Hume, 'one of the greatest pleasures of my life will be, to reflect that I owe them to you. To make another happy is to deserve to be happy one's self. May you, therefore, find in yourself the reward of all you have done for me!' He went on to say that for the reasons they had discussed – presumably to do with cost – he wished not to receive anything by post. When Hume had to write to him, could he send it via Davenport?

But what he saw as the slight of the pretended retour chaise was still gnawing at him, and, interestingly, he blamed Hume more than Davenport, penning a stiff reprimand to his patron:

> The affair of the carriage is not yet adjusted, because I know I was imposed on; it is a trifling fault, however, which may be only the effect of an obliging vanity, unless it should happen to be repeated. If you had a hand in it, I would advise you to give up, once for all, these little stratagems, which cannot have a good motive.

He closed with an oracular salutation. '*Je vous embrasse, mon cher Patron, avec le même Coeur que j'espère et désire trouver en vous.*' ('I embrace you, my dear patron, with the same love I hope and desire to find in you.') It is unlikely that Hume stopped to consider the phrasing.

Rousseau also immediately wrote to his new landlord, Davenport, gently reproving him, and pointing out that it could not have been a return chaise if the driver was going back to London with mail. (Davenport gave the game away by instructing the driver to wait.)

Another warm note to Hume followed a week later: 'It is freezing here since I arrived; it has snowed every day; the wind cuts one's face; yet in spite of these things I would rather live in the hole of one of the rabbits in this warren than in the finest apartment of London. Good-day, my dear patron, I embrace you and love you with all my heart.' In a postscript he mentioned that one of Mr Fitzherbert's servants had accompanied them on the Derby-to-Ashbourne leg after their chaise had an accident – the driver was drunk.

However, Rousseau had much preying on his mind beyond the affront of the retour chaise. He had begun slowly to work out the details of a plot against him. In his imagination, a vast conspiracy was taking shape in which Hume loomed up as the central figure.

A central piece of evidence was that spoof letter in the name of the King of Prussia, mentioned earlier. Rousseau seems to have read it early in April when it appeared in the London press, after having made the rounds in Paris in the new year.

My Dear Jean-Jacques,

You have renounced Geneva, your native soil. You have been driven from Switzerland, a country of which you have made such boast in your writings. In France you are outlawed: come then to me. I admire your talents, and amuse myself with your reverie; on which however, by the way, you bestow too much time and attention. It is high time to grow prudent and happy; you have made yourself sufficiently talked of for singularities little becoming a truly great man: show your enemies that you have sometimes common sense: this will vex them without hurting you. My dominions afford you a peaceful retreat: I am desirous to do you good, and will do it, if you can but think it such. But if you are determined to refuse my assistance, you may expect that I will say not a word about it to anyone. If you persist in perplexing your brains to find out new misfortunes, choose such as you like best; I am a king and can make you as miserable as you can wish; at the same time, I will engage to do that which your enemies never will, I will cease to persecute you, when you are no longer vain of persecution.

Your sincere friend,

FREDERIC

That the satire was the invention of that mad jester, that *fou moquer*, Horace Walpole, was common knowledge in the Republic of Letters. The spoof was conceived and composed by him, and then polished by his French acquaintances, between 12 and 27 December 1765, and was in circulation probably from 27 December, certainly from 1 January 1766. Walpole became the talk of Paris, and described the effect in a cluster of self-congratulatory letters to England, such as this to Conway, on 12 January 1766:

It would sound vain to tell you the honours and distinctions I receive, and how much I am in fashion; yet when they come from the handsomest women in France, and the most respectable in point of character, can one help being a little proud? If I was twenty years younger, I should wish they were not quite so respectable . . . Yet, you know, my present fame is owing to a very trifling composition, but which has made incredible noise. I was one evening at Madame Geoffrin's joking on Rousseau's affectations and contradictions, and said some things that diverted them. When I came home, I put them in a letter, and showed it next day to Helvétius, and the Duke de Nivernois, who were so pleased with it, that after telling me some faults in the language, which you may be sure there were, they encouraged me to let it be seen . . . The copies have spread like wildfire, *et me voici à la mode* . . . Here is the letter . . .

He sent copies of the letter to other regular correspondents. To one (John Chute, who worked with him on Strawberry Hill), he recounted why he felt moved to upbraid Rousseau – whom he regarded as a charlatan and hypocrite:

> I enclose a trifle that I wrote lately, which got about and has made enormous noise in a city where they run and cackle after an event, like a parcel of hens after an accidental husk of a grape . . . I am peevish that with his parts [Rousseau] should be such a mountebank; but what made me more peevish was, that after receiving Wilkes with the greatest civilities, he paid court to Mr Hume by complaining of Wilkes's visit and intrusion.

And to another (Anne Pitt), he archly deprecated his newfound fame: would she believe that, as news of the hoax letter swept the French capital, he became the fashion?

> Everybody would have a copy; the next thing was, everybody would see the author. Thus was I dandled about, with my little legs and arms shaking like a *pantin* (child's puppet).

However, not all the town revelled in his wit. Mme de Boufflers and Conti became enraged by it: in Walpole's words, he 'had the misfortune to give great offence *au Temple*.' On 7 January, Mme de Boufflers had even mailed a letter to Hume hoping to catch him at Calais. Missing him there, it was forwarded to London. She asked whether 'a letter from the King of Prussia that was circulating round Paris was true or false . . . They say [the letter] is full of irony.'

As we have seen, Hume must have raised this with Rousseau on or before 18 January, probably stirred into action by her mentioning it. Rousseau wrote to Mme de Boufflers that day, and Hume to her the next when he added the postscript, 'M. Rousseau says the letter of the King of Prussia is a forgery; and he suspects it to come from M. de Voltaire.' But by that time, she had already discovered it was a spoof. When, on 12 January, Walpole supped at Mme du Deffand's, his hostess said Mmes de Luxembourg and de Boufflers had both been there to complain about the letter: Mme de Boufflers said it was 'wicked to be so hard on an unfortunate and so ridicule him.' A fortnight later, *l'Idole du Temple* lined up the Prince de Conti to add weight to her finger wagging. Walpole found their earnestness comical and, according to the description he sent to Thomas Gray, played the clown:

> Madame de Boufflers, with a tone of sentiment, and the accents of lamenting humanity, abused me heartily and then complained to myself with the utmost softness. I acted contrition . . . I acted contrition, but had like to have spoiled all, by growing dreadfully tired of a second lecture from the Prince of Conti who took up the ball, and made himself the hero of a history wherein he had nothing to do. I listened, did not understand half he said (nor he neither), forgot the rest, said 'Yes' when I should have said 'No', yawned when I should have smiled, and was very penitent when I should have rejoiced at my pardon.

Walpole enclosed yet another copy. To the Reverend Mr Cole, on 28 February 1766, he also scorned Rousseau's idiosyncrasies and – a leitmotiv of the *philosophes*, this – questioned his genuineness. The King of Prussia letter was

> only a laugh at his affectations. I hear he does not succeed in England, where his singularities are no curiosity. Yet he must stay there, or give up all his pretensions. To quit a country where he may be at ease, and unpersecuted, will be owning that tranquillity is not what he seeks.

Walpole's handiwork was now making a splash in London, too. His distribution alone had guaranteed that a number of copies were circulating around the city. An early mention in the press appeared on 28–30 January in the *St. James's Chronicle*: 'A letter is handed about Paris, said to have been written by the King of Prussia, to the celebrated Rousseau.' The *British Chronicle* for 31 January soberly pointed out it had not yet been 'authenticated'.

Towards the end of January or beginning of February, Hume returned to the subject with Mme de Boufflers, supposing by that time she had learned Walpole was responsible: '[Walpole] is a very worthy man; he esteems and even admires Rousseau; yet he could not forbear, for the sake of a very indifferent joke, the turning him into ridicule, and saying harsh things about him. I am a little angry with him; and I hear you are a great deal; but the matter ought to be treated only as a piece of levity.'

'A piece of levity' or not, the spoof must have made Hume deeply uncomfortable – even beyond what might be natural when a companion is satirized accurately. We can conjecture that it was only with Mme de Boufflers's Calais letter, showing how public the King of Prussia hoax had become, that Hume was panicked into telling Rousseau of its existence. There is every reason to suppose that Hume was aware of the letter's true authorship from the outset, though he let Rousseau suspect first Voltaire, then d'Alembert.

The Scotsman was notably anxious lest Mme de Boufflers think he had contributed a key witticism to the bogus letter and, curiously, he had a (guilty?) need to have his memory vouched for. In mid-February, he asked Mme de Barbentane to assure Mme de Boufflers 'that Horace Walpole's letter was not founded on any pleasantry of mine; the only pleasantry in that letter came from his own mouth, in my company, at Lord Ossory's table; which My Lord remembers very well'. In his anxiety to disclaim responsibility, Hume had let slip that he was present at the satire's creation.

So the question arises, what precisely did Hume know of the letter and when did he know it?

Lord Ossory was one of two young men whom *le bon David* would summon as witnesses in his defence. The other was John Craufurd (often rendered in the modern 'Crawford'). Hume and Walpole dined with both regularly in Paris in the winter of 1765. Walpole told Thomas Brand on 19 October, 'The man I have liked best in Paris is an Englishman, Lord Ossory, who is one of the most sensible young men I ever saw.' He praised him, too, as one of the 'properest and most amiable young men I ever knew'. In fact, Ossory was a determined gambler and, with John Craufurd, a founder member of Almack's notorious club in Mayfair in 1764. Back in London, they put Hume up for membership. As for Craufurd, nicknamed 'Fish' for his inquisitive manner, he was a man about town, close to Mme du Deffand. Sitting relaxed in an easy chair, he looks out from his portrait with a cool, appraising gaze. He is probably the subject of a Paris police report that praises a young Briton's *sang-froid* on discovering his mistress cheating on him when he had paid her to be faithful for six months. (He became MP for a Scottish constituency in 1774.)

Hume's approach was to deny having had any sight of the satire while he was in Paris, and Walpole (glorying in his wit) backed him up. He confirmed, at Hume's request, that he had not shown it to Hume, even though they lived for a while in the same inn, because the Scotsman was Rousseau's host. Walpole wrote (on 26 July),

> I cannot be precise as to the time of my writing the King of Prussia's letter, but I do assure you with the utmost truth that

it was several days before you left Paris, & before
Rousseau's arrival there, of which I can give you a strong
proof; for I not only suppressed the letter while you stayed
there, out of delicacy to you; but it was the reason why, out
of delicacy to myself, I did not go to see him, as you often
proposed to me; thinking it wrong to go & make a cordial
visit to a man, with a letter in my pocket to laugh at him.

That was the line. However, Walpole's *Paris Journal*, which
provides a daily record of where Walpole went and with whom
he dined and supped in December 1765 and January 1766,
indicates that this was less than the whole truth.

As we record above, Hume told Mme de Barbantane that
'Horace Walpole's letter was not founded on any pleasantry of
mine; the only pleasantry in that letter came from his own
mouth, in my company, at Lord Ossory's table.' And what the
Journal shows is that the only occasion on which Hume dined
with Walpole and Lord Ossory was on 12 December when
Walpole entertained Hume, Ossory and Craufurd. That was
probably when the joke began. A few days before the dinner,
Hume must have received Rousseau's letter throwing himself
'into [Hume's] arms'; as the jesters enjoyed themselves, the
exile was on the road to Paris. The four men, no doubt
prompted by Walpole and fuelled by a good meal, poked fun at
the man shortly to be in Hume's charge.

Certainly in the Republic of Letters, Hume's role was bruit-
ed about. Even his dearest Parisian confidante, Mme de Boufflers, was convinced that a witticism of his had prompted the
most biting of the sarcasms. She levelled the accusation at
Hume on 25 July 1766:

I have heard it said, and perhaps it has been stated to
[Rousseau], that one of the best phrases in Mr Walpole's letter

belongs to you; that you had said by way of bantering, and speaking in the name of the King of Prussia: 'If you are in love with persecutions, I am King, and I can procure you all sorts.' . . . If this statement be founded in fact, and if Mr Rousseau has been informed of it; irritable, fiery, melancholy, and even proud, as he is said to be, can it be a matter of astonishment, that he should grow mad with vexation and rage?

'Fish' Craufurd was the likely bearer of this news, though he, too, maintained Hume's innocence in public. Hume may have guessed the source of the leak. In August 1766, he warned Mme du Deffand to avoid Craufurd: he was a good for nothing.

But even if Hume coined that taunt, had he seen the letter in which Walpole used it? And if he had not seen it, was he at least aware of it? Walpole made no secret of the spoof – far from it. He carried his *jeu d'esprit* across Paris to dinners and suppers, accepting various corrections to the French suggested by the Duc de Nivernois, Helvétius and Henault, with all of whom Hume mingled. And the *Journal* reveals that Hume had at least two direct opportunities to hear of it. On 24 December, he was at the dinner where, said Walpole, 'Helvétius was much diverted with [the letter], and pointed out one or two faults in the French.' On 1 January, at supper with Mme du Deffand and with her encouragement, the author read the letter aloud to the assembled company. Hume was present at this occasion as well. So it seems plausible that when Hume insisted he did not *see* the letter until London, he was sticking to the literal truth, while allowing this economy with the *verité* to give the impression of complete ignorance.

Meanwhile, the spoof continued to ripple through London society. On 13 March, Lady Hervey told Walpole that 'nothing ever was so genteel, so delicate and so just'. On 3 April, it appeared in the *St. James's Chronicle*, printed in both French and English. The *London Chronicle* followed on 5 April.

One of these papers – probably the *St. James's Chronicle* – even made its way to the wilds of the Derbyshire Peaks and into the hands of the victim. Sir Brooke Boothby recollected finding Rousseau 'in extreme agitation' in consequence. 'I endeavoured to console him by remarking that in England no one was exempt from such little babells [*sic*], but he would hear nothing. He was as certain that it was the production of d'Alembert as if he had seen him write it & that Hume was certainly his accomplice.'

Rousseau reached for his pen. In its 8–10 April edition, the *St. James's Chronicle* printed his response (in translation), more sorrow than anger, but with two far-reaching phrases. It was addressed to the printer, Henry Baldwin:

> Wootton 7 April 1766
> You have been wanting, Sir, in the respect which every private person owes to crowned heads, in publicly ascribing to the King of Prussia a letter full of extravagance and malice by which circumstance alone you should have known he could not be the author. You have even dared to transcribe his name, as if you had seen him write it with his own hand. I inform you, Sir, that this letter was fabricated at Paris; and, *what rends and grieves my heart, the impostor has his accomplices in England*. You owe it to the King of Prussia, to truth, and to me, to print the letter which I write to you, and which I sign, as an atonement for a fault with which you would doubtless reproach yourself severely, if you knew *to what base acts you have rendered yourself accessory*. I make you, Sir, my sincere salutations.' (Authors' italics.)

An overreaction, Hume thought. To Mme de Boufflers, he belittled the letter as 'full of passion, and indeed of extravagance'. But the *St. James's Chronicle* felt an editorial statement was required, apologetic in tone:

> The imposture was a very innocent one, and we do not imagine that readers were deceived by it. It was indeed nothing more than a harmless piece of raillery, not calculated to injure the philosopher in this country. It was handed about town for several weeks before it made its way into the *St. James's Chronicle*, and we are told that it was a *jeu d'esprit* of an English gentleman, now at Paris, well known in the *Catalogue of Noble Authors*.

The last comment was a scarcely veiled reference to Walpole. Meanwhile, the spoof letter and Rousseau's reply were picked up in other papers. And Rousseau's hurt response caught Grimm's satiric eye in Paris as juicy material for mockery in his Europe-wide cultural newsletter. 'If the monarch took these things as keenly as the author, and if Frederic was of the state of mind of Jean-Jacques, this letter could become the subject of a bloody war.'

Unfortunately for Rousseau, his anguished reply in the *St. James's Chronicle* served only to egg on his critics. A series of malevolent newspaper squibs were aimed in his direction. On 17–19 April, passages of a parody entitled in English *A Letter from M. Voltaire to M. Jean-Jacques Rousseau* and in French *Lettre de M. de Voltaire au docteur J. J. Pansophe* were printed in the *London Chronicle* and the *Lloyd's Evening Register* and noted in the *Gentleman's Magazine*:

> I am told, my good Doctor, that you have an intention of going into England. That is, in fact, the country of fine women and true philosophers. Those women and these philosophers will, perhaps, be curious of seeing you, and you will be careful to be seen. The news writers will keep an

exact register of all your actions and jests, and will talk of John James, as they do of the king's Elephants, or the queen's Zebra; the English love to amuse themselves with oddities of every kind, but this pleasure never amounts to esteem . . .

Voltaire (as was his wont) disclaimed authorship and, in fact, the lampoon appears to have been contrived by a M. Bordes of Lyon, though it has been included in Voltaire's collected works. Voltaire was certainly a reasonable enough assumption; it was in his style and he was overflowing with venom towards Rousseau.

Although nothing in the *Pansophe* pasquinade besmirched Rousseau personally, he saw it as evidence of his enemies colluding in Paris and London. But other letters in French followed the King of Prussia letter into the newspapers, and two did pierce their thin-skinned target.

The first (*St. James's Chronicle*, April 17–19) purported to come from a Quaker, 'Z.A.', thus allowing the author to adopt the familiar *tu* form with the Genevan. It chided him for getting upset over *une Bagatelle*: he was in the land of liberty, and liberty had its price; there were always people who abused it. 'But your words *grieving* and *rending* are too strong. And what piqued you was that your character was nailed down too well. It is a foolish vanity to believe oneself above charity.' The letter ended by quoting Voltaire (thus exacerbating the insult) on the propriety of accepting charity publicly without regrets: 'Think it over.' Signed, 'Z.A'.

Then (*St. James's Chronicle*, April 24–26) there was a Greek 'Tale' which opened with the words 'In Greece there was a charlatan', and concerned a pill salesman, 'the most singular man anyone had ever seen'. It concluded with a sentence about the charlatan's death: 'Some say from boredom and rancour, but most said simply that he stopped being singular since people stopped talking about him.' To Rousseau's mind, this mockery was 'still more cruel, if that were possible' than the King of Prussia satire.

The authorship of these hurtful letters is a matter of dispute, though one scholar, Frederick Pottle, has argued for Walpole. In Paris, preparing to return to London, Walpole had been following events avidly; he had whetted his pen again, but held the result back. He recorded his reaction on the day he read Rousseau's 'ridiculous' protest in the *St. James's Chronicle*:

> Before I went to bed, I wrote a letter to Rousseau, under the name of his own Émile, to laugh at his folly; but on reflection I suppressed this, as I had done a second letter in the name of the King of Prussia, in which I foretold the variety of events which would happen in England to interfere with the noise Rousseau hoped to make there, which would occasion his being forgotten and neglected, and which consequently would soon make him disgusted with our country. These events were, politics, Mr Pitt's return to power, horse-races, elections, &c. all easily foreseen, and which did happen of course, and which did continue to make Rousseau weary of the solitude which he pretended to seek, which he had found, and which he could not bear.

However, as seems the rule, while in the end Walpole 'suppressed' the 'Émile' epistle (though sending it in mid-April to Mme du Deffand), Hume had seen it within a month. On 16 May, he told Mme de Boufflers, 'Mr Walpole has wrote a reply, full of vivacity and wit, but sacrifices it to his humanity, and is resolved that no copy of it shall get abroad.'

Did Walpole leave matters there, or was the temptation to tease Rousseau irresistible?

The traffic was not all one way. Other letters in the papers supported Rousseau, including one (*St. James's Chronicle*, 3–6 May) that attacked Walpole by insinuation. Signed with the initial 'X', it assailed the 'scribe', now travelling, who had picked up some French and used it to 'throw ridicule on a very respectable man. – Respectable to the literary world by his writings – to the humane one by his misfortunes.' 'X' called on his brother scribblers to be contented with teizing [*sic*] one another. Opinions differ as to whether this was James Boswell's work but it appears to have prompted the last and most important of the letters in French hostile to Rousseau – a highly personal assault (*St. James's Chronicle*, 5–7 June), but addressed to 'X' and signed 'V.T.h.S.W.'. In other words, says Pottle, *Votre Très humble Serviteur Walpole*.

Adopting a restrained and polite tone, 'in all humility' V.T.h.S.W asked Rousseau's defender, 'X', to clear up several little difficulties that embarrassed 'V.T.h.S.W.'. (1) Had Rousseau not renounced the bourgeoisie of Geneva and then written the *Letters from the Mountain*? (2) Had the author of *La Nouvelle Héloïse* not treated his relatives and friends with *froideur* (not to say more) and often changed his friends and called them monsters? (3) Had the author of *Discours sur l'inegalité des conditions* not opened his door to the great and closed it to the humble?

And 'V.T.h.S.W.' closed with a final thrust: he knew that this extraordinary man lived by principles different from ordinary folk – but what were those principles?

All this was grist to a mill already turning. In mid-March, Rousseau had only the glimmerings of a plot against him. By 9 April, he had made up his mind and begun to assemble his case.

14
Flight from Reason

Wootton Hall: 'A solitary house . . . not very large but very suitable.'

The imagination was the first faculty of his mind and this faculty even absorbed all the others.

Mme de Staël

Early on at Wootton, Rousseau described himself as born again by a new baptism, having been soaked when crossing the sea. He had sloughed off his former self and had forgotten everything pertaining to that strange land, the Continent.

Yet all the new harmonies apparently suffusing this reborn soul were seamed with darker emotions. Rousseau sent instructions to Du Peyrou to be on his guard when dealing with Rousseau's papers. He must not hand over anything, even to those purporting to act in Rousseau's interests. Similar entreaties went in confidence to Richard Davenport. If Davenport had any letters for Rousseau, could he bring them himself to Wootton or send them directly on? Please would his landlord not give them to any third party for forwarding, other than his own staff. Security was more important than promptness. Davenport agreed, without querying the rationale.

The same day, 31 March 1766, Rousseau shared his swelling dread with François-Henri d'Ivernois, a Genevan merchant originally from France who had wormed his way into Rousseau's acquaintance in Môtiers. Rousseau had received a letter from d'Ivernois, but . . .

It had been opened and sealed again: it came to me via Mr Hume, who is thick as thieves with the son of Tronchin, 'the Juggler,' and lived in the same house with him, and also thick as thieves in Paris with my most dangerous enemies.

If he is not a knave, I shall have real amends to make to him in spirit. I owe him thanks for the trouble he has taken over me, in a land where I do not know the language. He is very concerned with my minor interests, but this does not benefit my reputation. I do not know how it happens, but the public papers, which before our arrival talked a great deal about me, and always with honour, have ceased to do so since he came to London, or speak only to my disadvantage. All my affairs, all my letters pass through his hands: those I write do not arrive; those I receive have been opened. Several other circumstances render me suspicious of his conduct; even his very zeal. I have not been able to uncover his intentions, but I cannot help thinking them sinister . . .

Rousseau asked d'Ivernois to pass his fears on to Du Peyrou. His friends should take precautions: not be in touch too frequently, and examine letters carefully, checking the seals, the dates, the hands through which they had passed. He had arranged a way for letters to be posted to him without his name appearing on the cover:

A Monsieur
Monsieur Davenport
A Wootton Ashborn bag
Derbyshire

The first week of April saw him complaining about his post to Mme de Boufflers. Letters did not reach their destination or were opened. There is an insinuation as to the culprit: 'In a country where, through ignorance of the language, a man is at the discretion of others, he must be fortunate in the choice of those to whom he gives his confidence; and to judge from experience, I would be wrong to count upon good luck.' Shortly after this, he sent his protest about the King of Prussia letter to the *St. James's Chronicle.*

To Walpole, the King of Prussia letter might have been a little *jeu d'esprit,* within the culture of vigorous satire of public figures by one another. But to Rousseau, antagonistic to that culture, the spoof was both exceptional and damaging. To a London bookseller, he claimed that publication of Du Peyrou's letters describing Rousseau's treatment in Neuchâtel had been held back because of the spoof, though he himself took little interest in the false letter, and 'I hope the black vapours, raised in London, will not disturb the serenity of the air I breathe here.'

If Rousseau felt serenity in spite of everything, it was the serenity of a man sure that he had grasped the truth, a truth he poured out in all its specifics before his chosen confidante – the woman who had forced her friendship on him so recently, Mme de Verdelin.

We can imagine Rousseau that day, 9 April 1766, in the silence of Wootton. Outside, the wild landscape still frozen. Inside, wrapped against the chill in the barely furnished rooms, the exile totally absorbed in reconstructing scene after scene of his life with Hume. At his feet, a peaceful Sultan keeps him company; at his shoulder snarls the creature identified by Grimm, which we might see as a second dog, the 'companion who will not suffer him to rest in peace'. Rousseau's pen flows irregularly, shaking with anger, pausing occasionally from panic or horror. The letter becomes a mess of crossings-out, insertions, additions written in the margins, and rejected phrases.

He begins by telling her that it was absolutely necessary she should understand this David Hume, to whom she had consigned him. 'Since our arrival here in England where I knew nobody else but him [Hume], somebody who is well informed

and knows about all my activities, constantly works in secret
to dishonour me here, and achieves this with a success that
astonishes me.'

In a tumbling stream of allegations, he starts the story in
Paris, where there had been distorted descriptions of his welcome there – the press inaccurately suggesting he had been
unable to appear in public. The papers had also reported that
he had needed Hume's protection to cross France, and that
Hume had obtained a passport for him. The fraudulent King of
Prussia letter, written by d'Alembert and circulated by Hume's
friend Walpole, had been treated as authentic. Every step had
been taken in London to make him and Mlle Le Vasseur the
objects of ridicule. In less than six weeks, all the newspapers
that at first spoke of him only in honourable terms had
changed to contempt. The Court and public had changed just
as quickly, and those with whom Hume was connected were
the most derisive. As for Hume himself, during the journey to
England Rousseau had spoken of his mistrust of the 'juggler'
Tronchin, but it turned out that Tronchin's son lodged with
Hume in London.

Later, during the overnight stay at Lisle Street, both hostesses
[Annie and Peggy Elliot] and servants exhibited hatred and
scorn for him; the welcome they offered Mlle Le Vasseur was
abominable. Anyone Hume met was almost certain to adopt a
disdainful and malevolent tone towards Rousseau; a hundred
times, in his very presence, Hume had twisted people against
him. What Hume's aim was, he could not say, but all
Rousseau's letters passed through his hands. Hume was always
avid to see and have them. Of those Rousseau wrote, few
arrived. Almost all those sent to him were opened, and any
which might have shed some light on his situation probably
suppressed.

Without drawing breath, Rousseau then went into much

more detail. First, he recounted Hume's muttering '*Je tiens Jean-Jacques Rousseau*' on the journey to Calais, in a voice that Rousseau would never forget, petrifying and ill-omened. Next, he related the events that led to the emotional paroxysm at their last meeting.

That night, 18 March, he had been at Hume's desk, writing to Mme de Chenonceaux. So desperate was Hume to discover what Rousseau was saying, he could barely restrain himself from reading it over his shoulder. Rousseau deliberately closed the letter. Thereupon, Hume hungrily asked for it, promising to post it the next day. But then Lord Nuneham arrived and, when Hume left the room, offered to send it in the French ambassador's packet. Rousseau accepted. Just as the peer took out his seal, Hume returned and volunteered his with such enthusiasm that it could not be refused. A servant was called and Nuneham handed over the letter to be dispatched to the ambassador. Rousseau said to himself that Hume would pursue the servant out of the room – which he did.

Finally, Rousseau led Mme de Verdelin from the practical world into a chthonic realm of shadows and hidden menace. During and after supper, Hume fixed Rousseau and Le Vasseur with a frightening look that no honest man would ever have encountered. A room had been prepared for Le Vasseur – which Rousseau labelled the 'kennel' (he erased the adjective 'filthy') – and after she retired to bed, he and Hume sat in silence for a while. Hume then resumed his staring, and although Rousseau tried to stare back, he was unable to meet the Scotsman's terrorizing glare. He sensed his spirit quail; he was filled with foreboding. Suddenly he was swept by remorse at having judged so great a man by appearances.

In tears, I threw myself in his arms, crying, 'No, David Hume is not a traitor; that is not possible; and if he was not

the best of men, he would have to be the blackest.' At this,
my man, instead of being moved to pity, or becoming angry,
or demanding explanations, remained calm, responded to
my transports with a few cold strokes, patting me on the
back exclaiming over and over again, 'My dear Sir! What is
it, my dear Sir?' I confess that this reception of my outpouring struck me more than everything else.

In contrast to Hume's account of this evening, Rousseau makes
no mention of the retour chaise. Possibly this was because his
outrage there was straightforward – he simply resented being
lied to. So matter of fact a transgression had no place in this
Gothic tale of psychic horror and one man's mastery over
another.

Another discrepancy is over the nature of Rousseau's apology.
In Hume's version, Rousseau is apologizing for his folly and ill-
behaviour; in Rousseau's version, the apology concerns
Hume's character. Whom should we believe? Unquestionably,
Rousseau's record of Hume's stilted reaction – so reminiscent
of the Scotsman's embarrassing inarticulateness when playing
the sultan in Paris to the two slaves – has the ring of veracity.

However, though he unburdened himself at length to Mme de
Verdelin, Rousseau did not tell her everything on his mind. He
had mulled over the Lisle Street happenings and, in particular,
Hume's detached response to his impassioned outburst. Why
had Hume not insisted on knowing what he meant by 'traitor'?
Or provided an explanation for his behaviour? As Hume's
honour and friendship surely demanded.

From this brooding emerged that letter to Hume from Wootton on 22 March. In Rousseau's mind, this was no routine epistle. The point was to put Hume to a trial. The expression of
Rousseau's gratitude was followed by an apparently loving

passage in which he urged Hume to preserve their friendship.

> Love me for myself who owes you so much; for yourself;
> love me for the good you have done me. I am conscious of
> the full value of your sincere friendship; I ardently wish it; I
> wish to return it with all mine, and I feel something in my
> heart to convince you one day that it is not at all without
> some value.

Rousseau crafted these superficially naive lines with intense care. His strategy was to make his suspicions overt, and thus give Hume a last chance to explain himself. Rousseau believed that this statement of doubt over Hume's feelings for him set Hume a simple test: if his *cher patron* found the passage natural, he was guilty; if he found it extraordinary, and requiring a response, he was innocent.

From Hume in reply came an apology for the 'cheat' over the retour chaise, while making plain the initiative was Davenport's. 'Mr Davenport himself repents of it, and *by my advice* [authors' italics] is resolved nevermore to form such a project.' But there was nothing on the main issue. Nothing on Rousseau's tormented heart. Indeed, Hume was standoffish: 'My good wishes attend you to whatever part of the world you may retreat; mixed with regret that I am so far distant from you.'

Over the next weeks, Rousseau reiterated his charges against Hume to several others, including Earl Marischal. Mme de Verdelin told Rousseau she was rocked by his assertions. The story had chilled her blood. Since reading it, she had found it difficult to order her thoughts and had been unable to close her eyes for more than two hours. She had burned his letter. She went through the allegations, attempting to soothe him. Hume was not capable of such things.

Earl Marischal declared himself astonished and disbelieving, though, given Rousseau's past persecution, he empathized with his vigilance. He then applied the same poultice as Mme de Verdelin – running through the allegations one by one in a vain attempt to dispel Rousseau's worries. And he advised Rousseau to say 'yes' to the royal pension, if it were ever offered.

That offer, as we have seen, was made on 2 May, and the royal pension finally brought Rousseau into direct confrontation with the blissfully unaware Hume.

When news of the King's agreement came via Conway, Hume had at once sent the general's letter on to Rousseau, recommending acceptance. Rousseau duly answered Conway on 12 May. Had he, as might have been expected, confined his response to an expression of humble thanks, Hume could have allowed himself a moment's self-congratulation. Instead, Rousseau's reply was streaked with paranoia. But the design was clear: a man in torment, he was making a plea to delay his decision.

In elegant phrases, the exile expressed thanks to both the King and Conway. However, he explained, he was too upset to think clearly: 'After so many misfortunes I had thought myself ready for all possible happenings. One has come upon me that I had not foreseen and that no honest man could have foreseen. It has affected me cruelly.' Consequently, no matter how important the issue, he lacked the presence of mind to think what action to take:

> So far from refusing the benefactions of the King from pride, as is imputed to me, I take them as something to glory in; and what is most painful is that I cannot do so in the eyes of the public. But when I actually receive them, I wish to be able to give up myself entirely to those sentiments they

inspire in me, and to have a heart filled only with gratitude for his Majesty's goodness and yours . . . Deign, therefore, Sir, to keep them for me for happier days.

Hume must have been relieved to see the issue of the pension heading towards a conclusion, with only the administrative arrangements to be finalized. He had spent some of his influence with Conway, and when the payment was eventually settled, he could consider his obligations to his charge at an end. As Professor Hugh Blair noted on 13 May, when thanking Hume for his entertaining anecdotes about Rousseau ('a high feast to all your friends'), 'Much as you loved him, you felt some deliverance upon his going away; for his whims and oddities could not fail to be sometimes a burden to you.'

That he was not, after all, free of the burden must have come as a profound shock to Hume when he called on Conway on 15 May to be handed Rousseau's letter. His surging frustration resounded through his missive to Mme de Boufflers the next day: '[Rousseau] has been guilty of an extravagance the most unaccountable and most blameable that is possible to be imagined.'

The exasperation is equally patent in the letter he tore off to Davenport:

> It is very remarkable that in the same instant when Mr Rousseau appears to you in so good humour, he represents himself to General Conway as overwhelmed with the deepest affliction on account of some most unexpected misfortune; and he even says that his profound melancholy deprives him, for the time, of the use of his understanding.

Even more remarkably, Rousseau had refused the King's bounty, though, Hume explodes,

> He had allowed Mr Conway to apply for it, had wrote to Lord Marischal to obtain his consent for accepting it, and

had given me the authority to notify his consent to Mr Conway; and though in all this he may seem to have used the
King ill, and Mr Conway and Lord Marischal, and me,
above all, he makes no apology for this conduct and never
writes me a word about it.

In his first flush of anger, Hume had understood Rousseau as
saying that he wanted to amend the pension's terms – in particular, to make it public. Preoccupied with government, Conway seems to have gone along with that construction.
However, others who read the letter (including Adam Smith)
recognized that this was a misreading. Rousseau was merely
attempting to explain why he felt unable to accept the pension
at that moment.

Much would flow from this misconstruing. In his letter to
Mme de Boufflers, Hume sounded ready to confront Rousseau:
'I shall write to him, and tell him that the affair is no longer an
object of deliberation . . . Was anything in the world so unaccountable? For the purposes of life and society, a little good
sense is surely better than all this genius, and a little good
humour than this extreme sensibility.' There could have been
no clearer statement of the rational sceptic's inability to
empathize with the man of sensibility. Philosophy had crossed
over into life.

By the next day, however, Hume had cooled down. He tried
to come to the rescue of his charge, writing that he and Conway hoped Rousseau would change his mind on the condition
of the pension's secrecy. Conway and his wife surmised that the
cause of Rousseau's profound melancholy was the King of
Prussia letter, said Hume. If so, they wanted him to know that
Mr Walpole was very sorry to have given such offence. 'That
idle piece of pleasantry was meant to be entirely secret, and the
publication of it was contrary to his intention and came from

accident. Mr Walpole has expressed the same sentiments to me.' Of course, all that was complete hogwash. In any case, from Rousseau there was no (immediate) response.

Bruised feelings aside, Hume was still convinced that Rousseau's prime concern was to renegotiate the terms of the pension with the King. So, on 19 June, he wrote to Rousseau again. From Rousseau's silence, he deduced that Rousseau was still adamant over the secrecy stipulation. Therefore he had approached Conway to see if the King would allow the pension to be made public. Conway would speak to the King if he were assured that Rousseau would accept and the King not be exposed to a humiliating second refusal. Would Rousseau give that consent as soon as possible?

But Hume's patience was wearing out. Although Rousseau could not have replied yet, Hume followed up on 21 June in formal terms, writing of himself in the third person and threatening to have nothing more to do with the pension: 'Mr Hume's compliments. He . . . begs as soon as convenient, an answer to his last, as he shall be obliged to leave London soon; and shall not then have it in his power to be any longer of service to him.'

This plea would have reached Wootton on 23 June. Its impact was immediate. That same day, Rousseau wrote 'the last letter you will receive from me'. In the words of one editor of Hume's correspondence, G. Birkbeck Hill,

In the midst of [Hume's] self-complacency, while he was, no doubt, flattering himself with the thought that he had attained the highest degree of merit which can be bestowed on any human creature, by possessing 'the sentiment of benevolence in an eminent degree', the fat good-humoured Epicurean of the North received, one day in June, a ruder shock than has perhaps ever tried a philosopher's philosophy.

15

Three Slaps

Je laisse un libre cours aux manœuvres de vos amis, — ... aux vôtres, et je vous abandonne avec ce peu de regret ma réputation durant ma vie, bien Sûr qu'un jour — on nous rendra justice à tous deux. Quant aux bons — offices en matière d'intérêt avec lesquels vous vous — masquez, je vous en remercie et vous en dispense. Je me dois de n'avoir plus de commerce avec vous, et de n'accepter, pas même à mon avantage, aucune affaire dont vous — Soyez le médiateur. Adieu, Monsieur, je vous Souhaite le plus vrai bonheur, mais comme nous ne devons plus — rien avoir à nous dire, voici la dernière lettre que — vous recevrez de moi.

Rousseau

Rousseau springs a surprise

Those who do not feel pain seldom think that it is felt.
Samuel Johnson

In the letter of 23 June that so amazed Hume, Rousseau's 341 words (in French) had a pitch of utter conviction and unanswerability. Rousseau had no further doubts about either Hume's conduct or the veracity of his own charges:

> I believed that my silence, interpreted by your conscience, had said enough; but since you purpose not to understand me, I shall speak. You have badly concealed yourself. I understand you, Sir, and you well know it.

No ancient mariner holding a wedding guest with his glittering eye could have been more compelling.

> Before we had any connection, quarrels or disputes; while we knew each other only by literary reputation, you hastened to offer me your friends and your assistance. Touched by your generosity, I threw myself in your arms; you brought me to England, apparently to procure a refuge for me, and in reality to dishonour me. You applied yourself to this noble endeavour with a zeal worthy of your heart and with an art worthy of your talents. Success did not require great effort; you live in the grand world, and I in retirement; the public love to be taken in and you are made for deceit. However, I know one man whom you will not deceive, you yourself. You know with what horror my heart rejected the first suspicion of your designs. Embracing you, my eyes filled with tears, I told you

that if you were not the best of men, you would have to be the blackest. In reflecting on your secret conduct, you sometimes say to yourself you are not the best of men; and I doubt that, with this notion, you will ever be the happiest.

I give your friends and you a free hand to carry on your manoeuvres; and with little regret I abandon to you my reputation during my lifetime, certain that, one day, justice will be done to both of us. As to your good offices in matters of interest, which you have used as a mask, I thank you for and excuse you from them. I ought not to have any further correspondence with you, or to accept any business, even to my advantage, in which you will be the mediator.

Adieu, Sir, I wish you the truest happiness; but as we ought not to have anything more to say to each other, this is the last letter you will receive from me.

JJ ROUSSEAU

Three days later (26 June), an upset and furious Hume was replying to Rousseau at length, his agitation coursing through every line. As he was conscious always of acting towards Rousseau in 'the most friendly part', and 'of having ever given you the most tender, the most active proofs of sincere affection, you may judge of my extreme surprise on perusing your epistle.' He went on to demand particulars of the accusations and the name of the 'calumniator' who, 'I must charitably suppose', had made them:

You owe this to me, you owe it to yourself, you owe it to truth and honour and justice and to everything that can be deemed sacred among men. As an innocent man; I will not say, as your friend; I will not say, as your benefactor; but I repeat it, as an innocent man, I claim the privilege of proving my innocence, and of refuting any scandalous lye which may have been invented against me.

Rather than write directly to his accuser, and presumably because he wanted proof of delivery, Hume addressed the letter to Davenport at Wootton, begging him to peruse the content before handing it over, and enclosing a duplicate of Rousseau's thunderbolt. He called for Davenport's aid in 'the most critical affair which, during the course of my whole life, I have been engaged in . . . You will be astonished, as I was, at the monstrous ingratitude, ferocity, and frenzy of the man.' His first concern was to have his nameless slanderer exposed, and in summoning Davenport to stand by his side, his tone became positively Shakespearean: 'If it were necessary, I should conjure you by all your regards to truth and justice to second my demand and make him sensible of the necessity he lies under of agreeing to it. He must himself pass for a liar and calumniator, if he does not comply.'

While ingratitude might be read into Rousseau's letter, the terms *ferocity* and *frenzy* scarcely matched its measured diction. Hume was the man possessed. Comically enough, this letter was opened by Davenport's agent, Mr Walton (who administered his estate), with Rousseau looking on. (If it had taken two days to reach Wootton from London, it must have arrived on 28 June, Rousseau's fifty-fourth birthday: an explosive present.) Seeing the copy of his own words, Rousseau resealed the packet and sent it on to Davenport by express. It was too long a story to narrate by mail, he said in a covering note. 'We can talk about it when we meet. In the meantime, read, ponder and see what you make of this affair.'

Somehow, a complete reversal of roles had taken place. Hume was convinced that Rousseau had devised a plot to dishonour him, and he now acted with the ferocity and frenzy of which he had accused his accuser.

On 27 June 1766, Hume wrote to d'Holbach in Paris, following it up with a second letter on 1 July. These letters, from which d'Holbach read extracts to an open-mouthed audience in his salon, promptly disappeared. The editor of Rousseau's *Correspondance complète*, Ralph Leigh, believed they were of such extraordinary violence as to have 'disconcerted even Rousseau's most unremitting enemies'. Two missives Hume dispatched to d'Alembert in the second half of July also vanished – only extracts have survived. The assumption must be that *le bon David's* friends destroyed them in the interests of his good name. In the salons of the French Enlightenment, they did not approve of reason becoming the ugly creature of the passions. Hume's anger, together with his failure to comprehend the sophisticated manners governing the Republic of Letters, as exemplified in Mme de Boufflers's *Rule of Life*, had driven him to breach the conventions.

According to Amélie Suard, the wife of Hume's French translator, she and her husband were at Mme Necker's salon when someone bustled in from d'Holbach's and reported that d'Holbach had just received a letter from Hume which began with the words: 'My dear baron, Rousseau is a scoundrel.'

Hume retracted all the decent things he had ever said about Rousseau. He regretted keenly ever having taken an interest in the ex-citizen of Geneva, because he had indeed nursed a viper in his bosom. (Just as d'Holbach had warned him.) He rehearsed all the efforts he had made to gain a pension for the exile and fulminated that Rousseau's snub was simply a declaration of war and the first signal of a campaign designed to dishonour him. What is more, he had proof that Rousseau must have planned this campaign for two months. His strategy was to let Hume pursue the pension on a verbal assent and then summarily and ostentatiously to refuse it. Rousseau would thus ingratiate himself with the opposition parties while compromising Hume with the King and the people. (Hume could have had no grounds at all for this: there was no evidence of

Rousseau's interest in the machinations of London politics.)

A letter to Hume from one of his admirers and translators, Mme de Meinières, on 7 July, is suffused with the same bewilderment and shock with which Hume's anguished tidings were received in Paris. She opened sweepingly: she wrote not just as one whose life he had profoundly influenced, but as a citizen who desired the destruction of fanaticism and ignorance, and the glorious union of philosophers and men of letters. Did he want the baron to publish his letter? Was Hume going to publish it? All France waited with bated breath. No one doubted that Rousseau was ungrateful, wild, capricious, vain. But, and here she quoted Hume directly, that he was the *blackest and most atrocious villain that ever disgraced human nature*, and that one could lavish on him the descriptions *of the lying, the ferocity, of the rascal* – that was new.

Notably, Hume had shared his rage and distress with his French contacts before any other. Notably, too, he selected d'Holbach, unyieldingly antagonistic to Rousseau, rather than his passionate devotee Mme de Boufflers, who was also a Rousseau supporter and whom Hume was allowing to continue under the illusion that he intended to return to Paris to live in the apartment she had arranged for him in the Temple. (As 'grand priest to the Idol of the Temple', sniffed Mme du Deffand.)

However, the Scotsman was in a stew of anxiety for his reputation in Britain, too. On the first day of July, he wrote to Professor Blair 'earnestly desiring' him not to show anyone the letters he had sent him about Rousseau and to retrieve any copies. Indeed, how embarrassing their so-recent encomiums must have seemed when the subject had been revealed as 'surely the blackest and most atrocious villain, beyond comparison, that now exists in the world and I am heartily ashamed of anything I ever wrote in his favour'. There is the first glimpse of

Hume's intentions and his awareness of the related perils: 'I know you will pity me when I tell you that I am afraid I must publish this to the whole world in a pamphlet which must contain an account of the whole affair between us . . . You know how dangerous any controversy on a disputable point would be with a man of his talents.' Hume's *Concise Account* of the dispute was some months and many twists and turns away from publication.

Three days later, Hume sent a similar message to Davenport, asking if Davenport could unearth copies of his letters to Rousseau: 'It would be of no consequence for me to have copies of them, were he not the most dangerous man in the world on account of his malice and his talents: I cannot take too many precautions against him.'

The idea of putting his side of the affair into the public domain continued to germinate. Thanks to Hume's circle, Rousseau's *démarche* was instantly the talk of *le tout Paris*. In one of his letters to d'Holbach, the contents of which were relayed around town, Hume spoke of a pamphlet to instruct the public in all Rousseau's 'atrocities'.

On both sides of the Channel, Hume's flabbergasted friends now rallied to his support, all compassion on his abused philanthropy but all caution on publication. On 6 July, Julie de L'Espinasse and d'Alembert wrote a joint letter, indicative of how eager they were to be involved. De L'Espinasse began, 'What atrocities has [Rousseau] committed against you?' They had heard something about it from the baron. She asked for a summary of Hume's reply to these atrocities – not out of curiosity or doubt but to be ready to defend him against Rousseau fanatics, many of whom were held in high public esteem. She surrendered the pen to an impatient d'Alembert. What had gone on? He, too, desperately wanted to be better informed so that he could persuade people of what he was already persuaded, that Rousseau had truly wronged Hume. However, he counselled Hume to think twice before subjecting his woes to public scrutiny: these sorts of quarrels only encouraged the zealots and gave the indifferent an excuse to blackguard men of letters.

Adam Smith adopted the same line, introducing a note of political realism. He also wrote from Paris (where he was enjoying the grand tour as tutor to the Duke of Buccleuch): 'I am thoroughly convinced that Rousseau is as great a rascal as you & as every man here believe him to be; yet let me beg of you not to think of publishing any thing to the world upon the very great impertinence which he has been guilty of to you.' By refusing the pension, Rousseau might have exposed Hume to some ridicule in the eyes of the Court and ministry; however, said Smith, within three weeks *le bon David* would again be recognized as the man of honour he was:

> To write against him, is, you may depend on it, the very thing he wishes you to do. He is in danger of falling into obscurity in England and he hopes to make himself considerable by provoking an illustrious adversary. He will have a great party. The church, the Whigs, the Jacobites, the whole wise English nation, will love to mortify a Scotchman, and to applaud a man who has refused a pension from the King.

On 7 July, the original recipient of Hume's distress (and the man who had assured it maximum publicity), d'Holbach, finally replied in person, sympathetic over Hume's plight but joining with the others in trying to temper the broiling emotions of the exemplar of moderation.

He pointed out that Hume was not used to this mischief making. Readers of Hume's *History* expected more history to come, not pamphlets to correct the incorrigible. Now that the dust had settled a bit, no doubt Hume would agree with the baron, and all with whom he had shared the news, that he should avoid an endless literary dogfight. He must not be embarrassed at having been duped through his goodness of heart. He should leave polemic to those who had no better way of passing the time. His French friends had let well alone when attacked by Rousseau. Hume would come to share this judgement when his serenity returned. He should remember that he was David Hume: his name was known and respected, and no one could injure it. However, if in spite of their guidance he did decide to publish something, he should send it to Mr Suard at the *Gazette de France*.

D'Holbach also answered a query. Hume, pursuing his investigations into Rousseau's resources and seemingly intent on demonstrating that the exile was not as poor as he claimed, had asked the baron to verify that Rousseau had received several thousand francs from the Maréchal de Luxembourg. D'Holbach reported back that he had heard from a friend of the banker Rougemont how money was sent to Rousseau in Môtiers through the Maréchal de Luxembourg's *valet de chambre*, the confidential servant La Roche. Once, La Roche had handed over ten thousand *louis, about the sum Hume had mentioned* (authors' italics).

Hume had been told by Mme de Meinières of the buzz he had stirred up in Paris – and of splits emerging within the Republic of Letters:

> Rousseau's followers claim that it was his refusal [of the pension] delivered with all his usual haughtiness that seemed like an insult, and that is all there is to it. Your friends believe and say that the refusal had grave consequences and that Rousseau had accompanied it with some base trick . . . Your team will triumph over his team.

Was Hume's aim the triumph of his team? Could he let rumour and scandal circulate unchecked in the city where he had enjoyed such veneration only half a year before? Would Rousseau's supporters let the matter rest? Should Hume's supporters not be armed? However, there was more to his dilemma than such rational calculations.

Hume was not only beside himself with fury but also stricken with conspiracy sickness. He told Davenport that Rousseau had all along pursued, 'from ostentation, an opportunity of refusing a pension from the King, and at the same time, of picking a quarrel with me, in order to cancel at once all his past obligations.'

Secluded in Wootton, Rousseau had also been occupying himself with the affair. On 10 July, he sent Hume the detailed case his mortified patron had insisted upon so ill-advisedly.

The exile began by explaining that he was sick and in no condition to write. However, Hume wanted an explanation and so must have it. Then Rousseau unrolled the indictment in sixty-three lengthy paragraphs. Of course, he had already laid the foundations in his letter to Mme de Verdelin, but he must have taken pains to compose this philippic; its elegantly written final version belies the roughest of rough drafts.

At the commencement, he promoted the idea of himself as a man apart, implying that he was not involved in the quotidian politicking of Hume's life. His world was one of feeling, of self-knowledge, a world that enabled him to rise above the need for legal proof of his allegations. From that basis, he could answer Hume's confident demand for the name of his accuser. 'That accuser, Sir, is the only man in the world whose testimony I should admit against you: it is yourself.'

He began at the beginning, with his quitting Switzerland. The narrative then followed the general course mapped out to

Mme de Verdelin, with the stylistic quirk that Rousseau treated Hume in the third person throughout. 'I received a letter
from Mr Hume . . . "I went to Paris to join Mr Hume . . .' Possibly Rousseau envisaged sending the letter to others, perhaps
Conway, but this literary device was a powerful one, severing
their relationship while putting Hume at arm's length from the
reader as well as from Rousseau himself.

The structure is also conceived with a novelist's eye for
drama. The episode of Hume's 'four terrifying words' (on their
journey to England) is alluded to midway, though out of its
chronological order, but the words are not spelled out until
almost the end when they can be deployed against Hume to
devastating effect. '*Je tiens J.-J. Rousseau*' becomes successively
the capstone of the author's argument, his petrifying nightly vis-
itation, and his instrument of emotionally charged repetition:

> The critical situation to which he had now reduced me,
> recalled strongly to my mind the four words that I men-
> tioned above and which I heard him say and repeat at a time
> when I had not really understood their force . . . Not a night
> passes but I think I hear I have you J.-J. Rousseau ring in my
> ears, as if he had just pronounced them. Yes, Mr Hume, you
> have me, I know, but only by those things that are external
> to me . . . You have me by my reputation, and perhaps my
> security . . . Yes, Mr Hume, you have me by all the ties of this
> life, but you do not have me by my virtue or my courage . . .

Rousseau also brought a fine craftsmanship to a dramatized
mockery of his victim. He records how he metaphorically
'slapped' his patron's face three times, but Hume did not feel
it. Contemporaries thought this pillorying of Hume inspired,
executed with the lightest of touches. Jean-François Marmontel, the popular author of novels, plays and verse, praised
the 'sublime insolence' of 'this trick of raillery'.

He first 'slapped' Hume's face, Rousseau recorded, when he failed to write to his benefactor after the King of Prussia letter was published in London – in adversity, he had turned elsewhere. The second slap came with Rousseau's assertion (in his 7 April letter to the *St. James's Chronicle*) that the spoof's author in Paris 'had an accomplice in London and that was what rendered his heart'. This had to mean Hume, but his protector pretended to believe that the only cause of Rousseau's distress over the spoof was his vanity: 'Vain or not, I was mortally afflicted; he knew it and wrote not a word.' The third slap was delivered when Rousseau replied directly to Conway over the pension, not rejecting it but excusing himself for the present, and not to Hume, who had undertaken the negotiations. 'Third blow on the cheek of my patron, and if he does not feel it, that is assuredly his fault. He feels nothing.'

In concluding the long indictment, Rousseau framed a per-oration in which he contemplated the possibility that he, not Hume, was in the wrong. It is easy to hear this powerful appeal being spoken to judge and jury:

> You make me desire to be that despicable object. Yes, the situation in which I would see myself reduced, trampled pros-trate at your feet, crying out for mercy, and doing everything to obtain it; publishing aloud my own unworthiness, and paying the most brilliant homage to your virtues, would be a state of blossoming and joy to my heart after the state of suf-focation and death where you have placed it. If innocent, Hume should justify himself; if guilty, adieu for ever.

It is unsurprising that such prose scared Hume. Hume's own written style has a beautiful lucidity; it is never meretricious, and his theoretical writings are scattered with plain and unpre-tentious illustrations. (Samuel Johnson condemned Hume for revelling in reasonableness: 'He had a vanity in being thought easy,' he said to Boswell.) Narrating history, the Scot had a facility both for engaging his readers' sympathies and for creating comedy. But he could never match Rousseau's rhetorical force, poetic gifts and sense of theatre.

Taking the indictment as a whole, the effect is Gothic, as hidden enemies cynically plot the fall of the innocent, and seemingly harmless actions carry a subterranean danger. When digesting it, Hume might have laughed over the contortions the plot demanded and wept over his erstwhile friend's torments. He might have chosen to dismiss Rousseau as either a lunatic or an imbecile, recalling John Locke's distinction between the reasoning of a madman and a fool: the fool reasons incorrectly on correct premises, while a madman reasons correctly on absurd premises. Instead, what he did was furiously to annotate Rousseau's allegations, discovering 'twelve lyes' to be communicated to the public in his pre-emptive campaign to shield himself from the eloquence of the most powerful writer in Europe.

16
Twelve Lies

This world is a comedy to those who think and a tragedy to those that feel.

Horace Walpole

To a philosopher and historian the madness and imbecility and wickedness of mankind ought to appear ordinary events.

David Hume

He might not have believed in an afterlife, but Hume had been worrying about posterity. In a long and detailed note composed between 15 and 25 July for Mme de Meinières, who had begged to know if he had intended d'Holbach to publicize his letter, he explained his 'many reasons for not concealing the affair':

> I know that Rousseau is writing very busily at present, and I have grounds to think that he intends to fall equally on Voltaire & on me. He himself had told me, that he was composing his memoirs, in which justice would be equally done to his own character, to that of his friends, and to that of his enemies. As I had passed so wonderfully from the former class to the latter, I must expect to make a fine figure.

However, he continued, the arrival of Rousseau's detailed indictment – 'which had been extorted from him by the authority of Mr Davenport' – had put his mind at rest. That Rousseau might print the indictment

> gives me no manner of concern. The letter will really be a high panegyric on me; because there is no one who will not distinguish the facts which he acknowledges, and the chimeras which his madness and malice have invented . . . I own that I was somewhat anxious about the affair till I

received this mad letter, but now I am quite at my ease.

Quite at his ease maybe, but the story Hume relayed to Mme de Meinières is notable for the gloss he put on it. For example, Hume claims Rousseau had described him as 'the greatest villain alive, *le plus noir de tous les hommes*'. But this was not the entire, carefully conditional expression that Rousseau had used. How Rousseau had insulted Hume was gossip in London. In a letter from the capital on 18 July, Garrick repeated that Rousseau had called Hume '*noir*, black, and a *coquin*, knave' (both untrue).

While Hume claimed to be sighing with relief after absorbing Rousseau's indictment, he was, in fact, preoccupied with the probability of his accuser publishing it. So on 15 July he reported to Hugh Blair that Rousseau's extended condemnation was 'a perfect frenzy. It would make a good eighteen penny pamphlet; and I fancy he intends to publish it.' Writing to Davenport on the same date, Hume increased the cover price, perhaps in deference to his correspondent's wealth: it became a two shillings pamphlet, but remained 'a perfect frenzy'. He had a word of acid advice for Rousseau's landlord:

> It is, that you would continue the charitable work you have begun, till he be shut up altogether in Bedlam, or till he quarrel with you and run away from you. If he show any disposition to write me a penitenial [*sic*] letter, you may encourage it; not that I think it of any consequence to me, but because it will ease his mind and set him at rest.

The Blair and Davenport correspondence is significant in revealing Hume's dread that, at the very least, a lethal pamphlet was being hatched at Wootton. Hume sought d'Alembert's guidance on his response. Once he had replied to Rousseau, dealing with his accusations in the indictment, should he stand by with arms folded and await attack? That would be his instinct, as he abhorred quarrels, especially in public. On the other hand, Rousseau was hard at work, and would probably fall on Hume with the insolence and audacity of his letter. He was also preparing his memoirs, where Hume would play a pretty role. Suppose those memoirs appeared after Hume's death? Or indeed after Rousseau's?

Frenzied or not, Rousseau's peerless rhetoric commanded Hume's objective respect. However absurd the logic of Rousseau's case might be, there was no denying the wicked mockery of those 'three slaps' and the beauty and power of his final paragraphs. As Hume told Mme de Meinières, 'Would you believe it, that in a piece so full of frenzy, malice, impertinence, and lyes, there are many strokes of genius and eloquence, and the conclusion of it is remarkably sublime.'

With Rousseau isolated in the stillness of Wootton, Hume pondered his reply amid the tumult of Leicester Fields. This he did not send to Rousseau until 22 July.

Curiously, he took up only one accusation in the indictment, relating to the dramatic events on the evening before Rousseau left for Staffordshire. In his rebuttal, Hume reconnected these to the retour-chaise affair, recording how he justified Davenport's deceit while insisting he himself had had no part in it. In this retelling, Rousseau's silence followed, then his bedewing of Hume with tears, and the emotional outburst. One or other must be a liar, protested Hume, as their accounts were diametrically opposed: 'You imagine, perhaps, that because the incident passed privately, without any witness, the question will lie between the credibility of your assertion and mine.' But Hume had three proofs. First, a letter from Rousseau confirming Hume's account; secondly, Hume had told Davenport the story the next day 'with a view to preventing such good-natured arti-

fices for the future'; thirdly, as he thought the story 'much to
your honour', he had also conveyed it to friends, including
Mme de Boufflers.

Hume ended uncompromisingly; while his account was consistent and rational, Rousseau's was devoid of all common sense:

> I shall only add in general, that I enjoyed, about a month
> ago, an uncommon pleasure, when I reflected, that, thro'
> many difficulties and by most assiduous care and pains, I
> had, beyond my most sanguine expectations, provided for
> your repose, honour, and fortune. But I soon felt a very sen-
> sible uneasiness, when I found, that you had, wantonly and
> voluntarily, thrown away all these advantages, and was the
> declared enemy of your own repose, fortune, and honour. I
> cannot be surprised after this, that you are my enemy. Adieu,
> and for ever.

The tone is triumphalist. But, for all that, Hume's letter is
unconvincing and again raises some awkward questions about
his good faith. In the indictment, Rousseau does not refer to
the retour chaise at all. He is solely concerned with Hume's
staring that filled him with 'inexpressible terror'. Moreover,
Hume is simply wrong if, when he refers to a letter from
Rousseau confirming his account, he means the one from
Wootton on 22 March designed to test Hume by offering him
the chance to respond to the word 'traitor'. In that, Rousseau
reproves him over the chaise, but by no stretch of interpretation can it be seen to deal with, let alone corroborate, Hume's
version of the evening. As for the letter to Mme de Boufflers
about the turbulent and tearful night in Lisle Street, while this
has Hume attesting to Rousseau's 'extreme sensibility and
good heart', the main objective seems to be to show himself in
a favourable light to his dear friend, and all the other ladies to
whom he allows her to pass on the story.

Hume did not let the matter drop with this limited reply to Rousseau. Scrutinizing Rousseau's indictment, he identified twelve lies (in fact more, but he 'gave' Rousseau some repetitions) that must be among the most curious of marginalia. Hume's comments, which can be read in a duplicate in the Royal Library at Windsor, are penned in his spidery writing with care and precision; they are at the heart of the *Concise Account*, his published version of the affair.

For Hume, every detail had to be addressed. In uncovering the conspiracy, Rousseau accorded the most trivial incidents equal probative value with the most wounding. No happening was by chance or without significance. To misquote T. S. Eliot slightly, 'In the sordid particulars, the unearthly design appears.' And only by confronting and disputing the sordid particulars could Hume confront and dispute the underlying narrative – his alleged plot against Rousseau.

The 'First Lye' was identified in the second sentence. Rousseau remarked that Hume could have had an explanation of his case against Hume a long time ago but did not want it, so he, Rousseau, remained silent. Hume's riposte: 'M. Rousseau never gave me the least opportunity of demanding an explication [*sic*]. If he ever entertained any of those black and absurd suspicions, of which the letter is so full, he always concealed them as long as we lived together.' However, this claim is not completely accurate if, during that turbulent evening in Lisle Street, Rousseau really did blurt out, '[Hume] is not a traitor.'

The 'Second and Third Lyes' were Rousseau's complaint that on arrival in London he had been treated rudely by an unnamed gentleman and his brother. Another lie then emerged from Rousseau's declared suspicion of flattery and his describing Hume as flattering him in a suspect way. Rousseau added an insightful example. 'I shall mention only one which made me smile: every time I came to see him he took care to have a volume of *Eloisa* [*Héloïse*] upon his table; as if I did not know enough of Mr Hume's taste, to be well assured that of all the books in the world, *Eloisa* must be one of the most tiresome to him.' Hume struck back. Rousseau 'never objected to any civilities which I paid him; and he expressed indeed a general satisfaction at every part of my conduct. Here is therefore a lye which I will throw into the dozen.'

Significantly, Rousseau's critique on the flattery charge adds, 'I could have wished he had sometimes substituted, in the place of such gross encomiums, the style of a friend; but I never found in his language anything which favoured of true friendship, not even in his manner of speaking of me to others in his presence.'

The story moves on to the evening before the departure for Wootton. At the point where Rousseau ejaculates, 'No, no, David Hume is not a traitor; if he is not the best of men, he must be the worst', Hume notes, 'This is the fourth lye: the most studied and most premeditated of the whole.'

The next lie follows from this scene, with Rousseau in the country 'afflicted with the most cruel uncertainty, and ignorant what to think of a man whom I ought to love', and writing Hume the entrapment letter, 'which he ought to have found very natural, if he were guilty; but extraordinary, if he were innocent'. 'Fifth lye: See the letter itself, dated 22 March page 13, where there is a most unreserved cordiality, not the least appearance of suspicion.'

Rousseau goes on to ask what *éclaircissement*, illumination, his letter produced in Hume. 'None.' Hume entirely failed to detect the state of Rousseau's heart, his torment. This was to be expected. 'For when one had ventured to declare to a man's face, *I am tempted to believe you a traitor*, and he has not the curiosity to ask you *For what?*, it may be depended on he will never have such curiosity as long as he lives: and it is easy to judge of this man from this slight evidence.' Hume was curt: 'A repetition of the fourth lie; and consequently equivalent to a sixth.'

The seventh lie is Rousseau's claim that Hume questioned his *gouvernante* about his occupations, resources, acquaintances, their names, situations, places of abode – all up to the limits of importunity ... 'and with the most Jesuitical address, he would ask the same questions of us separately'. Rousseau thought it was unbecoming in a philosopher. 'Seventh lye. I never had but one *tête à tête* with his *gouvernante*. It was about half an hour on her first arrival. It was not likely I could have any other subject of conversation with her but about him.' (But bearing in mind his avid search for Rousseau's true income, we might wonder what aspect of her master's life he chose to discuss.)

The eighth and ninth lies concern the delay in publishing both a letter on his stay in Montmorency as well as Du Peyrou's correspondence about his persecution. Rousseau maintained that Hume had had oversight of these projects, which were stymied by the King of Prussia letter. 'Lye, lye,' scrawled Hume.

Having traversed much other ground, including the spoof letter, Rousseau had reached the moment his enemies judged right for their *grand coup*. It came with the *St. James's Chronicle* letter of 5–7 June signed by 'V.T.h.S.W.' that sniped at Rousseau, questioning how his door was open to the rich and closed to the poor. 'Had there remained in me the least doubt, it would have been impossible to have harboured it after perusing this piece, as it contained facts unknown to anybody but Mr Hume, though exaggerated, it is true, in order to render them odious to the public.' Hume's was an unconvincing rejoinder: 'I never saw the piece either before or after publication. I am not sure, that it even existed but in Mr Rousseau's imagination or assertion. None of my acquaintances whom I have spoken to, ever saw it or heard of it.' The improbability of that last assertion is noteworthy and tends to undermine Hume's own denial – he knew no one aware of a leading paper's sharp and witty exchanges about Rousseau? What about Walpole, with whom Hume was in touch over the affair?

The tenth lie arose out of another claim in this *St. James's Chronicle* letter, that Rousseau gave a cold reception to his only living relative outside Geneva. Rousseau took this to mean his cousin. Hume must have been the source, asserted Rousseau, as the cousin, his 'station in life confining him to the conversation of persons in commerce', had no contacts with men of letters or article writers. 'Tenth lye: I was not present when Mr Rousseau received his cousin. I afterward saw them together, and only for a moment, on the terrace at Buckingham Street.' (But then from whom did the letter-writer, presumably Walpole, obtain all these details?)

The eleventh lie was a repetition of the fourth. For the twelfth lie, we return to Roye and the four deadly words on the boat to England: '*Je tiens J.-J. Rousseau.*' Rousseau describes his being seized with terror and taking a moment before he could laugh at his reaction. Against this phrase, Hume wrote, 'Without scruples, I may set down this as a twelfth lye and a swinging one it is.' (At this point, Hume seems to have abandoned all logic: if he was asleep, how could he have known Rousseau was lying?)

The twelve lies are not the only comments Hume made about Rousseau's text as he went through it, pen hovering over the margins. Rousseau brought into his evidence the Ramsay portrait, his relationship with Davenport, a missed dinner at the British Museum, meals sent into Rousseau's Buckingham Street lodging, and the presence of the young Tronchin in Lisle Street. Hume begged the reader's pardon for his dealing with such silly and trivial matters.

For Rousseau, the plot comes into full view with the King of Prussia letter and the pension. Only then did he grasp that he had been lured to England, and had fallen prey to 'the treachery of a false friend . . . the circumstance that filled my too susceptible heart with deadly sorrow'. Hume responded, 'This false friend is, undoubtedly, myself. But what is the treachery? What harm have I done, or could I do to M. Rousseau? On the supposition of my entering into a project to ruin him how could I think to bring it about by the services I did him?' Publication of the spoof was unavoidable, after copies were dispersed in Paris and London. That Hume was completely innocent of everything to do with the spoof could be seen from a letter submitted by Walpole and attached to this response.

Hume also had to deal with Rousseau's climax: the revelation that the trap had closed in on him, and that all the evidence led back to the arch plotter (Hume). The letter in the press that questioned the Genevan's coldness to his cousin also said that he was apt to change his friends. Not only must Hume have furnished the materials for the piece, *he must also have intended Rousseau to realise this*. But why?

> Nothing is more clear. To raise my resentment to the highest point, so that he might bring on, even more sensationally, the blow he was preparing. He knew, that to make me commit a number of follies, he had only to put me in a passion. We are now arrived at the critical moment, which is to show whether he reasoned well or badly.

As Ralph Leigh remarks, whatever one thinks of the blind illogicality of Rousseau's case, one has to admire the ingenuity with which he makes his enemies responsible for his own follies.

The 'critical' moment was the offer of the pension and Hume's 'skill' in convincing Conway that it was the condition of secrecy that held Rousseau back from accepting. This was 'the end and object of all his labours . . . Already . . . he had treated me as a brutal man, and a monster of ingratitude. But he wanted to do still more. He thinks his measures well taken, and no proofs can be made to appear against him. He demands an explanation: he shall have it, and here it is.'

Understandably baffled by Rousseau's visions of phantasmagorical manoeuvrings, Hume noted, 'How should I have known of these nonsensical suspicions? Mr Davenport, the only person of my acquaintance who saw Mr Rousseau, assures me he was completely ignorant of them.'

In Rousseau's mind, the diabolical subtlety of Hume's plan was clear; it left him no way out. (We could see this as a perverted tribute to Hume's intellect.) If he knew of Hume's treacherous acts, then Rousseau could not accept Hume's help without becoming tainted, a scoundrel himself. If he refused his help, he would have to give an explanation and so would be ruined in the eyes of men. To achieve this, his inescapable dishonour, Hume had brought him to England under the guise of friendship.

Hume left this without comment. Doubtless, he felt that, on such fantasy, none was necessary.

But there was a simple threnody running through Rousseau's darkly surreal imaginings that Hume could not hear. It told of the exile's anguish at his inability to discover in Hume a true friend and at his patron's failure to respond to his distress.

Hume was left debating his next move. He had, he believed, destroyed Rousseau's case. Should he publish? To what end?

17

Willing to Wound

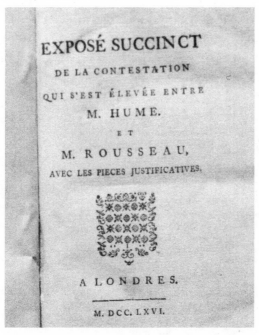

EXPOSÉ SUCCINCT

DE LA CONTESTATION

QUI S'EST ÉLEVÉE ENTRE

M. HUME.

ET

M. ROUSSEAU,

AVEC LES PIECES JUSTIFICATIVES.

A LONDRES.

M. DCC. LXVI.

Hume believed he was 'but little susceptible of enmity'

You can't make an eagle out of a butterfly . . . It is enough, it seems to me, that all the men of letters give him his just deserts, and moreover that his biggest punishment is to be forgotten.
Voltaire, writing about Jean-Jacques Rousseau

The quality, the most necessary for the execution of any useful enterprise, is discretion.
David Hume

In determining how best to deal with Rousseau, Hume faced two linked problems. He had to decide whether to publish his account of the dispute and he had to preserve the support of his highly placed friends in London and Paris. The option of attempting a rapprochement with his tormented former charge – perhaps involving a visit to Wootton, embraces, tears and a passionate affirmation of friendship – seems not to have occurred to him.

Rousseau must have anticipated that Hume would refuse to let the matter drop. In the middle of July 1766, François Coindet, a young Swiss friend who worked for the banker Jacques Necker and had assisted with the illustrations for *Héloïse*, warned Rousseau that his enemies were spreading poison about him in Paris. He specifically mentioned the two violent letters Hume had written to d'Holbach and reported that Hume intended to publish his version of all that had passed between them.

Meanwhile, as part of his preparation for possible publication, Hume turned to his supposedly closest Parisian friend, Mme de Boufflers, writing to her on 15 July after a two-month gap; 'This is a deliberate and a cool plan to stab me,' he lamented. And he asked for her 'consolation and advice' in this distressing and perplexing affair:

> Should I give the whole account to the public, as I am
> advised by several of my friends, particularly Lord Hertford
> and General Conway, I utterly ruin this unhappy man.
> [There is no evidence of such advice.] Everyone must turn
> their back on so false, so ungrateful, so malicious, and so
> dangerous a mortal. I know not indeed any place above
> ground where he could hide his shame; and such a situation
> must run him into madness and despair.

He could not resolve to commit such cruelty, Hume continued.
On the other hand:

> It is extremely dangerous for me to be entirely silent. He is at
> present composing a book, in which it is very likely he may
> fall on me with some atrocious lie . . . My present intention
> therefore is to write a narrative of the whole affair . . . in the
> form of a letter to General Conway.

Hume explained that he had already passed the story on to his
friends in London and that he '*wrote some hint of it* to Baron
De Holbach'. He had also asked d'Holbach to examine the
banker Rougemont's books 'with his own eyes. *I know not but
the inserting [of] that story may be to my purpose.*' (Authors'
italics.) He then chided her for 'always forgetting' his request
to investigate Rousseau's finances herself. 'Perhaps you have
done it, but have concealed the issue from me, as not being
willing to disgust me with my good friend.'

Seemingly, Rousseau's attack had produced a curious blind-
ness in this sympathetic and impartial historian. Until now he
had withheld from Mme de Boufflers that he had also commissioned d'Holbach to delve into Rousseau's resources. And to
describe his writing d'Holbach 'some hint' of his clash with
Rousseau hardly captures the fierce tenor of his letters.

Perhaps Hume anticipated her feeling affronted: after all, she saw herself as his soul mate, and yet he had contacted d'Holbach first. In any case, misleading her in this way was naive. In practice, given how inclusive and gossipy a social circle she moved in and what status she enjoyed, the chance of her not having heard of the d'Holbach letters was slim. In fact, Mme de Boufflers had already complained to Julie de L'Espinasse of Hume's leaving her in ignorance; had he told her about the affair, she would have kept it to herself, as d'Holbach should have done.

Hume's strategy was now fixed on those Parisians who already disliked and distrusted his adversary, and he dispatched a full history of his involvement with Rousseau to d'Alembert.

In the third week of July, Paris became Hume's campaign headquarters, with a meeting *chez* Mlle de L'Espinasse of practically all his Parisian friends. By chance, they congregated just as d'Alembert received Hume's most recent bulletin: it included Hume's plan to send an account to a chosen few. These brilliant Enlightenment spirits – exponents of the supremacy of reason and exactly the people Hume wanted to share his thoughts – formed themselves into an ad hoc advisory committee, Turgot, l'Abbé Morellet, Marmontel, among them. All were burning to learn the latest and to counsel Hume on tactics.

D'Alembert reported their initial conclusions to the anxious Scot: everybody, including he and Julie de L'Espinasse, now thought the story must be made public. If the matter had not made such a sensation, and if Hume had not complained in so lively a manner, he would have continued to advise discretion. But now the public was so taken with the quarrel, and things were so advanced, Hume ought quickly to put the truth before them.

Plainly, however, shock at Hume's berserk letters to d'Holbach had not worn off. The message from the advisory committee was unanimous and unambiguous: 'Practise the greatest moderation, but at the same time the greatest clarity and the greatest detail.' Hume should explain that he was publishing at that moment in order to give Rousseau the chance to reply. He should then go into detail, but stick to the simple facts, with no bitterness, without insult, without even reflecting on Rousseau's character or writings. He must not repeat too often how he was Rousseau's benefactor; everyone knew that already.

D'Alembert added that it was also put about that Rousseau suspected Hume of a hand in what d'Alembert called 'Mr. Valpole's' King of Prussia letter. D'Alembert disapproved of the spoof: to torment an unfortunate being who had done you no ill was cruel. It was essential Hume proved he had nothing to do with this rotten deed (d'Alembert was quite sure he did not). D'Alembert then advised Hume against merely sending five or six copies to selected supporters. This would seem like an underhand trick, a *coup fourré*, unworthy of him, and would not put Rousseau in his place.

On receipt of this advice, Hume asked Walpole for full details of his King of Prussia letter: 'Though I do not intend to publish, I am collecting all the original pieces, and I shall connect them by a concise narrative.' Walpole responded almost by return, on 26 July, from Arlington Street, as we have seen, exonerating Hume from involvement. The Englishman was quite unrepentant, adding that he had a hearty contempt for 'the moutebank' Rousseau.

However, not all voices were tuned in a chorus for publication.

On 22 July, while taking the waters with her lover Conti at Pougues-les-eaux, an ancient spa some 220 kilometres south of Paris, Mme de Boufflers began a memorable epistle to Hume. In her indignation, and with notable insight, she offered her friend a finely worked judgement on the affair. He could not have asked for guidance that was more sensitive – or less welcome.

D'Alembert had forwarded Hume's newest letter for her perusal:

> I confess that it has surprised and afflicted me to the last degree. What! You recommend to [d'Alembert] to communicate [Hume's account of Rousseau's behaviour], not only to your friends in Paris (a definition at once very vague and very extensive), but to M. de Voltaire, with whom you have very slight connections, and with whose principles you are so well acquainted.

She also firmly rebuked him for asking d'Holbach to investigate Rousseau's means:

> What use do you intend to make of the new inquiries with which you have charged M. D'Olbach? You have not apparently the design of writing anything against this unfortunate man. You will not become his denunciator, after having been his protector . . .

She had discussed matters with Adam Smith, she recorded. She and Smith believed that Hume had misread Rousseau's letter refusing the pension, and Smith suggested Hume should re-read it to Conway.

> It does not seem to us, that he is refusing the pension, nor that he wants it made public. He begs that it may be deferred till the tranquillity of his soul, disturbed by violent sorrow, is re-established. In his ill-temper, your mistake, which he supposed was intentional, must have put the finishing stroke to his misfortunes, by souring his mind, and completely upsetting his reason.

Even so, Hume should have demonstrated his superiority by not involving himself further and by acting with 'generous pity' towards Rousseau.

Hume was now cornered. The violence of his language and the severity of his allegations, she told him, the liberty he gave to d'Holbach to tell the world, the engagement of his Parisian supporters in managing the affair, the promise to supply evidence of Rousseau's plotting against him – all these made it nigh impossible for Hume to avoid publication. Paradoxically, his lack of moderation had put his reputation more at risk than Rousseau's; the injured innocent had become the vicious attacker. Some of Hume's friends, Mme de Boufflers maintained, feared for him.

She could have meant Turgot. The meeting *chez* de L' Espinasse had left this enlightened statesman uneasy. On 23 July, he wrote the first of a number of letters rehearsing his doubts and tactfully providing Hume with another approach: it was a subtle exercise in the diplomacy of dissuasion. His first opinion, he said, had been not to publish, and he had come round to the common view only after reviewing all the circumstances. For in the eyes of Rousseau's numerous partisans, Hume had become the accuser and, as such, obliged to justify himself. Rousseau's accusations were so wild that no one would give any credence to them. So the only reason for publishing was to show that Hume's own counter-accusations of villainy, of baseness, and of atrocity were justified. If he had the proofs of Rousseau's manoeuvering, then they must be declared, even though bringing down a man of talent was sad or regrettable; the hypocrite's mask must be ripped off, the truth exposed.

'If [Hume] had the proofs . . .' But did he? What could they possibly have been? Turgot had identified Hume's 'proofs' as the weak point in his case and was delicately proposing an honourable retreat. Only four days later, he composed another long letter, for his hesitation over Hume's course had been reinforced. He surmised that the real cause of Rousseau's fury was

Hume's quip (the Prussian King could supply all the persecution Rousseau needed) as borrowed by Walpole, and the subsequent correspondence in the London press. In the country, living, as he was, a solitary life, Rousseau's imagination had been ignited. The misreading of his pension letter by Hume and Conway seemed to demonstrate Hume's treachery. So, Rousseau's actions were not premeditated, Turgot concluded. Violent, impetuous, defiant, yes. But not villainy.

However, Hume's obsessive rage had blinded him to all other possibilities: come what may, he would expose Rousseau. If, in July, he had been genuinely seeking advice about publication, by August he had made up his mind. The conundrum was how to publish while retaining his reputation as *le bon David* and the confidence of those advising him against publication.

Replying to Turgot on 4 August, Hume asked rhetorically, 'What epithet could you give to a man like this, when you must allow, that it is safer to take a basilisk or a rattle-snake into your bosom than to have the least intercourse with him?'

He brushed aside the notion that he himself was in any way responsible. His feelings had not abated by late September when he unleashed another extravagantly brutal and unbending letter to Turgot, whom he accused of 'a great partiality' towards Rousseau. Referring to Rousseau's seal, *Vitam impendere vero* ('Consecrating my life to the truth'), Hume went on,

> You say indeed that he cannot properly deserve the severe epithets with which I have honoured him; because it is probable that he had not calmly formed the deliberate purpose of quarrelling with me and calumniating me: He was only actuated by the sourness and melancholy of his temper. Add by the pride and malignity of his heart: Add, that he sacrifices every regard to truth and honour, in order to gratify his malice: Add, that his ferocity is directed against a man who is his

benefactor . . . I really believe him one of the worst and most depraved of men.

He ended this passage with a violent metaphor intended to dispose of a comment from Turgot that Rousseau's letter to Hume did not hurt Hume, but Hume's complaints against Rousseau had irreparably damaged Rousseau's character. 'To this I reply that the case is similar as if an assassin had fired a pistol at me, and missed me; while I, to prevent his firing another pistol, run him through the body. It is always happy when the harm falls on the first aggressor.' It is with relief that we see Hume turn from this ranting against Rousseau to a rational and incisive discussion of whether it is better to impose taxes on land or consumption. (He argues, convincingly, for consumption.)

The Republic of Letters advisory committee now performed a volte-face, one inspired, oddly, by news of Rousseau's long letter – the detailed indictment in which Hume had identified twelve lies. A report of it that Hume sent to Paris produced the response that this was not the appropriate time for publication; the committee was as comforted by its irrefragable absurdity as Hume professed to be. On 4 August, d'Alembert reassured Hume that when he read this account of Rousseau's accusations, his first reaction was to admire the rhetoric, but his second was to laugh and shrug his shoulders. Rousseau was a lunatic, a dangerous lunatic, fit for Bedlam. However, he wanted only to be talked about, whatever the cost, and to ensure this did not happen was the worst punishment one could inflict on him. Do not let that stop you sending me a copy of the big letter [Rousseau's indictment] and all the correspondence, d'Alembert added; it is a curious collection and good to have.

D'Alembert had also decided the time had come for him to inform Rousseau directly that he had played no part in the

King of Prussia letter. He wrote a short note that he asked Hume 'to throw to the wild beast across his barricade'. (True to form, Hume did not send it on to Rousseau.)

Hume now sought a solution to his publication problem by simply putting the decision into the hands of others. He dispatched two packets with all the papers to the powerful financial administrator Jean-Charles Trudaine de Montigny, asking him to peruse them and to advise, then forward the papers to d'Alembert. He included 'a short narrative to connect the letters' and left it to his French friends to determine what to do with them: 'I am really at a loss what use to make of this collection.' It was an approach either dictated by the need not to cross the anti-publication coterie or else testifying to a willingness to wound but not strike. To de Montigny, he claimed his moral character was at stake, if apparently only in Paris: 'At London a publication would be considered entirely superfluous.' He wanted the papers read as widely as possible, even if they were not to be published, and he welcomed opinion . . .

Opinion there came – the first from a guest at the Trudaine de Montigny château, Mme de Saint-Maur. M. de Montigny had received the papers from Hume, and de Saint-Maur and five other guests had sat up together with them – an all-night reading party – excited by the 'bizarre denouement' to the Hume–Rousseau relationship. (M. de Montigny had retired early and would see the papers on the morrow.) No one doubted the excellent David Hume. So, they all concurred, it was futile to publish. (Publication seemed futile in another sense: within a short time, everyone in the Republic of Letters appeared to have read the full account.)

Across the Republic of Letters, sympathy was almost all on Hume's side. But after seeing Rousseau's case for themselves, they concluded that Hume had over-reacted to ludicrous charges. Perhaps a sensitivity to the persecuted Genevan's evident distress equally dictated holding back. Even d'Holbach, who had so signally lacked discretion, was cautious: if forced to break his silence, then Hume was not to go beyond a simple exposition of the facts, with the proofs he must have in hand. From Hume's fellow countryman Earl Marischal came a plea for restraint: 'It will be good and humane in you, and like *le bon David*, not to answer.' In September, d'Alembert informed Hume he had read the *gros paquet*. Rousseau's indictment left him unmoved.

Meanwhile, Hume had given the papers to the King and Queen, or rather, as he told de Barbentane at the end of August,

> The King and Queen of England expressed a strong desire to see these papers and I was obliged to put them into their hand. They read them with avidity, and entertain the same sentiment that must strike everyone. The King's opinion confirms me in my conviction not to give them to the public unless I be forced to it by some attack on the side of my adversary, which it will therefore be wisdom in him to avoid.

(The copy in the Royal Archive at Windsor has a handwritten inscription on the cover: '? Sent to the King about 1767'.) The phrase 'confirms me in my conviction not to give them to the public' is curious when he had abdicated responsibility for publication to his French supporters.

Hume had now left London for his home at James's Court in Edinburgh. On his way to Scotland, on 2 September, he wrote to Davenport with yet another version of events and of his intentions. He disclosed that he had made three copies of the papers: one he had deposited with a sure hand at Paris, one with Lord Hertford, and one he had kept. 'These will remain in reserve, till Rousseau attacks me, which I expect every day . . . There is scarce a person in Europe, who does not look upon

him at present as very mad or very wicked or as both; and if the
public voice were not apt to be soon obliterated, I might rest
my defence upon it.' None the less, Hume asked Davenport to
continue his good offices to the exile: 'Notwithstanding his
atrocious conduct towards me, I should be very sorry to see
him abandoned by all the world.'

So the question of publication was apparently deferred indefi-
nitely. But if Hume still wanted to publish, by a supreme irony
Rousseau came to his aid.

On 2 August, Rousseau wrote to the Paris publisher, Pierre
Guy. The letter showed clearly how his paranoia was still
seething, and it gave Hume just the rationale (or pretext) he
needed.

Rousseau had heard about the uproar in Paris, he told Guy.
He felt as if twenty *poignards* were being stabbed in his breast.
Alone, he could do nothing to combat the hydra-headed league
formed against him. Destroy one of their calumnies and twenty
more would arise. Rather, he should leave it to the public to
judge, remain quiet, and try to live and die in peace. 'They say
that Mr Hume has called me the lowest of the low and a villain.
If I knew how to reply to such language, I would deserve his
description.' He then summed up his story in a brilliant, stirring, Manichaean paragraph. It was a question of two men, one
of whom took the other to England, almost against his will; one
of whom was ill, friendless, isolated by language, in retreat; the
other active, with friends at Court, moving in the grand world,
well connected with the press. And the latter allied himself with
the mortal enemies of the former. He had heard Hume would
publish. So be it. Let him at least do it faithfully.

Although Rousseau had forbidden Guy to publicize his letter, news of it naturally leaked out: the rumour was that
Rousseau had challenged Hume to publish, had dared him to

do so honestly. By mid-August, Hume had heard about it through d'Holbach.

In September, a translated extract of Rousseau's letter appeared in the *London Chronicle* and the *Lloyd's Evening Post*. The *London Chronicle* also carried an earlier report, datelined Paris, 26 August:

> The Sieur John James Rousseau hath written to several persons in this city, and amongst others to a bookseller, whom he acquaints that he is not ignorant of there being a considerable party formed against him, of which Mr. H– is the chief; but he defies his enemy to dare, as he has threatened, to publish their correspondence, as he has wherewith to confound the English philosopher. However, we dare not yet condemn Mr. H–.

The challenge was in the public domain. On 7 September d'Holbach told Hume that Rousseau's many fanatics and supporters were interpreting Hume's silence as guilt, so open justification had become necessary. None the less, he still recommended moderation, simply facts and proofs. The authors of the *Gazette littéraire* were offering to be his publishers: he could not be in better hands. Turgot wrote similarly advising publication and also urging just the facts. 'The more moderate you are, the worse Rousseau will appear,' he advised.

Let d'Alembert know he was free to edit the papers to suit 'the latitude of Paris', Hume requested Adam Smith, on 9 September. In the various collections of correspondence, there is no specific fiat from Hume for d'Alembert to set publication in motion, but this Smith letter looks like Hume's way of prodding d'Alembert on. On 6 October, less than a month after that message via Smith, d'Alembert informed *le bon David* that his intentions (stated presumably in the original packet) had been fulfilled.

Editing, he said, had been entrusted to Jean-Báptiste-Antoine Suard, editor of the *Gazette littéraire*. Suard had translated the paper and made a few changes on Hume's instruction. A preface had been added to say, in accordance with Hume's wishes, how reluctant the Scotsman had been to publicize the quarrel but why he felt compelled to do so. Publication would be in eight to ten days in the name of his friends, not just d'Alembert, as he was a participant in the quarrel. D'Alembert had included his declaration disavowing all knowledge of Walpole's letter, though it would have been better, he said, if Hume had sent the original disavowal on to Rousseau. Mme de Boufflers and Mme de Verdelin did not wish to be named and would not be.

Thus was born the *Exposé succinct de la contestation qui s'est élevée entre M. Hume et M. Rousseau avec des pièces justificatives*.

While he had a free hand, d'Alembert's own target was now 'Valpole's' letter. He wanted to put himself in the clear. He also wanted to savage Walpole for ridiculing Rousseau, a man who had done Walpole no harm. Walpole should eternally reproach himself, he told Hume.

On his own initiative, Suard suppressed the sharper remarks about Rousseau that d'Alembert slipped into the text; he did not exclude critical comments by d'Alembert about Walpole's *jeu d'esprit*.

Suard and d'Alembert disagreed on an epigraph: should it be Tacitus or Seneca? Neither, the editor decided, but at the end of the main text a passage of Seneca was inserted from *De Beneficiis*, Book VII, chapter 29. The choice is revealing:

I have wasted a good deed. And yet, can we ever say that we have wasted what we consider sacred? A good deed is one of these things; even if there is a bad return, it was a good investment. The beneficiary is not the sort of man we hoped; let us remain what we have been, and not become like him.

Decoded, the text offers humane reproach as much as reassurance to the injured and vengeful Hume: his good deed should have been its own reward. It seems fairly to represent the ambiguity of the Scot's *philosophe* friends towards Rousseau's bizarre conduct and Hume's own violent response.

According to d'Alembert, the clash created the least stir in London of all the capitals of Europe. Travellers from England confirmed that. All the same, though he had earlier reckoned it superfluous, Hume arranged the details of an English edition with his publisher, William Strahan, in October. The English text should follow the French, he insisted, since he had allowed the French to make such alterations as they thought fit. He would deposit the original letters in the British Museum; this was in response to Rousseau's taunt that Hume dare not publish them. (The Museum declined the deposit.) Commercial considerations were not far away: 'The whole will compose a pretty large pamphlet, which, I fancy, the curiosity of the public will make tolerably saleable.'

His satisfaction with the French version did not last. He was soon instructing Strahan to utilize the original English text where possible, and he made changes up to the middle of November and the publishing of *A Concise and Genuine Account of the Dispute between Mr. Hume and Mr. Rousseau; with the Letters that passed between them during their Controversy. As also the Letters of the Hon. Mr. Walpole and Mr. D'Alembert, relative to this extraordinary affair. Translated from the French. London. Printed for T. Becket and P. A. De Hondt near Surrey-street, in the Strand.* MDCCLXVI.

At the end of the *Account*, Hume anticipated twenty-first-century public relations, quoting the thoughts of 'friends' on the case. Some blamed Rousseau's vanity and ostentation. Some viewed his conduct in a more compassionate light, with Rousseau as an object of pity. Others supposed domineering pride and ingratitude to be the basis of his character, but that 'his brain has received a sensible shake, and that his judgement has been set afloat – carried to every side by the current of his humours and his passions'. Still others believed that he was 'in a middle state between sober reason and total frenzy'.

Hume told the *Account*'s readers that he was of the latter opinion – adding his doubts as to whether Rousseau was ever more in his senses than at present. 'It is an old remark, that great wits are near allied to madness, and even in those frantic letters, which he has wrote to me, there are evidently strong traces of his wonted genius and eloquence.'

So Hume had his publication, but had he retained the support of his friends?

18

Love Me, Love My Dog

Finally, a figure of fun: Rousseau becomes a Yahoo

Our reputation, our character, our name, are considerations of vast weight and importance.
David Hume

The celebrated J.-J. Rousseau . . . the celebrated Historian . . . the celebrated quarrel.
1820 introduction to Hume's private correspondence

It suited Hume to present publication of the *Exposé* as somehow done without his volition, as certainly not what he had wanted, almost against his will – yes, even forced upon him.

He wrote from Edinburgh to Horace Walpole on 30 October:

A few days ago I had a letter from M. d'Alembert, by which I learn that he and my other friends at Paris had determined to publish an account of my rupture with Rousseau, in consequence of a general discretionary power which I had given them . . . My Parisian friends are to accompany the whole with a preface, giving an account of my reluctance to this publication, but of the necessity which they found of *extorting my consent* [authors' italics]. It appears particularly, that my antagonist had wrote letters of defiance against me all over Europe, and said that the letter he wrote me was so confounding to me, that I would not dare to shew it to any one without falsifying it. These letters were likely to make [an] impression, and my silence might be construed into a proof of guilt.

Again in November, he emphasized to Walpole with what unwillingness he had released his account: 'Had I found one man of my opinion, I should have persevered in my refusal.'

Ironically enough, Walpole was just such a man, as he vigorously pointed out to Hume, having received the pamphlet. He was surprised; after all, Hume had been against publication before leaving London for Edinburgh. It was also contrary to the advice of his best friends, not to speak of his own nature. Indeed:

> I am sorry you have let yourself be over-persuaded, and so are all that I have seen who wish you well . . . You add, that they told you Rousseau had sent letters of defiance against you all over Europe. Good God! My dear Sir, could you pay any regard to such fustian? All Europe laughs at being dragged every day into these idle quarrels, with which Europe only wipes its b–s–e [backside].

Elsewhere, Hume's protestations seemed to carry equally little weight. This publishing was greeted with shock and regret. In November, his English patron, Hertford, dropped him an intriguing line thanking him for the copy of 'the printed dispute'. Hertford had been in Paris, 'but you will not imagine I waited till this time to see it, a paper which was in everybody's hands . . . I was however surprised to find it in print after what you had told me but when I see the King again in private I will acquaint him with your reasons.' The note reinforces doubts that Hertford and Conway had advised publication; indeed, the former ambassador appears to have told the King that Hume would not publish.

Meanwhile, Voltaire was relishing the opportunity to go for Rousseau. On 1 November, Grimm recorded: 'M. Voltaire has had printed a little letter addressed to M. Hume, where he has given the *coup de grâce* to poor Jean-Jacques. This letter had been very successful in Paris, and it has possibly done more harm to M. Rousseau than M. Hume's pamphlet.' (It was reprinted in London.) 'If [Rousseau] should need it,' wrote Voltaire, 'one should throw him a hunk of bread on the dunghill where he lies gnashing his teeth at the human race.

But it was necessary to show him up for what he is so as to enable those who might feed him to guard against his bites.' While Hume had endeavoured to co-opt George III on his side, Voltaire attempted in vain to enlist Rousseau's mighty admirer, Frederick the Great. 'You ask me', wrote the King, 'what I think of him? I think he is unhappy and to be pitied . . . Only depraved souls kick a man when he is down.'

Sitting it out, but not down, in Wootton, Rousseau could congratulate himself both that Hume had been unmasked and that he, the exile, was enduring his tormentors with noble patience. They could do and say what they liked while he awaited death. As for the alleged plotter in chief, in mid-November Rousseau wrote to a friend, 'For myself, I have nothing to say to Mr Hume, except that I find him too insulting for a good man, and too noisy for a philosopher.'

In Britain, while sympathy with Hume and indignation against Rousseau were widespread, they were far from universal. Hume's account circulated in the press. The *Gentleman's Magazine*, *London Magazine*, the *St. James's Chronicle*, the *London Chronicle,* and the *Monthly Review* for November printed long extracts from the *Exposé*. 'You can't conceive how much you are put in the right and Rousseau in the wrong by everybody here [in London],' wrote the classicist and politician Robert Wood, who had been instrumental in Hume's going to Paris.

The *Monthly Review* article was sandwiched between a collection of 'squibbs and crackers' on Pitt's elevation to the peerage and details of a plan to set up a free university for all-comers. It offered its report, it declared, to gratify the curiosity of the many readers who would have heard of the 'late quarrel between these two celebrated geniuses'. Although it pledged to present the narrative without comment, it could not resist a few lines. 'It appears with the clearest evidence that

Mr *Hume* has acted the part of a generous and disinterested friend to Mr ROUSSEAU: in regard to the conduct of the latter, humanity seems to dictate silence.'

So the *Review* decided not to publish the fifty pages of Rousseau's indictment, though the editor was not hostile to Rousseau. The problem was his 'extreme sensibility [that] renders him peculiarly liable to entertain suspicions even of his best friends.' What was required was not condemnation but 'compassion towards an unfortunate man, whose peculiar temper and constitution of mind must, we fear, render him unhappy in every situation'.

Nobody was emerging well from the episode. The editor did not temper his outright condemnation of Walpole. His part in the affair

appears neither consistent with humanity nor with politeness. By an ill-judged piece of pleasantry he endeavours to expose Mr Rousseau to public ridicule, and when he finds that this gives great uneasiness to a poor unfortunate man, who had never done him any injury, instead of expressing any concern on this account, he publishes to the world that he has a thorough contempt for him, and represents him as an object of detestation.

It was altogether unworthy of him.

Rousseau had champions in Britain. The Zürich-born painter Henry Fuseli published *A Defence of Mr. Rousseau, against the Aspersions of Mr. Hume, Mons. Voltaire, and their Associates.* 8vo. 1s 6d Bladon, which was scorned by the *Monthly Review* as 'a bare-faced catch-penny job. The author is an impertinent intruder into a controversy of which he appears to know nothing more than what every reader might gather from the *Concise Account*.'

Several readers, after digesting the contents of the *Concise*

Account, were sufficiently up in arms to write in to the press, under pseudonyms including 'Emilius', 'Crito', and 'A. Bystander'. In the 27–29 November edition of the *St. James's Chronicle*, a letter from 'An Orthodox Hospitable Old Englishman' chided Hume: 'If [his] heart had ever been indeed the friend of Rousseau, his philosophy and coolness might have treated Mr Rousseau as a man under a strong and great mistake; this would have been more for Mr Hume's glory . . . to go on imputing all kinds of bad motives shows that a philosopher when provoked is not a better man at bottom than the poor mere bigot of religion.' 'A.O.H.O.E.' also rebuked Walpole for 'an indecent and barbarous piece . . . M. Rousseau is a persecuted and an unfortunate stranger. I neither know him nor Hume, nor H.W. but humanity obliges me to wish that poor Rousseau may not be made uneasy here, but left in as much peace as possible.' Other correspondents also took up the cudgels for Rousseau: one recurring theme was the lack of hospitality and respect accorded the exile, which shamed the British nation. There was poetical support in the 9–11 December *St. James's Chronicle*:

> Rousseau, be firm! Though malice, like Voltaire,
> And superstitious pride, like D'Alembert,
> Though mad presumption Walpole's form assume,
> And base-born treachery appear like Hume,
> Yet droop not thou; the spectres gathering round,
> These night drawn phantoms, want the power to wound.
> Fair truth shall chase th'unreal forms away,
> And reason's piercing beams restore the day;
> Britain shall snatch the exile to her breast,
> And conscious virtue soothe his soul to rest.

A parody of this verse appeared in the next issue. Rousseau was mocked in a burlesque indictment that made the round of periodicals, while another correspondent asked what could be expected from such deists and infidels. Newspaper readers were clearly enjoying the affair – not quite the outcome Hume had in mind.

Although he came in for as much abuse and reproof as Rousseau, in February 1767, Hume informed Mme de Bouf- flers that there had been

> a great deal of raillery on the incident, thrown out in the public papers, but all against that unhappy man . . . There is even a print engraved of it: M. Rousseau is represented as a yahoo, newly caught in the woods; I am represented as a farmer, who caresses him and offers him some oats to eat, which he refuses in a rage; Voltaire and d'Alembert are whipping him up behind; and Horace Walpole making him horns of *papier maché*. The idea is not altogether absurd.

(It had been printed in the *Public Advertiser* in January 1767: in his *Journal*, Boswell stated that the design for the cartoon was his.)

Across the Channel, in Hume's principal market for his dossier, outrage over Rousseau's treatment of Hume was tempered by some hard assessments about Hume's tactics and motives. Besides, Hume had ignored or misjudged the likelihood of his case simply being swept into the established pro- and anti-Rousseau factions.

Turgot's sense of decorum had plainly been offended. In September, he expressed his pity over Rousseau's indictment, viewing it as more madness than villainy, telling Hume, 'Your letter harmed him, his did not harm you.' Some of Hume's circle, he noted, regretted that Hume had not simply composed a letter to Rousseau, rather than involving his friends in Paris.

Turgot's elegantly expressed reservations were not exceptional. In October, Grimm penned a mocking account of the quarrel – 'excellent fodder for the idle'. A declaration of war between Europe's two big powers could not have made more noise in Paris, he said, though in London, they were foolish enough to be occupied more with the change of ministry and Pitt becoming Earl of Chatham. Grimm continued,

> I do not know why it says in the preface that Mr Hume, in making the process public, only conceded with a great deal of repugnance to the importuning of his friends. No doubt, he means Mr Hume's friends in England; because I know many who have written to him precisely to dissuade him from making this quarrel public. In effect, if you are forced to plead your cause in public, I sympathise with you with all my heart; if you take it into your head unnecessarily to make such a decision, I will think you a fool.

Grimm then recounted his own breach with Rousseau nine years earlier: an affair 'even sillier' than Hume's. Rousseau's was the only friendship he had lost in his life without any regrets. None the less, he had always behaved with decency and respect towards Rousseau: not to do so would be against his nature. So he could confidently say how he would have acted in Hume's place:

> On receiving the gentle and honest letter of June 23, so unexpected, I, fat David Hume, would have first rubbed my eyes; then, my gaze would have become as fixed and prolonged as ever on that terrible and memorable day when David looked at Jean-Jacques; but this surprised movement over, I would have put the letter in my pocket. The next day, I would have written to my friend Jean-Jacques, to thank him for the good opinion with which he had honoured me, and the complexion he had given my services and my most tender care, and

then I would have wished him good night for all his glorious life . . .

But neither on that day, nor any other, would Grimm have published what was no business of the general public. Anyone who read about the affair, he wrote, must feel 'a deep pity for this unfortunate Jean-Jacques' and his life of 'madness and painful tumult'. It was at this point that Grimm added percipiently, 'Where can he end his days in peace? It seems plain that he takes with him a companion who will not suffer him to rest in peace.' In Paris, tracts, letters, pamphlets proliferated in Rousseau's defence, though Grimm recorded that they were 'detestable, written by rascals one does not know, driven to write by idleness and perhaps hunger. No one has a single new fact to allege.'

If Hume had hoped the published account would decisively swing the public to his side, he must have been disappointed. The character of Rousseau as an artist and a man, his standing as a hunted exile, his hurt at the King of Prussia letter, Hume's coldness and extravagant reaction – all these were well understood by readers. Even when criticizing Rousseau in corrosive letters to the press, they were inclined to find fault on both sides. And, of course, Hume had succeeded in keeping the affair alive: it ran and ran.

However, there were also serious repercussions in his personal relations. Hume's ties with his passionate friend Mme de Boufflers were stretched to breaking point. In her fine letter of 22 July from Pougues-les-eaux, she had told him that his communicating first with d'Holbach had trenched on the friendship he had promised her. The public thought that in propagating the complaints and abetting Hume's indignation, d'Holbach had rendered Hume a bad service. Why had Hume deprived himself of the noblest possible revenge on Rousseau, 'to wit, that of overwhelming him with your superiority, of dazzling him with the lustre of that very virtue, which he wilfully misconceives?'

Rousseau's letter was atrocious, she agreed, but the impossibility of his ever obliterating this folly would constitute the eternal torment of his life. 'Do not, however, believe that he is capable of artifice, or of falsehood; that he is either an impostor, or a villain. His anger is unfounded, but it is real, I have no doubt of it.' And it was just improbable that Rousseau had set out to injure and dishonour Hume in a premeditated way.

Mme de Boufflers then broke off the letter for three days to travel the sixty-four leagues to Paris. Although she nowhere states it explicitly, the impression she gives is that anxiety over Hume's mania had driven her back to the capital to be closer to events. When this advocate of magnanimous spirit and zealous moderation picked up her pen again, anxiety had transmuted into fury. She could not counsel him: 'You are too confirmed in your own opinion, too much engaged, too much supported in your anger, to listen to me.' With a note of disappointment, she pointed out how many in Paris would be only too happy to see him behave like an ordinary being. She had no energy to write more on this sad subject, other than what her conscience and friendship obliged her.

Mme de Boufflers regarded the violation of the rules of civilized behaviour as gross, and she did not let Rousseau escape unscathed. On 27 July, she rebuked him for the disgraceful letter he had sent Hume: she had never seen anything like it. All his friends were in consternation and reduced to silence. What could be said on his behalf after a letter so unworthy of him? That Hume was a traitor was utterly implausible. Even if true, Rousseau had acted precipitously, had not justified his suspicions, had not asked the advice of anybody in France. He should never forget that Hume had rendered him real assistance. Quoting Rousseau back to himself, she reminded him that 'the bonds of friendship are entitled to respect, even after they are rent asunder'. Conti, Luxembourg and de Boufflers awaited an explanation. He should not delay. 'Let us know, at least, how we may excuse, if we cannot entirely exculpate you.'

Rousseau did not counter Mme de Boufflers's reproaches until a month later, and then in injured and truculent terms. Hume had compelled him to explain himself and he had done so in great detail. It was not a question of suspicions but of facts, not of judgement of Hume's character but of his conduct. In his letter to Hume, he had been as mild as he could, considering how he suffered. As for Hume, 'At the same time that in reply to this self-same letter he wrote to me in decent, even in courteous terms, he wrote to M. D'Holbach, and to the world at large, in terms rather different. He has filled Paris, France, the gazettes and the whole of Europe, with things which my pen is not competent to write, and which it never shall repeat.' True, the ties of friendship were to be respected even after they were broken. But what if they had never existed in the first place? If Hume's services, which he had acknowledged, 'were as much for display as reality, if they were nothing more than so many snares, which concealed the blackest designs, I do not see that they call for extraordinary gratitude.'

Mme de Boufflers did not reply. Perhaps she recognized that some of his remarks about Hume were justified, but her silence must have hurt Rousseau. An even heavier blow was to follow – struck by his second father, Earl Marischal.

The elderly Earl's deciding to confine his correspondence with Rousseau to essentials stemmed directly from the row. He was shocked by his 'son' Rousseau's conduct: henceforth, relations between them would be distant. Rousseau was bitterly upset and in agitated distress. As Christmas 1766 approached, he delivered a passionate appeal. Of all the misfortunes that had crushed him, this was the worst. Let Milord at least write once a month to say he was well. If the Earl adhered to his 'cruel decision', Rousseau would die.

Meanwhile, on 12 August, Hume had finally responded to Mme de Boufflers's fusillade. He opened with a fawning apology: 'I kiss the rod which beats me, and give you as sincere thanks for your admonitions, as I ever did for any of your civilities and services.' He then attempted an excuse for not having alerted her to his quarrel with Rousseau first. He had believed her to be one hundred leagues from Paris:

> I wrote to Baron D'Holbach, without either recommending or expecting secrecy: but I thought this story, like others, would be told to eight or ten people; in a week or two, twenty or thirty more might hear it, and it would require three months before it would reach you at Pougues. I little imagined that a private story, told to a private gentleman, could run over a whole kingdom in a moment.

But his main consideration from the outset was Rousseau's forthcoming memoirs. If Hume had kept quiet about this, what other lies might his enemy concoct?

This marked the end (perhaps welcomed by Hume) of their closeness, though the final straw came the following year when she realized that even if Hume returned to France, he had no intention of lodging in the Temple in the bright, pretty apartment she had set up for him. Her letters appear to have been so spiky at this point that Hume threw them away. Correspondence continued in a desultory manner, but she was quick to find his letters irritating.

Hume's bond with Walpole was affected, too. Walpole was irked over the treatment of the statement he supplied Hume for use in the *Exposé* and he made his feelings, as well as the facts, clear in print, drawing up a narrative of his role in the quarrel, dated Paris, 13 September 1767. He had willingly supplied a letter that cleared Hume of involvement in the King of Prussia spoof, but had used the opportunity to spell out his strong opposition to Hume's publishing. Hume had then selectively quoted:

> I am sorry to say, that on this occasion Mr Hume did not act quite fairly by me. In the beginning of my letter, I laughed at his learned friends, who wished him to publish, which, as I told him, was only to gratify their own spleen to Rousseau. I had no spleen to him, I had laughed at his affectation, but had tried to serve him; and above all things, I despised the childish quarrel of pedants and pretended philosophers. This commencement of my letter was therefore a dissuasive against printing. Could I imagine that Mr Hume would make use of part of my letter, and suffer it to be printed – and even without asking my consent?

In London, the reprinted French edition sold out while 750 copies of the English re-translation had been bought by mid-November. But none of this caused any real problems for the protagonists with their public. Rousseau's opera *Le Devin du village* was published in a translation as *The Cunning Man* by the composer, organist and musical historian Dr Charles Burney. The piece was produced at the Drury Lane Theatre, in late November to a generally favourable reception, though on the second night, Scottish supporters of Hume barracked it from the parterre, much to the exasperation of the English spectators. In all, *The Cunning Man* had over a dozen performances and would have had more but for the illness of the lead soprano.

Hume returned to diplomacy in February 1767 as Conway's under-secretary of state (deputy secretary). At Westminster, Rockingham had been sacked after barely a year, never having gained royal favour. In July 1766, he was replaced by Pitt, who went to the House of Lords as Earl of Chatham. The King was anxious to keep Conway in office throughout, telling the General that the government depended on *his* conducting the business of the Commons. By the end of the year, George had become even more effusive and appreciative: 'I am certain I can rely on your zeal, at all times, to carry on my affairs, as I have no one desire but what tends to the happiness of my people.' (Small wonder the King was so complaisant over Conway's overtures on Rousseau's pension.) So, urged on by Walpole, Conway remained in the secretary of state's office under Pitt/Chatham and his successor, Grafton, too.

Hume's invitation to serve Conway had come through Lord Hertford. He knew that Hume had resolved not to be occupied, but, at Walpole's suggestion, asked Lady Hertford to try to change his mind. On 1 March 1767, Hume gave Mme de Boufflers a slightly contrived version of his return to public life. He had thought of declining the job, 'but I own, I could not find terms to express my refusal of a request made by persons to whose friendship I had been so much obliged.' There was no danger of his being ensnared by Court favour and the pursuit of riches. On the contrary, 'I feel myself at present like a banished man in a strange country; I mean, not as I was while with you in Paris, but as I should be in Westphalia or Lithuania or any place the least to my fancy in the world.'

If that was true, he and his adversary had something in common. In far away Staffordshire, Rousseau and his *gouvernante* were feeling that Wootton had become the place least to their fancy in the world. Yet initially it had seemed the ideal retreat.

19
Friends in Arcadia

Rousseau's grotto: he turned it into his confessional

I am commencing an undertaking without precedent.
Jean-Jacques Rousseau, *Confessions*

*A perfect solitude is, perhaps, the greatest punishment
we can suffer.*
David Hume

Plots apart, settling in to Wootton, looking out over the wild Staffordshire countryside, Rousseau was conscious of his creative life being at a critical juncture. He had emigrated from the Republic of Letters for good:

> Authors, warrants, books, that field fuming with glory that makes one shed tears, all such things are the follies of the other world in which I take no more part and which I shall hasten to forget . . . during the fifteen years that I have had the misfortune to exercise the melancholy art of being a man of letters I have not contracted any of the vices of that profession, envy, jealousy, the spirit of intrigue, and charlatanry have not once come near my heart. I do not feel myself even embittered by persecutions and by misfortunes, and I quit the career as whole of heart as I entered it.

The message of his withdrawal from a life of letters was reiterated to Mme de Boufflers, who, he felt, had nagged him about abandoning his muse:

> I wish to obey you in everything; but for heaven's sake speak no more about writing books, or even about the people who write them. We have a hundred times more books on morality than is necessary, and we are no better off for them. You fear for the effect on me of idleness and boredom from my withdrawal from the world: you are mistaken, Madame, for

I am never less bored or less idle than when I am alone.

Alone and in Arcadia, as the description of Wootton Hall he
had sent to Mme de Luze on arrival made clear:

> At the bottom of the valley, which serves both as a warren
> and as a pasture, one hears the murmuring of a brook which
> comes running down from a neighbouring mountain and is
> parallel to the house, and its little turnings and waterfalls
> bear in such a direction that from the windows and the ter-
> race the eye can follow its course a long way. The valley is
> lined, in places, with rocks and trees where one finds deli-
> cious haunts, and now and again these places are far enough
> away from the stream itself to offer some pleasant walks
> along its banks, sheltered from the winds and even from the
> rain, so that in the worst weather in the world I go tranquilly
> botanising under the rocks with the sheep and the rabbits.

During fine weather, he could wander for miles in the limestone
hills, following the course of the river Dove, through water-
meadows and by its sharp gorges and cascades. It was (and is
still) one of the loveliest parts of Britain, rich in hazel and
hawthorn, birch and osier. In summer, honeysuckle and wild
roses sweeten the air. The steep-sided valleys – the dales – are
carpeted with ash woods, or bare to the skies with scrub or
grassland. Perhaps, in his wanderings, Rousseau added to the
richness of the flora. He was a collector of plants: an early
nineteenth-century guide to the region makes a claim that 'the
fickle and whimsical Rousseau' sowed 'the seeds of some curious foreign flowers in the neighbourhood'.

Rousseau was in two simultaneous worlds. In one, he was
exposed to betrayal and conspiracy and trailed by the companion
seen by Grimm, the second dog 'who will not suffer him to rest in
peace'. Safe within his other world, he was living the life he had

long sought, a blissful existence in nature, away from the impurity, the competitiveness, the triviality, the lack of authenticity of the city that he always characterized by black vapours.

On most of Rousseau's walks, to his evident pleasure, he was unlikely to encounter another living soul. In any case, were he to, he could retreat behind a language barrier. The minister from Ellaston village stopped by early on to welcome the exile, and Rousseau reported to Hume, with apparent glee, the meeting's discomforting silence. 'Seeing that I would speak only French to him, he did not wish to talk to me in English, so that the interview passed with almost not a word spoken.' Even if he learned English, Rousseau told Hume, he would still speak only French to local people who knew nothing of the language. (In fact, he seemed to have a good passive knowledge, reading letters written to him in English by Hume and Davenport.) So far as Davenport's servants were concerned, 'Mlle Le Vasseur serves me as interpreter, and her fingers speak better than my tongue.'

A number of legends grew up around Rousseau's limited contact with country folk. Local lore had it that some mistook him for a king driven from his realm. It was said that he wandered at night over the Weaver Hills ('when the fairies were out'). Near by, at Stanton, was a lead mine, and Rousseau is thought to have made the acquaintance of workers there: his accounts show him donating money to the lead miners in August 1766, an intriguing action, given his ambiguous attitude to accepting gifts from others.

In 1840, the social historian William Howitt went to Wootton in search of memories of Rousseau and in *Visits to Remarkable Places* documented the clear recollections from some of the oldest inhabitants of the area, transcribing their strong Staffordshire accent:

What, owd Ross Hall? Ay know him did I, well enough.

Ah've seen him monny an' monny a time, every day welly, coming and going ins comical cap an' ploddy gown, a gathering his yarbs. Yes there war a lady – they cawd her Madam Zell, but whether how war his wife or not, ah dunna know. Folks said how warna.

Howitt gives the only evidence of Le Vasseur speaking English. Davenport's housekeeper was beaten by her husband and the outcry brought some villagers running up: 'Madam Zell in a state of great excitement said in her few words of English to some young women – "Never marry! Never marry! You see! You see!"'

Another of his stories has it that when Rousseau was out one day, a man approached him to enquire if he was a botanist. This was Erasmus Darwin, physician, scientist, educationist, standard-bearer for the Industrial Revolution, and leading member of the pathfinding Lunar Society of enlightened scientific thinkers (also grandfather of Charles). Apparently, Darwin had learned when Rousseau was due to pass a particular spot. Immediately recognizing that the encounter was not by chance, Rousseau was so wary that Darwin never came near him again.

Away from the world of betrayal and conspiracy, Rousseau's life was one of playfulness, sociability and charm. Intimacy with Hume had been out of the question, but Rousseau could relax with a Wootton neighbour, a stiff, reticent and, it seems, endearingly grumpy sixty-seven-year-old. The relationship between Bernard Granville and the fiery Genevan was both touching and incongruous, though (initially) Rousseau regarded it as purely superficial. 'I talk merely about inconsequential things with the only neighbour with whom I converse – because he's the only one who speaks French.'

Granville lived some two miles from Wootton Hall at Calwich Abbey, which he had purchased four decades earlier. The mansion was in a valley with the river Dove only 200 yards away and the grounds were constantly flooded.

A man of substantial means, Granville dedicated time and money to improving his gardens; he put in a lake, for example, with a wooded island in its centre connected to the bank by a pretty little bridge. At the front of the house was a bowling green. According to Granville's younger sister, Mrs Mary Delany, the estate was 'said to out-do any of the wonders of the Peak'.

Granville's other passion – shared with Rousseau – was music. In a room dedicated to it he had an organ that had been chosen for him by the composer George Frideric Handel, a neighbour of Mary Delany's in London.

Of Mary Delany, Edmund Burke said, 'she was the truly great woman of fashion, not only of the present, but of all ages.' Then sixty-six, she still retained her irrepressible vitality, her bright eyes, and her wave of curly hair. She had the reputation for being deeply spiritual as well as cultured and artistic. George III and Queen Charlotte welcomed her at Court.

Rousseau was introduced to Granville's wider family. Among his nieces and nephews, Granville's favourite was another Mary, born in 1746. This Mary was a frequent visitor to Calwich, especially after the death of her mother, Granville's sister, Anne Dewes, in 1761. She had been given a traditional upbringing, learning dance, deportment, lacework, and French – she was confident enough to write to Rousseau in his own language.

Rousseau obviously warmed to Mary, in an avuncular way, addressing her in letters as his *belle voisine*, his lovely neighbour. The (rather childish) twenty-year-old appears to have taken in her stride the attention paid her by her uncle's unlikely neighbour and international celebrity. On one occasion, she embroidered a collar for Sultan, receiving in return a gallant and comical note of thanks: 'My lovely neighbour, you make me unjust and jealous for the first time in my life: I could not see, without envy, the chains with which you would honour my Sultan, and I stole from him the privilege of wearing them first.'

Although Rousseau treated her with nothing more than affection, his mere proximity was enough to make Mrs Delany apprehensive. She was not familiar with Rousseau's oeuvre as 'I avoid engaging in books from whose subtlety I might perhaps receive some prejudice', but she was uneasy about Rousseau's influence. 'Now for a word about Monsieur Rousseau, who has gained so much of your admiration. His writings are ingenious, no doubt, and were they weeded from the false and erroneous sentiments that are blended through his works (as I have been told), they would be as valuable as they are entertaining.'

Mrs Delany then played a role in successfully dissuading a wealthy Irish landowner, the Marchioness of Kildare, from approaching Rousseau. Although the Marchioness, too, had not read *Émile*, she was of the opinion, until Mrs Delany convinced her otherwise, that the educational innovator might be the perfect tutor for her eldest son.

In winter, apart from Rousseau, Calwich had few visitors. But from June there was an endless stream of guests who came for the vistas, the vigorous walks, the clean air, and to admire Granville's landscaping. They included Brooke Boothby from Ashbourne and Margaret Cavendish Bentinck, the Duchess of Portland.

The Duchess was an intimate friend of Mary Delany's and another remarkable woman. Widow of the second Duke of Portland, she combined a sharp intellect with an obsession for collecting that extended from *objets d'art* to natural history, from the Portland Vase to sea shells (she was a serial snail-slayer: a thousand died at her fair hands). But her true zeal was for botany, and she was acquainted with all the prominent botanists of the day.

If the Duchess had heard the talk in London society of Rousseau's maligning Hume's name, it seems not to have made an impression on her. Rousseau appeared to be a normal, if strangely dressed, enthusiast for botany. She went with him into the Peak District on an expedition, and from that time on Rousseau occasionally puffed himself as '*Herboriste de la duchesse de Portland*'. They flattered each other in correspondence, and the Duchess sent her Swiss acquaintance seeds and plants – including, in August 1766, some 'great tufted wood vetch [found] growing upon a high bank'. He thanked her, on 3 September 1766: 'If I had not had any love of botany, the plants M. Granville has sent me from you would have given it to me.' The natural world suffused his soul with a 'precious serenity'. Botany was conducive to wisdom and virtue, 'chaining the passions with bonds of flowers'. The Duchess was charmed by the grace of expression.

Back at Wootton Hall there were few distractions, and to those who met him, Rousseau seemed in high spirits. Davenport put in occasional appearances, and Rousseau assisted him in clearing and cutting back the woods. Once or twice he showed up with his granddaughter Phoebe, of whom he was very fond, and grandson Davies. Davenport and Rousseau played chess, though the old gentleman could not put up much resistance. Rousseau engaged in good-natured banter, pretending Davenport lost to him intentionally.

During August, Rousseau and Le Vasseur visited Davenport at Davenport Hall in Cheshire. Brooke Boothby dropped in at Wootton now and again, encounters that meant so much to him that in his portrait by Joseph Wright of Derby he is holding a volume of Rousseau. In his mid-twenties, he had been at a military academy in Caen, so was fluent in French.

However, the only regular, day-to-day company was provided

by Davenport's servants, with whom Rousseau delighted in not being able to communicate. Taking care of his and his *gouvernante*'s needs were the steward Benjamin Walton, John Cowper and his housekeeper wife, the watchman Samuel Finne. There was also Davenport's near-blind, nonagenarian former nurse; she and Le Vasseur quarrelled incessantly.

Besides his botany, the local social life, and his counter-measures against plotters out to destroy him, what else was there to keep the fugitive occupied?

He continued to take an active interest in Genevan politics, siding with the *Représentants*, the Party of Liberty as he called them, who were pushing to extend rights and prosperity among the population. Their opponents condemned this struggle as a threat to the city's unity. France backed the existing political settlement – in effect, the oligarchy – and put the city under an increasingly tight blockade. From Wootton, Rousseau sent moral and financial support to its beleaguered citizens. In January 1767, he wrote to François-Henri d'Ivernois praising the *Représentants*, comparing their valour to the courage displayed by Roman senators about to be killed by Gauls.

However, once he had adapted to Staffordshire, Rousseau reverted to what he knew best, the pen, although he had chided Mme de Boufflers for her stress on his continuing to work. Davenport relayed to Hume that he found his tenant 'busy writing; and it should be some large affair, from the quantity of paper he bought'. (News Hume greeted with terror.)

After the weather improved, a favourite haunt was in the shade under a stand of trees known as Twenty Oaks, not far from Wootton Hall. Another choice nook was a small, u-shaped grotto, about six square metres in size, situated adjacent to the main house, and built into the solid, sandstone rock. Even Rousseau, slight as he was, would have had to squeeze through the low, narrow, wooden doorway. Inside were a stone seat, a fireplace in the corner, and a small, open window looking out on to a passageway leading to the basement of the main building. Here Rousseau composed a major section of a book accepted today as a landmark in literature. We could say of it what Rousseau's biographer, John Morley, said of *On the Social Contract*: it ranked in history as an act, not a book.

'I wrote the first part,' says Rousseau, 'with pleasure and gratification, and at my ease.' And indeed, the opening half of his autobiography, the *Confessions*, is full of sunny vignettes and happy reminiscences, though, as we have seen, his early life had its share of hurt, even torment, which he picked over in masochistic detail: 'All the memories which I had to recall were for me so many fresh enjoyments. I turned back to them incessantly with renewed pleasure, and I was able to revise my descriptions until I was satisfied with them, without feeling in the least bored.'

Rousseau began the *Confessions* well before coming to Wootton, and completed them well after he had left, in 1770. But he laboured over much of Part I of the book while he was in England. That part, which conducts the reader through his life up to his going to Paris in 1742, contains six 'books', or chapters, as does the notably darker Part II. So feared by Hume, the autobiography stops abruptly just short of Rousseau's setting out for Strasbourg. The next stage of his life was reserved for Part III, never to be written. (Although in Part I he does refer to a visit made 'a few days ago' to Davenport, where something occurred to remind him of learning arithmetic as a child.)

Rousseau's last thought in the *Confessions* was to record a statement he made after reading his work to a group of five aristocrats (whom he carefully names). He avowed to them the truth of what he had written. Anyone who challenged it was guilty of a lie or imposture. Anyone who examined his life and who could still believe him a dishonourable man deserved to be stifled. Thus, in the final act, the watchmaker's son from Geneva presents himself as justified in the high court of honour.

The title was surely a nod to St Augustine's *Confessions*, but, in Rousseau's more subversive version, the truth about one's character and actions could be arrived at through introspection alone, and without needing any recourse to God.

The memoirs ('the history of my soul') are still in print more than two centuries later, the text pored over by academics and biographers. Epochal claims are made for it – that it heralds the breakdown of the distinction between public and private, the dawn of our confessional era in which declaration of guilt itself becomes a virtue that helps cleanse the soul and diminish the offence, that it instigates a path of self-regard that ineluctably leads to the voluntary revelations of reality television shows, that it opens the way to particularism and the rejection of universal values that it announces a radically new culture in which emotional truth is to be accorded a higher value than external evidence, that it is pioneering in its stress on the significance of childhood, both as a stage in our life of interest for its own sake, and for its impact on the formation of character.

This social and moral priority given to emotional honesty is crucial, though there is also a strong element of self-justification. Certainly there are dozens of factual inaccuracies in the *Confessions* – scholars have established that Rousseau gets dates wrong and, on occasion, mixes up the chronology of events. On the whole, these particulars are trivial, though sometimes the error colours our judgement of an episode. For example, Rousseau says that he was first spanked aged eight, and the feeling of sensuality it gave him made him 'desirous of experiencing it again'. In fact, he was eleven (with all the turmoil of approaching adolescence) – knowledge of which transforms our reading of the scene. But in chronicling his early life, Rousseau often had little more to rely on than his memory; it is not surprising that he makes a few mistakes. It is far more surprising that he makes so few.

What caused such a furore – and distress to supporters such as Mme de Boufflers – was the book's brazen openness about the author and his cast of characters. While there is a line of autobiographies stretching back to St Augustine, one must remember that at the time there was still no established genre of literary autobiography. Though this was the great age of untrammelled biography, the word 'autobiography' was not used until a *Monthly Review* article in 1797. The first person to proclaim the work's uniqueness was Jean-Jacques himself, and he did so on the very first line: 'I am commencing an undertaking, hitherto without precedent, and which will never find an imitator. My purpose is to display to my fellows a man entirely true to nature – and that man is myself.'

He wrote that he was going to expose his life to the world, 'vile and despicable when my behaviour was such, as good, generous and noble when I was so'. And he was true to his word – the vile episodes he recounted included stealing, being sexually assaulted and visiting brothels, flashing at women in Turin (the latter presented as pathetically comic for the perpetrator). He also goes into the moral 'crime' that many found unforgivable: the abandoning of his five children to the Paris foundling hospital.

The *Confessions* is not all excitement. Indeed, it took some self-absorption to imagine that the humdrum details of his life, his diurnal comings and goings, his friendships and feuds, his emotional highs and lows, would be of interest to anybody but himself. The *Monthly Review*, shortly after the *Confessions* was first published, barked that Rousseau was 'a man whose vanity and presumption so imposed on his understanding, as to lead him to imagine that mankind would lend a ready ear to the most trifling, to the most dull, to the most impertinent, to the most disgusting relations, because they concerned ROUSSEAU!'

Some passages are inescapably Pooterish, but Rousseau sees himself in these pages as not just a man; he represents humanity, in all its moral, emotional and physical complexity. The unremitting wholeness of the portrait lifts the *Confessions* into a class of its own and sets the standard of revelation for generations to come. It contains flashes of brilliant illumination and insight. It can be tender, tragic, poignant and poetic. There are moments of charged sensuality. There are moments of sheer joy. There is drama, there is gossip and bitchiness. There are times when Rousseau is brave, others when he is cowardly; times when he is embittered, others when he is generous. There are moments when it is unclear whether the reader is expected to laugh or cry. Thus, early on he describes the death of Mme de Vercellis, in whose household he worked. 'At last, speaking no more, and already in the agonies of death, she broke wind loudly. "Good!" she said, turning round. "A woman who can fart is not dead!" These were the last words she uttered.' (Rousseau also recorded that she was a woman of ability and judgement 'who died like a philosopher'.)

The unsparingly open Rousseau presented here does not exempt the reader from his nightmare world – one far removed from the soulful contemplation of tufted wood vetch and the delightful exchanges with his *belle voisine*. In Part II of the book, a thread of secret foes and plots lurking behind the mask of comradeship, a sense of gloom and foreboding, evoke a Gothic mood in what is held out as honest recollection. In this world, the innocent narrator is helpless against the schemes of his adversaries, as in this extract from Book 10, when he moved to Montmorency: 'My heart clung still to attachments which gave my enemies countless holds on me; and the feeble rays that penetrated to my retreat served only to show me the darkness of the mysteries that were hidden from me.'

If Wootton presented the exile with the pastoral joy and peace of Arcadia, its rustic beauties did not ensure Rousseau a refuge from that darkness.

20

Where Has My Wild Philosopher Fled?

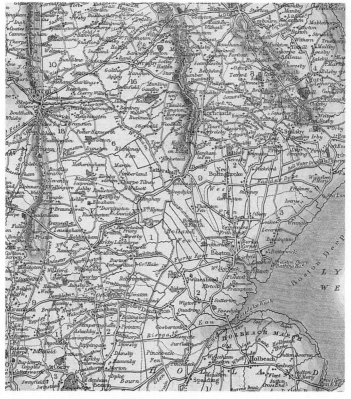

Rousseau's flight from Wootton led him post-haste to 'one of the most cursed disagreeable places in England'

*If all men had but the tenth part of Mr Rousseau's goodness
of heart, we should have a much better and much more
peaceable world.*
Richard Davenport

*I have always made one prayer to God, a very short one. Here
it is: 'My God, make our enemies very ridiculous!' God has
granted it to me.*
Voltaire, writing about Jean-Jacques Rousseau

The exiles were enduring a second cold spring in Staffordshire.
The mists and incessant rain made Wootton Hall seem more
cut off than ever. The two Englishmen to whom Rousseau was
most attached, Davenport and Granville, were away. Granville
had gone to Bath; Davenport was in London. Rousseau's *gouvernante* was increasingly restless. Not only was the damp air
making her ill, life at Wootton for this Parisian former kitchen
maid had become the torture of solitary confinement. This
bleak isolation was reinforced by constant battles with the
house servants. Le Vasseur claimed to have discovered Davenport's nonagenarian former nurse stirring cinders into their
meals. She and the nurse continued to bicker (presumably with
limited comprehension) from morning until night.

After the turn of the year, as winter lingered on, Rousseau
made no secret of his yearning to leave. As early as February,
he had conferred with Davenport about the sale of his library,
and on 12 March, with Davenport's help, he sold it *en bloc* to
Vincent-Louis Dutens, an Anglican priest, an associate of Mme
de Boufflers, and an unusual figure in being a Frenchman who
served occasionally in the British diplomatic service. In return,
Dutens gave him an annuity of £10.

In mid-March, Rousseau mulled over the possibility of

removing to London or Chiswick. Le Vasseur's health might
benefit. To Dutens he remarked that he would rather put himself at the mercy of all the devils in hell than that of English
servants. In London or the suburbs, they could find a *pension*
with an English-speaking French or Swiss domestic to run
their errands. It was the only way to be sure of peace and
independence.

In a letter to Davenport, Rousseau reminded his landlord
that he had deprived him of his house for a year, thanked him
effusively for his hospitality, and asked for his assistance in
moving. The plan was to leave most of their effects and just
take their 'togs' in one small box for the coach; the main items
would be safer at Wootton than being transported hither and
thither.

Davenport was anxious that his guest should not be abandoned. He offered another of his houses in Cheshire, Calvely
(in his family since the fifteenth century), three times the size of
Wootton, with cows and a large garden and in 'remarkably
soft air', healthier for Le Vasseur. However, if Rousseau was set
on going to London, he volunteered help to get him there and
search for lodgings. But, by the end of the month, he was again
urging Rousseau and Le Vasseur to stay in the country: 'I wish
to God you would let me send her along with you to Calvely.'
Rousseau declined. He wanted his own household. As for Le
Vasseur, she was still deteriorating (it was not surprising given
her sad existence) and hoped in London there would be people
to talk to. Her request was perfectly reasonable; after all, she
had left family and friends to be at his side.

Davenport had also asked his tenant's permission to revive
the question of a royal pension. Rousseau agreed: if the favour
came only from the King and his ministers, he would accept at
once. He would implacably reject it if it were owed to the solic-
itations of anyone else. He was never to discover that when

Davenport approached Conway, Conway consulted Hume. The Scot endorsed the idea. In his words to Blair, he had 'exhorted [Conway] to do so charitable an action'.

Conway arranged the pension even though he was entangled in the low politics of Chatham's administration, moderating American policy, and negotiating over proposals for a parliamentary inquiry into the East India Company (and the regulation of its income). He officially informed Davenport of the King's approval for a pension of £100 per annum on 18 March 1767 (by which point Davenport had braved Rousseau's wrath by telling him that Hume had been appointed under-secretary to Conway):

> I found in His M. an immediate readiness to comply with my application, that neither M. Rousseau's former refusal, *nor any other circumstances which have since happened* [authors' italics] might prevent the effect of His M.'s intended bounty. You'll therefore be so good as to acquaint M. Rousseau with what has past & with the pleasure I had in being thus employed to procure any degree of ease and satisfaction to a person of Monsr R's distinguished talents.

In making his recommendation to the noble Conway, *le bon David* had had to rise above his feelings about Rousseau, though rancour still permeates his own account of the episode. While exaggerating his part in the re-granting of the pension, he relayed to friends (wrongly) that 'the King was very much prejudiced against Rousseau', and that Rousseau's change of mind proved the 'suspicion which I always entertained' that he thought he had sufficient interest to obtain the pension by himself, and 'that he only picked a quarrel with me in order to free himself from the humiliating burden of gratitude towards me. His motives, therefore, were much blacker than many seem to apprehend them.'

Hume was presumably unaware that in January the then prime minister, the Duke of Grafton, had remitted the duty on Rousseau's books from France and, as Davenport reported to his tenant, 'has ordered this to be done immediately & he wishes that it may be represented to Mr Rousseau as a compliment intended by the King in showing him this little mark of DISTINCTION.'

In passing on the pension news, Davenport judged it wise to gloss over Hume's role. He told Rousseau that the pension came only from the King himself and his immediate ministers.

He judged well. His tenant had certainly not put the Hume 'plot' behind him: a February note to Brooke Boothby refers to 'the treachery of M. Hume' and 'his secret intrigues'. He asked Boothby, who was in Marseille, to send 'a small twig of an olive tree with the flower well preserved in a book: this would give me great pleasure, if only because of the augury'. An augury of what? Did Rousseau imagine himself in a Gethsemane?

He still pined for authentic friendship as he defined it, mourning the rupture with Earl Marischal, behind which he detected the manoeuvrings of both *le bon David* and the son of the *jongleur* (Tronchin). In mid-March, he complained to Marischal that the Earl had never specified Rousseau's wrong-doing. In any case, the accused man was not the real Rousseau, he said. Someone had given a phantom his name.

Davenport's kindliness was a poor substitute for *bona fide* friendship. To Du Peyrou, Rousseau lamented that though 'Mr Davenport renders me great services with much affection and zeal, he never says anything to me, never replies to my out-pourings of feeling. I never saw in my whole life a man so reserved, so profoundly mysterious. I believe him to be a gen-tleman: but he is an intimate friend of good David; that's all I know.' Only Sultan could offer him that transparent and pure fullness of love. And all the while, Rousseau could hear his other dog snarling.

Dark fantasies of plotters and hidden hands still held the exile in their grip. After a letter from Du Peyrou had been misdirected to Rousseau's cousin and sent on to him opened, Rousseau informed Du Peyrou in April 1767 that his 'dear cousin' was in league with his enemies. On all sides there were traps awaiting him: 'Oh destiny, O my friend, pray for me. I have not merited the misfortunes which are crushing me.' Spies had been dispatched to steal his papers; their preservation was now of the utmost importance. Although he was under constant surveillance from those who would stop them escaping, and all his post was monitored, providence had sent a friend of Du Peyrou's into Rousseau's neighbourhood. This man would arrange for a courier to collect the papers which could then be forwarded on to Du Peyrou.

This providential figure was Jean-François-Maximilien Cerjat. He lived in Louth in Lincolnshire – a small market town, with a large fulling-mill (for treating cloth) – and was in the Ashbourne area in January 1767. (Mysteriously, a phrase in one of Hume's letters shows that he had heard that Rousseau was intending to stay with a friend in Lincolnshire. Perhaps Rousseau's fears were not altogether unfounded.)

At this point, Davenport promised his tenant that he would visit Wootton after he had spent Easter week with his daughter in Warwickshire. It meant, he explained, that he would be at Wootton on 26 April at the earliest.

In fact, on leaving his daughter, Davenport did not go straight to Rousseau but diverted to his Cheshire seat, Davenport Hall, arriving there on 27 April. He had intended to stay for only a couple of days, but was laid low by gout, unable to stir two yards. In recompense, he invited Rousseau and his *gouvernante* to Davenport Hall: he would send horses for the four-wheeled chaise that was already there. However, it was 4 May before he put this down on paper. In the meantime, his absence from Wootton was unexplained.

Rousseau determined to leave. Perhaps he now included Davenport among his foes. A more plausible theory is that his decision was precipitated by another row between Le Vasseur and the nurse. Relations with the servants had finally imploded just when the exiles were relying on Davenport's presence to impose order. In a note to his niece, Mary Dewes, ten days later, Bernard Granville was under the impression that the servants had driven the exiles away, even naming the guilty woman.

> Mr Rousseau left last week, went for London, but I think he purposed making Chiswick the place of his abode for the summer. Mrs Cowper, Mr Davenport's housekeeper, behaved in so brutish a manner to him that it occasioned his sudden departure from this country – a sad loss to me; I would fain have had him come and stay at Calwich, but could not prevail. If chance should bring him your way, tell him how I mourn the loss of such a neighbour . . .

That problems with the servants triggered their departure is indicated from the opening of the note Rousseau left for Davenport, written on 30 April. It started abrasively, but was by no means the blistering tirade commonly reported.

First, he rebuked Davenport for allowing his servants to mistreat his two foreign guests. As master of the house, he should have known what was going on at Wootton Hall, particularly as it involved his hospitality to strangers. If he did not know, he was at fault; it would be even worse if knew and did nothing about it.

But Davenport's least excusable fault was forgetting his pledge to come to Wootton, establishing himself at Davenport Hall without bothering to consider the state of the man awaiting him. That was unbearable:

Tomorrow, Sir, I leave your house . . . I am not ignorant of the ambushes which threaten me, nor of my powerlessness in protecting myself from them. It only remains for me to finish with courage a career passed with honour. It is easy to oppress me, but it is difficult to degrade me. That is what reassures me against the dangers I will run.

There was also a practical component to the letter. Their few household effects, plus the proceeds of the sale of Rousseau's engravings and books, would serve as security for their expenses since December. He warmly thanked Davenport for his noble hospitality and said if it had finished as it had begun, he would have carried away the most tender and everlasting memories: 'I will often regret the dwelling I am leaving, but I will regret much more having had so amiable a host, and not having been able to make him a friend.'

The rush to depart is shown by his adding postscripts about what they were leaving behind: three full trunks with the keys in; books for Dutens 'on the commode in the little room', some not worth selling but others would compensate for them; some botanical works and a collection of music that Phoebe Davenport 'will find excellent if she cultivates that art and that I ask her to keep in memory of me'. Finally, he remembered to say he had put Davenport's books in a chest.

Rousseau, Le Vasseur and Sultan then disappeared, travelling with the minimum of baggage and barely enough to pay their way with postboys, innkeepers and coachmen on the long journey that lay ahead, a 150-mile haul across the heart of England, over the flat terrain of the east Midlands, into the wetlands of Lincolnshire. The Ashbourne postboy was dubious: should not Mr Rousseau wait for his landlord, Richard Davenport, to discuss this arduous trek into strange territory? There was no question of it.

Beforehand, Rousseau had discarded several gowns, which he dispersed in the village among the poor. Hume and Walpole both record him as no longer wearing his Armenian costume, maybe with the idea of travelling incognito. He was in 'an old French dress'. Perhaps, in divesting himself of the costume of exile, Rousseau was also consciously breaking with the recent past. Later, Hume could not resist a sour quip to Blair: he had not left all his baggage – he did, after all, take Le Vasseur.

Meanwhile, on 2 May, Hume, unaware of Rousseau's movements, supplied Davenport with an update on the administration of Rousseau's pension: 'I hope he will enjoy this mark of His Majesty's bounty with tranquillity and peace of mind.' Davenport replied with details of Rousseau's departure, prompting an 'I told you so' from Hume. 'I cannot say I am the least surprised . . . So you are a traitor, too, it seems; pray, do you speak in your sleep?' Later, he said to Mme de Boufflers – wrongly – that Rousseau had accused Davenport of being Hume's accomplice in the plot against him.

Granville was not alone in supposing London to be Rousseau's objective. Davenport supposed so, too. Having discovered his philosopher had flown, he made inquiries at Rousseau's bankers in the City of London and with the pastor of the Swiss Church in Soho, to whom Rousseau had contributed money for the relief of Geneva. Hume told Davenport that though Rousseau was probably already in the capital (doubtless to publish his damaging memoirs), 'I fancy he dares not approach a house in which he expects to meet with me.'

Nothing is known about Rousseau's life in those few days of May 1767. The first news we have of the runaways after they left Wootton on 1 May is an extraordinary letter from Rousseau to the Lord Chancellor, Lord Camden, dated 'A Spalding in Lincoshire [sic] le 5 May 1767', in which Rousseau put himself under the protection of the first minister of the law. He was, he told Camden, detained in Spalding by the impossibility of travelling on alone without danger, and sought an official guide to conduct them at his own expense directly to Dover. Camden's secretary replied on his behalf that the least postboy could shepherd him without the need for extra security measures.

The drive across England had clearly exacerbated Rousseau's paranoia. But why did he toil all the way to Spalding?

There are two significant facts from which Rousseau's objective and hence his itinerary can be conjectured. One is his plan to entrust his papers to Jean-François-Maximilien Cerjat, whose home was in Louth to the north of Spalding. The other is that between Louth and Spalding is the east-coast port of Boston.

The most likely sequence of events is that from Wootton Rousseau headed straight to Louth, either to deliver his papers for Cerjat to send on or else to pick them up if Cerjat had them already. From there, Rousseau travelled the short distance to Boston. In Boston, he discovered there were no ships for France, and concluded his enemies had stopped them to entrap him. Only at this point did he determine to go to Dover, pausing in a state of panic at the first substantial town towards the south coast, Spalding, to request his escort.

In 1767, Spalding was a trading centre, the conduit for exports, such as corn and coleseed, and for various imports including timber. Its population was barely three thousand. The river Welland flows through the town. In that year, its waters were swollen by torrential rain.

Driving into the town across the flat landscape of the Fens, past the wind engines or watermills draining off water from the surrounding farms, Rousseau, Le Vasseur and Sultan headed for lodgings in the White Hart, crossing the marketplace, with its pillory known locally as White Willey, and passing under the arch dividing the two wings of the inn. Two centuries earlier, Mary Queen of Scots had occupied a room in the White Hart – not necessarily a good precedent.

Well within living memory, in nearby Peterborough, a mother and daughter had been burned as witches for causing bad weather. The sudden appearance of the small, dark Swiss and his French housekeeper might have roused an ugly reception from the Spalding townsfolk. However, its provincial gentry were not ignorant of the outside world. For improving conversation, they could resort to the Gentlemen's Society, which boasted of members 'in every branch of knowledge'. If Rousseau had been invited in, he might have spotted Hume's *History* among the recently acquired books.

For the Society's members, Rousseau's arrival must have been a sensational talking point: the news soon reached London. The president was the vicar of Spalding Parish Church, forty-three-year-old John Dinham. He had been educated at Eton and Cambridge, was an avid reader, and well connected. A family man, he wore a ring on which was a tiny portrait of his wife. He was a close friend of William Fitzherbert, the MP (and now Lord of Trade) who had been Rousseau's original link to Davenport. Fitzherbert had also been involved in settling the pension.

Much later in the year, Hume reported to Adam Smith a conversation between Dinham and Fitzherbert in which the vicar described how 'he had passed several hours a day with Rousseau; that he was cheerful, good-humoured, easy, and enjoyed himself perfectly well, without the least complaint of any kind'. At the time, Hume painted a somewhat different picture to Davenport, who had been desperately trying to locate his missing tenant.

It had taken a while to track Rousseau down. It was not until 11 May that he addressed his former landlord in what, charitably interpreted, was a grudging expression of affection and gratitude, though stated with his usual directness and honesty: 'I preferred liberty to a residence in your house. But I infinitely prefer a residence in your house to any other form of captivity, and I prefer every other kind of captivity to that in which I am, which is horrible and unendurable.'

Postal delays meant that Davenport did not receive this note until 18 May. His generosity and sympathy were undiminished. Having expressed his amazement at Rousseau's speaking of Wootton as captivity, he wrote to his erstwhile guest that he was sending a boy over with twenty guineas. Rousseau should hire a carriage and come back to Wootton. 'I was never at Spalding, but I have always understood it to be one of the most cursed disagreeable places in England . . . For God's sake return out of it as soon as you can.' On the same day, he informed Hume that Rousseau had resurfaced: 'I was quite moved to read his mournful epistle . . . Poor Rousseau writes of nothing but his misery, illness, afflictions; in a word, of his being the most unfortunate man that ever existed.'

In fact, Hume had already discovered his foe's whereabouts and, in one of a series of crossed letters, had written to Davenport on 16 May. Davenport, he said, had probably heard from Fitzherbert that his 'wild philosopher' had appeared at Spalding, whence he had written an extravagant letter to the Chancellor. 'In short, he is plainly mad, after having been long maddish; and your good offices, with those of Mr Conway, not to mention mine, being joined to the total want of persecution in this country, have pushed him beyond all bounds of patience.' Hume's phrase 'want of persecutions' caught the eye of Ralph Leigh, the editor of Rousseau's correspondence: 'The echo of the King of Prussia letter makes one think.'

Shortly thereafter, details of Rousseau's tragic missive to the Lord Chancellor found their way into the press, which was taking a renewed interest in Rousseau's activities. The May 16–19 edition of the *London Chronicle* carried the following notice:

> Mr Rousseau, it now appears, is at Spalding in Lincolnshire; from whence he hath written a most extraordinary letter to the Lord Chancellor, demanding that a messenger may be sent down to that place to conduct him in safety to Dover, for which, he says, there is an absolute necessity. And this act of hospitality he requests, as the last he shall ever require from a country, which he is henceforth determined to abandon for ever.

Rousseau lingered in Spalding for nine days, a town with few distractions besides a nearby racecourse and a Tuesday market with only three stalls, two of which sold nothing but gingerbread.

Having discarded his gowns in Wootton, Rousseau had a blue coat made. Once the favoured guest of French nobility, he was now approached by the local surgeon and librarian of the Gentlemen's Society, Edmund Jessop. Jessop penned a long, florid note in Latin, expressing his desire to discuss one of the Genevan's publications which, though condemned by many, merited approbation in Jessop's view. Rousseau took his time before delivering a rebarbative response:

> You address me as a literary man, sir, in a literary language, on subjects of literature. You load me with eulogies so pompous that they are ironical, and you think to intoxicate me with such incense. You are mistaken, sir, on all these matters. I am not a man of letters. I was so once, to my misfortune, but I have long since ceased to be.

And he went further:

> Excessive eulogy has never flattered me . . . You style your-
> self a surgeon. If you had spoken to me of botany, and of the
> plants your country produces, you would have given me
> pleasure, and I should have been able to discourse with you
> on that.

The next day, Rousseau, Le Vasseur and Sultan left for Dover:
he could not wait to reach the sea. Their resources were so
strained that the philosopher was forced to sell his silver cutlery
to pay their way.

Fortunately, if they travelled non-stop, Dover was only two
days away. There was a twice-weekly coach, 'The Flying
Machine', which departed from an inn in Boston, stopped off
in Spalding, and then sped the 99.5 miles through Peterborough to the Spread Eagle inn in Gracechurch Street in the heart
of the City of London. From there, it was a day's run to the
coast on a direct route that went via Dartford, Rochester, Sit-
tingbourne and Canterbury.

In Dover on or about 18 May, Rousseau composed two letters, one to Davenport, the other to Conway, which began in
tiny characters that steadily grew in size as the missive went on.

When he saw the sea, he told his former landlord, he realized
he was free to cross it, and even considered returning to Wootton. It was only when he happened upon a newspaper article
(about his leaving Wootton) that he was forced to change his
plans. Having assumed that Davenport was the source for this
piece, Rousseau issued a sorrowful rebuke. He restated his
belief that friendship imposed its duties even when broken.

The press had indeed picked up Rousseau's flight. There
were poems and ditties, including one in the *Lloyd's Evening
Post* about Rousseau turning his arse on God. The *London*

Chronicle accused him of abusing 'his protector and friend . . . the ingenious Mr Hume' who had conducted him to the land of liberty. Rousseau's pride, caprice and ingratitude were 'unbecoming in a man of his singular talents and genius'. The *Gentleman's Magazine* spoke of his quitting Wootton in a very abrupt manner and abusing his benefactor 'in the most ungenerous terms'. Where they obtained this information, we can only guess. Certainly not from the gout-ridden benefactor.

In seven pages to Conway, Rousseau's other letter rehearsed the plot against him, adding that it was so extensive that the state must be involved. Perhaps the aim was to prevent the publication of his memoirs. However, he assured Conway that he did not believe him to be personally implicated. Conway had been deceived by Rousseau's enemies. He warned Conway against any attempt by the state to have him assassinated: he, Rousseau, was (unfortunately) so well known that his death or disappearance would inevitably prompt investigation. He proposed an agreement: if he were allowed to leave the country in peace, he promised in return that he would abandon his memoirs and not mention a word of his complaints nor utter one word against Hume – or always to speak of him with honour.

The most interesting aspect of Rousseau's proposal is how he undertook, if challenged, to explain his previous accusations. A flash of true insight shines through. He would blame them on his bad humour and the effect on him of the mistrust and offence brought on by his misfortunes. He admitted to 'too many unjust suspicions with which to reproach myself'. All the preceding sentences are in the third person – on how 'he' would abandon his memoirs and 'he' would explain 'his' accusations. The confession of unjust suspicions alone is in the first person, giving it a plangent reality.

Conway showed Hume the letter and, according to Hume,

thought it 'the composition of a whimsical man not a mad-man'. Hume then told Davenport, '[Rousseau] says that all the world in England are prejudiced against him; for which, how-ever, he knows no reason, except his behaviour to me, in which he confesses he might be to blame.' Writing to Turgot, Hume quoted Rousseau directly, but, intriguingly, given the *mea culpa*, omitted the phrase 'unjust suspicions'.

In fact, Rousseau and Le Vasseur had already booked their passage to France, though their boat remained in harbour because of strong winds. This was a routine problem in Dover. Boats had to travel through a series of sluices and then a slen-der constructed throat – a design which made the harbour impassable whenever a storm coincided with a neap tide (the point at which high water is at its lowest level).

For forty-eight hours Rousseau brooded on his situation. He stood on a hillock and addressed an uncomprehending crowd. One version of his leaving had him at dinner with a local man whom he suddenly suspected of being about to detain him on Conway's instructions. Rousseau rushed to the ship. Another told how, at his lodgings, on 21 May, he was served a meal with parsley, which he suspected was hemlock (though as a botanist he would be familiar with the plant). He rushed from the room, made for his ship, and hid in a cabin. Nobody, not even his *gouvernante*, was now beyond distrust. They sailed that night, reaching France in the morning.

Rousseau had bolted in a pitiable state, but the Scot was unre-lenting. In the first week of October 1767, he gave an account of Rousseau's flight to Adam Smith, summing it up:

> Thus, you see, he is a composition of whim, affectation, wickedness, vanity, and inquietude, with a very small, if any, ingredient of madness. He is always complaining of his

health; yet I have scarce ever seen a more robust little man of his years. He was tired in England; *where he was neither persecuted nor caressed* [authors' italics]: he resolved, therefore, to leave it; and having no pretence, he is obliged to contrive all those absurdities, which, he himself, extravagant as he is, gives no credit to . . . The ruling qualities above mentioned, together with ingratitude, ferocity, and lying, I need not mention eloquence and invention, form the whole of the composition.

Hume relayed to Smith – the tone is of barely restrained glee – how Hume's friends in Paris and the public were shunning him:

He endeavoured to regain his credit by acknowledging to everybody his fault with regard to me: but all in vain . . . He has had the satisfaction, during a time, of being much talked of, for his late transactions; the thing in the world he most desires: but it has been at the expense of being consigned to perpetual neglect and oblivion.

But, on the day Rousseau set foot again in France, Hume sat down to write to his French friends about the final act of this drama. And he appeared then to be concerned for Rousseau's fate, though making the serpentine suggestion that Rousseau was insane and therefore outside the law.

To Mme de Boufflers, he counselled that if she heard of Rousseau being caught and arrested, she might 'employ [her] credit in restoring him to his liberty, by representing him in his true colours, as a real and complete madman, who is an object of compassion, and can be dangerous to nobody.' At greater length, he suggested to Turgot, while giving a (heavily anti-Rousseau) account of his flight, that, 'If he could be settled in any safe and quiet retreat, under a discreet keeper, he has wherewithal to bear all charges for his support . . .' He added, 'It would be proper that his *gouvernante* should enter into the scheme, tho' I find that Mr Davenport had entertained no very advantageous idea of her character or conduct while they lived with him.' Nothing in Davenport's correspondence, at least, supports that.

Turgot's reply tactfully avoided the idea of a retreat with a keeper, brushing it aside with the quip that Rousseau's state of madness was preferable to his former less exalted state of ingratitude. He gave a list of people who would help Rousseau, including de Boufflers and Conti, de Montigny and de Malesherbes. (So much for Rousseau being shunned.) He did not think the French were so barbarous as to arrest Rousseau.

Thus the affair ended just where it began, with Hume involved in schemes to save Rousseau. However, in the context of Hume's unforgiving mood – his distortions, his assertions of madness – this final 'assistance' appears more tainted by vengeance than moved by charity.

21

After the Storm

Peace at last

31

After the Storm

Divine man, you have taught me to know myself.
Maximilien Robespierre

Rousseau was mad but influential, Hume was sane but had no followers.
Bertrand Russell

When Rousseau disembarked in Calais on 20 May, the Paris *parlement*'s order for his arrest was still in force. Warned about this by Conti, he accepted the hospitality of the prince at his château near Gisors, a medieval city in Normandy dominated by an eleventh-century fortress. There he lived incognito, adopting the name 'Renou'.

He was preoccupied by his memoirs and was still suffering bouts of paranoia. Towards the end of Part II he hinted at the nightmare that lay ahead when he left Switzerland. Presumably referring to Mme de Boufflers and Mme de Verdelin, he recalled, 'I thought I was setting out for Berlin [when] I was in fact leaving for England, and the two ladies who were trying to control me, after having driven me by weight of intrigue from Switzerland, where I was not sufficiently in their power, finally managed to deliver me over to their friend [Hume].'

There were also long periods of serenity. In mid-June, Hume's 'absolute lunatic' wrote a polite, restrained and balanced letter to Davenport thanking him for everything he had done and asking him to settle an account and to forward his post and trunks to his bankers. He hoped to see Davenport in France one day.

Replying on 4 July, Davenport attended to the business matters and added, 'The only thing I ever took amiss was your saying that I put a paragraph in the newspapers concerning your leaving Wootton, which upon my honour I neither directly nor indirectly did.' The house was always at Rousseau's service if he came to England again. Davenport's granddaughter Phoebe insisted 'she will abhor Wootton since she knows you are not there'. And 'It will give me more pleasure than you even can imagine to hear from you, pray don't refuse me that satisfaction, & if I can be of any sort of service depend on me.' Later the same month, he wrote again, having finally managed to get over to Wootton. He calculated he owed Rousseau £21 9s and had sent it to Rougement. The house seemed 'horrid dull' without its tenants. Phoebe sent a thousand thanks for the music he had left but said 'she had much rather hear you play the pieces yourself'. The old gentleman sent his compliments to Le Vasseur: he was particularly obliged to her, he said, as 'I have the satisfaction of bearing about me everyday, the marks of her favour'. This possibly referred to a pair of stockings she had knitted at his request.

The warm correspondence with Davenport continued on both sides as though Rousseau's year in Wootton had passed entirely without incident. Phoebe had the stuff, Rousseau thought, 'to make her the most adorable woman in England'. However, as he counselled all guardians, he advised Davenport to raise her outside the household. In December he wrote again:

> You want to know how I spend my time. Just about as at Wootton. I dwell in a very pleasant place where I live as solitary as possible, munching my hay as usual, fearing nothing, desiring nothing . . . I have 'my Host' [Du Peyrou] here who is convalescing, and with whom I play chess: he does not play so well as yourself, but on the other hand he is not so obliging as to allow himself to lose when he can win.

As for Davenport, there was a note of unmistakable regret when the old gentleman said he missed Rousseau.

In the summer of 1768, suspecting the domestic staff to be agents of Hume, Rousseau, with Conti's continued assistance, fled the château. He went, via the Temple, to Lyon and Grenoble, where his *maman*, Mme de Warens, was buried. On 29 April 1768 at Bourgoin, near Lyon, he finally married Le Vasseur, his loyal partner of twenty-three years, aiming to regularize her position. Two minutes before the secular ceremony Le Vasseur still had no idea what was happening. In a short speech, Rousseau explained his decision as rewarding her long devotion. Afterwards she took satisfaction in calling Rousseau 'my husband', though within a year Rousseau was complaining that she had become fed up with his morose moods and that sometimes a day would pass without their exchanging a single word.

Rousseau was seriously contemplating Davenport's invitation to return to Wootton (a plan he ditched for fear that Walpole was now plotting against him). Meanwhile, he continued to wander and to botanize. In 1769, one walk 'with three gentlemen' went disastrously wrong when the weather suddenly turned for the worse. Then 'one of our gentlemen was bitten by a dog [and] Sultan was half massacred by another dog: he disappeared and I thought him dead of his wounds or eaten by the wolf, and I was absolutely confounded on my return here to find him tranquil and perfectly healed . . .'

In 1770, Rousseau moved back to Paris and resumed the vocation that had sustained him throughout his life, copying music. He was asked by a group of dissident Polish aristocrats, and consented, to write the *Considerations on the Government of Poland* (published posthumously in 1782). Brooke Boothby was among those to visit him in Paris: 'When one day I vainly endeavoured to argued [*sic*] with him on his insane notions [of being constantly persecuted], I imprudently asked him if I was included amongst his oppressors. His eyes darting fire, - "Do not force me [to reply]", he said .' Courageously, Brooke Boothby raised the issue of the pension from George III. It had been authorized, but Rousseau had still not given instructions as to how it should be paid. Considerable arrears had built up. Rousseau's response was that as he had spoken of his treatment in England in 'an unfavourable manner', the first thing he required was a public apology. (It is not obvious who was supposed to deliver it.) Nevertheless, at home, he is said to have displayed a portrait of George III.

For a period, Rousseau's educational theories were all the rage, not only in France and England, but in Switzerland, Germany, and Ireland, too. Scores of pedagogical treatises were produced, almost all of them bearing his imprint. Parents who experimented by raising their children on Rousseau-ian principles experienced mixed results, some reporting that they produced a disconcerting wildness in their guinea pigs. It is possible that Davenport intentionally brought up his orphaned grandson Davies along Rousseau-ian lines. The boy turned out well, but fretted that he had received insufficient formal education, and did not like to hear the name of Rousseau mentioned.

In Paris during 1770–71, Rousseau gave readings – sometimes for up to seventeen hours – from the *Confessions*. His erstwhile friend, Mme d'Épinay, feeling defamed by his portrayal of her as a schemer and gossip, eventually persuaded the police to prohibit them. His readings elicited polarized reactions. Some listeners wept and kissed Rousseau's hand during passages of high emotional drama. Others were revolted. Mme de Boufflers totally repudiated him after reading the book on publication. The memoirs were 'like those of a farmyard worker or even lower, disagreeable, as well as tedious, thoroughly insane and spiteful in the most disgusting manner. I cannot get over it that I used to make a cult . . . of this filthy animal.'

Also posthumously published was the insanely brilliant *Rousseau Juge de Jean-Jacques*, which had gestated over several years. In these split-personality dialogues between Rousseau and Jean-Jacques, Rousseau is judge, jury and defendant as the author's deeds and personality are forensically examined and extracts from his writings used as evidence against him. Rousseau convicts himself on several counts, including being weak willed and following his whims, rather than being influenced by his duty. (Here he also has second thoughts on Ramsay's portrait of him, accusing Hume of having contrived the painting out of sheer malice and ensuring that in every respect – posture, clothes, Ramsay's palette – the sitter emerged as dark and monstrous with, in Rousseau's characterization, 'the face of a frightful cyclops'.)

When the work was completed in 1776, Rousseau was desperate to forestall any attempt by his foes to suppress it. On 24 February, he tried to place the manuscript on the high altar of Notre Dame, as though seeking sanctuary for it. The plan went awry: the gate dividing the choir from the nave was shut. According to an early biographer, Henry Grey Graham, Rousseau then 'wildly rushed from the church feeling God had joined with man in the conspiracy against him and wandered till darkness and fatigue drove him home.'

This disturbed state was not to endure. In his last years, Rousseau again achieved a degree of equanimity. *Reveries of a Solitary Walker,* composed between 1776 and 1778, revealed a man who seems finally at ease with himself, no longer raging at an unjust world or the corrupt and vain *philosophes*. His portrayal of nature, seen afresh as transcendental and sublime, would have a profound impact on novelists and poets. But the thinker who had read the truth of his and Hume's character from his heart now conceded in the *Reveries* that 'the real and basic motives of most of my actions are not as clear to me as I had long supposed'.

England was not forgotten. Despite the rawness of his experiences there, Rousseau continued to remain in touch with his friends from Wootton. In 1769, he had sent the Duchess of Portland seeds and plants. And three years later, on 17 April 1772, he wrote to her again, this time to thank her for news of Miss Dewes's forthcoming marriage: 'I rejoice therein with all my heart, and I rejoice both for her who is so well suited to make a good man happy and to be happy herself and for her worthy uncle whom the happy outcome of this marriage will bless with joy in his latter days.'

In May 1778, Rousseau and Thérèse, his wife, retired to a cottage on an aristocratic estate in Ermenonville, north of the capital (belonging to the last in his long line of patrician benefactors, the Marquis de Girardin). There Rousseau died on 2 July. Although the surgeons determined the cause had been apoplexy, rumours abounded that he had taken his own life. This seems unlikely: there is no record of Rousseau ever having contemplated suicide, even when the restless dog in his shadow growled most menacingly.

He was buried on an islet in a lake in Ermenonville. But five years after the Revolution, the French National Assembly determined that his remains should lie in a place of honour in Paris. On 9 October 1794, to the strains of his own music, Rousseau's body was disinterred and began the journey to the city on which he had turned his back in life. Crowds paid tribute at every village. A great torchlit procession greeted him in the capital. There, on the morning of 11 October, the coffin was placed in the Panthéon in the heart of revolutionary Paris, and, in a curious irony, positioned next to the body of his archenemy, Voltaire. Thérèse, who outlived Rousseau by twenty-three years, was on hand to witness her husband's nationalization: to the revolutionaries, her husband had come to embody the principles of liberty, equality and fraternity.

Therese Le Vasseur: lover, guardian, constant companion, she outlived
Rousseau by twenty-three years

As for *le bon David*, until illness consumed him, his final years
were comfortable, uneventful, and, unlike Rousseau's, almost
totally unproductive.

On his fifty-seventh birthday, 26 April 1768, he wrote to
Mme de Boufflers to inform her that Conway was leaving the
secretary of state's office and so, therefore, was he. Subsequent
letters to France explained his decision not to return to Paris:
the King, who had granted him a pension, was expecting him
to continue with his *History*. But to *l'Idole du Temple* he gave

another reason. He had a 'strong desire of enjoying' her society, but 'the truth is, I have, and ever had a prodigious reluctance to change my place of abode.' There had been a report in the newspapers that he would be going over to France 'in his former station'. The story, he said, had no basis in fact.

The Rousseau episode, which Hume still believed had threatened to ruin his name, ate away at him, and he kept a vigilant eye on news of his adversary. Having discovered that Rousseau had taken flight from Conti's château, he was unable to resist another attack. Rousseau, he wrote to Mme de Boufflers, 'is surely the most singular and most incomprehensible, and at the same time the most unhappy man that ever was born.' She told Hume untruthfully, perhaps to spare him embarrassment, that she had had no dealings with Rousseau since their row.

By the summer of 1769, Hume was back in Edinburgh for what was, effectively, the start of his retirement. It was a period of quiet contentment: he had his health, a revenue of £1,000 a year, 'and though somewhat stricken in years . . . the prospect of enjoying long my ease and of seeing my reputation increase'. He entertained regularly and lavishly, delighting in his (as he saw them) superb cooking skills. He claimed to Sir Gilbert Elliot that his sheep-head broth was so delicious that one of his guests spoke about it 'for eight days after'.

He described himself as having 'done with all ambition', but he still wanted to polish his *History*, regarded then as the real jewel of all his works. Much of his spare time was devoted to revising it. In 1770, new editions came out. In his own words to Elliot, the thrust of the changes had been to 'soften or expunge many villainous, seditious Whig strokes'. The early editions had been 'too full of . . . foolish English prejudices'. Meanwhile, there was the constant hospitality: Benjamin Franklin paid a visit in 1771.

In 1772, Hume moved to a new, small house ('a large house for an author'), whose construction he had supervised. Oddly, on display in his parlour were Allan Ramsay's portraits of both himself and Rousseau. Hume had 'totally and finally retired from the world', he insisted to Mme de Boufflers, and 'with a resolution never more to appear on the scene in any shape. This purpose arose, not from discontent, but from satiety. I have now no object but to *sit down and think, and die in peace.*'

Dying in peace would require tremendous fortitude. In the spring of 1775, he was affected by a bowel disorder. He could not know it, but he had cancer of the intestines. On 8 February 1776, he confessed to Adam Smith that he had lost five stone. He had aches and diarrhoea. Smith's classic *Wealth of Nations* appeared in March, and Hume wrote to congratulate him. The weight of expectation for Smith's book had made Hume nervous but, after reading it, he was 'much relieved'. Still, he remained sceptical of its winning a wide readership.

The cancer was coursing through his body. By the middle of 1776, he was so thin that he needed a cushion to sit. He wrote his short autobiography, *My Own Life*, in April 1776 and appointed Smith his literary executor with instructions to publish *Dialogues on Natural Religion,* which he had been reluctant to expose to the public for fear of disturbance to his quiet life: 'I consider an observation of [the seventeenth-century author, the Duc de la] Rochefoucauld, that a wind, though it extinguishes a candle, blows up a fire.' He told Smith that if he lived a few years longer, 'I shall publish them myself.' After Smith baulked at assuming responsibility for the explosive text, Hume added a codicil leaving his manuscripts and instructions to publish with Strahan.

He had no doubt that death was near. His physician updated Smith on the historian's health:

. . . which is so bad that I am quite melancholy upon it, and as I hear that you intend a visit to this country soon, I wish, if possible, to hasten your coming that he may have the comfort of your company so much the sooner. He has been declining several years, and this in a slow and gradual manner, until about twelve month ago, since when the progress of his disorder has been more rapid.

On 4 July 1776, the thirteen American colonies made their unanimous Declaration of Independence in Philadelphia; it was also the day of Hume's last dinner party. Three days later Boswell, who was contemplating writing Hume's biography, came to see him. The formerly *gros David* was 'lean, ghastly, and quite of an earthy appearance'. But what disturbed Boswell more was Hume's stubborn refusal, even in his final days, to take solace in God and concede the possibility of an afterlife. Worse still, Hume was disdainful of believers, remarking that 'when he heard a man was religious, he concluded he was a rascal'. Boswell did not think he was joking.

On 12 August 1776, Hume dispatched his last revisions to Strahan:

Please to make with your pen the following correction. In the second volume of my philosophical pieces, p. 245 l. 1 and 2, eraze these words, *that there is such a sentiment in human nature as benevolence*. This, Dear Sir, is the last correction I shall probably trouble you with: For Dr Black has promised me, that all shall be over with me in a very little time: This promise he makes by his power of prediction, not that of prescription. And indeed I consider it as good news: For of late, within these few weeks, my infirmities have so multiplied, that my life has become rather a burden to me. Adieu, then, my good and old friend. P.S. In the same page l. 4, instead of *possession of it* read *sentiment of benevolence*.

He still had to bid adieu to the woman in Paris to whom he had been so close, Mme de Boufflers. Her lover, the Prince of Conti, died on 2 August, and in receipt of this sad news, Hume summoned the strength to commiserate. On 20 August, he sent his final letter, in simple and direct language, eschewing his former elaborate courtesies:

> My reflection carried me immediately to your situation in this melancholy incident . . . Pray write me some particulars; but in such terms that you need not care, in case of decease, into whose hands your letter may fall . . . I see death approach gradually, without any anxiety or regret. I salute you, with great affection and regard, for the last time.
>
> DAVID HUME

He died five days later, at around 4 p.m. and was buried in the nearby Old Carlton cemetery. Robert Adam designed his classical cylindrical mausoleum. Not long before his death, he had told Adam Smith that he had been reading Lucian's *Dialogues of the Dead,* and that among all the excuses made to avoid stepping into Charon's boat, he could find none that fitted him:

> I could not well imagine what excuse I could make to Charon in order to obtain a little delay. I have done everything of consequence which I ever meant to do; and I could at no time expect to leave my relations and friends in a better situation than that in which I am now likely to leave them. I therefore have all reason to die contented.

Smith published his remarks, though there is some debate over whether the economist toned them down, removing some of his friend's more strident anti-Christian sentiments. None the less, he quotes Hume saying, 'Have a little patience, good Charon: I have been endeavouring to open the eyes of the public. If I live a few years longer, I may have the satisfaction of seeing the downfall of some of the prevailing systems of superstition.' It was provocative enough to raise hackles. Boswell wished Dr Johnson would 'knock Hume's and Smith's heads together, and make vain and ostentatious infidelity exceedingly ridiculous'. Both Johnson and Burke thought Hume's courage in the face of death was a mask; that his real agenda was to display his virtuous life and tranquil death as evidence that morality had nothing to do with religious faith. Johnson scoffed that Hume was 'a man who has so much conceit as to tell all mankind that they have been bubbled [deceived] for ages, and he is the wise man who sees better than they.'

Our two protagonists shared one noteworthy devotee. In 1762, with Rousseau in Môtiers and Hume about to move to Paris, in the isolated Prussian city of Königsberg, a thirty-eight-year-old lecturer devoured Rousseau's works as they were published. According to one anecdote, the fastidious Immanuel Kant, whose daily routine was so rigid and undeviating that people set their watches by him, became so absorbed in *Émile* that he bewildered his neighbours by forgetting to take his usual post-lunch constitutional. Kant was alert to the seductive dangers of Rousseau's language: he worried that its beauty distracted from his ideas; to penetrate these ideas he read and re-read him. Rousseau understood, he thought, the paradox of autonomy – that freedom meant conformity to a rule. As he was writing his own masterpiece, the *Critique of Pure Reason*, he had a single portrait in his house – of Jean-Jacques Rousseau.

As for Hume, Kant said the Scot had 'woken him from his dogmatic slumber'. Kant's preoccupation with cause and effect, which he thought the basis of all scientific knowledge, was provoked by Hume's sceptical reflections. Unable to accept Hume's scepticism about causation, he sought to demonstrate how a proposition such as 'every event has a cause' could be known *a priori* (i.e. could be known independent of experience), even though it was a synthetic proposition (not true or false by virtue of its terms). 'Water boils at 100 degrees Celsius' is a synthetic proposition. 'All bachelors are unmarried' is an analytic one, true by definition.

With the exception of Nietzsche, probably no philosopher's posthumous reputation has fluctuated quite so dramatically as Rousseau's. The *Confessions* was initially decried – 'pompous' and 'obscene' being the general judgement. Yet, within a decade, sentiment was already becoming more positive. The work is now established as a literary masterpiece.

Rousseau's political legacy has been much more contentious. Although he himself was no advocate of rebellion, his name became inextricably bound up with the French Revolution. Its makers on all sides drew on his works to justify their actions, most famously Robespierre, who ideologically embraced Rousseau (along with such Romans as Cato) and executed with zeal his understanding of 'the general will of the people' – in his own phrase *une volonté une*, 'one single will'. Nevertheless, two years before Robespierre grasped power, Edmund Burke had responded to the revolutionaries' worship of Rousseau with a brilliant and far-sighted diatribe, *A Letter to a Member of the National Assembly*. 'Everyone knows that there is a great dispute among leaders [of the National Assembly] which of them is the best resemblance to Rousseau.' The truth was, he said, they all resembled him. And Burke accused them of adopting the worst of Rousseau's vices, vanity, 'that makes the whole man false'. 'We have had the great professor and founder of *the philosophy of vanity* in England . . . He left no doubt in my mind that he entertained no principle to influence his heart or guide his understanding but vanity. With that he was possessed to a degree little short of madness.'

Rousseau's influence on later generations is indubitable (though not always positive). He can be seen as father of the Romantic movement, and even a great-grandfather of the Green movement. The Romantics were inspired by his confirmation of the worth of each and every one of us, however ordinary, by his emphasis on equality, on knowledge of the inner self, on a spiritual connection with nature, as well as by his imagination and the depth of his feelings.

In 1816, George Byron and Percy Shelley went on a pilgrimage to Lake Geneva, carrying with them *Héloïse*. Shelley described Rousseau as 'a sublime genius'. Mary Shelley had studied Rousseau, and his writings inspired *Frankenstein*: the monster becomes corrupted by his association with society. Schiller, Stendhal (for whom Rousseau was 'the noblest soul and the greatest genius that ever was'), de Tocqueville and Schopenhauer were all admirers. To Hazlitt, he was a new Prometheus. Lytton Strachey said of the *Confessions* that it 'started the vast current in literature and sentiment which is still flowing'. A youthful Leo Tolstoy took to wearing a medal on which was engraved Rousseau's portrait; he read all of Rousseau's works, but was captivated in particular by *Héloïse*, *Émile* and the *Confessions*.

In the twentieth century, Rousseau was charged with offering intellectual justification for totalitarianism. But if his posthumous reputation has ridden a helter-skelter – one moment he is a benevolent patron of equality and liberty, the next the warped mastermind of tyranny – Hume's has steadily climbed, though with only the occasional hiatus. In America, the influence of his less theoretical writings (his essays and *History*) should not be overlooked. Among the United States founding fathers, for instance, James Madison was a staunch disciple, his version of federalism traceable to Hume's thinking. Many American luminaries consumed Hume's *History*, including Samuel Adams, George Washington and Benjamin Rush (though Thomas Jefferson despised the work, labelling Hume a 'conceited Scotchman').

In the nineteenth century, the historian began to make way for the philosopher. Hume's *History* ceased to be the standard text, superseded by, among others, Thomas Macaulay's. Meanwhile, the *Treatise*, the book that fell 'dead born', came to be recognized as an enduring masterpiece. By the twentieth century, Hume's standing as one of the most significant thinkers of all time became firmly entrenched: there remains ongoing engagement with his sceptical conundrums, which still fascinate and unsettle, tease and bewitch. His philosophical style is hailed as an exemplar of clarity and a model of ingenuity. Bertrand Russell, an empiricist in the Humean tradition, acknowledged Hume's supreme importance in his *A History of Western Philosophy*. The Vienna Circle, which for a time before World War II dominated the world of philosophy, was a legatee of the eighteenth-century Scot. This group of mathematicians, logicians and philosophers dismissed much of aesthetics, morality and religion as meaningless metaphysics; to be meaningful, propositions had either to be verifiable through experience or true by definition. Two centuries earlier, Hume had famously concluded his *An Enquiry Concerning Human Understanding*:

> If we take in our hand any volume: of divinity or school metaphysics, for instance: let us ask, *Does it contain any abstract reasoning concerning quantity or number?* No. *Does it contain any experimental reasoning concerning matter of fact and existence?* No. Commit it then to the flames: for it can contain nothing but sophistry and illusion.

Members of the Circle grappled with Hume's conundrum about induction, as did the Viennese-born Professor Sir Karl Popper. In his book about Hume, the philosopher Sir Freddie Ayer could confidently assert that Hume was the greatest of all British philosophers. Beyond the confined world of academic philosophy, Albert Einstein revered Hume, giving credit to the philosopher for transforming his powers of critical reasoning and ultimately with being a catalyst in his discovery of the theory of relativity. In a 1915 letter to the founder of the Vienna Circle, Moritz Schlick, Einstein revealed that just before his fundamental insight, he studied Hume's treatise 'with eagerness and admiration'.

22

The Truth Will Out

Rousseau and true friend

A man is not a rogue and rascal and lyar because he draws a false inference.
David Hume

Rousseau was not a wicked man; he was an unfortunate, a distracted, a deeply sensitive, a strangely complex creature; and above all else, he possessed one quality which cut him off from his contemporaries, which set an immense gulf betwixt him and them: he was modern.
Lytton Strachey

At the end of his long tribute to 'our most excellent, and never-to-be-forgotten friend', Adam Smith put David Hume forward as the exemplar of 'as perfectly wise and virtuous man as perhaps the nature of human frailty will permit.' If so, why, in the quarrel with Jean-Jacques Rousseau, did Hume act so far out of character?

The answer must begin with Paris. Paris was the one arena where Hume had been an unmitigated triumph. In Paris, he had been treated with 'perfect veneration', esteemed by the *philosophes*, swooned over by salon hostesses. After a career marked by official hostility, qualified success and outright disappointment, France was the country in which he had been embraced and acclaimed, and not just for his work but for his character. He was *le bon David*, decent, honest, virtuous, just, wise. Mme de Boufflers, the woman who led the field in passionate reverence for Hume, begged him to save this persecuted and distressed author, Rousseau. How could *le bon David* possibly let her down? Hume's early, effulgent letters of love for Rousseau are quite out of keeping with his normal plain, direct style: he was visualizing himself through the gaze of others (an instance of what Rousseau would call *amour propre*).

But, a single man with no dependents and few obligations, Hume had neither wanted nor expected to chaperone Rousseau to safety. Perhaps, if Rousseau had travelled to England without him, as Hume intended, the Scot would have absented himself entirely, just as he had from Mme de Boufflers on her visit to England. No clinging devotee then, no clinging exile now. And, indeed, it was not just the bothersome Rousseau; with Le Vasseur and Sultan in tow, Hume suddenly acquired responsibility for a family. He had also passed from being the celebrated Mr Hume to being the escort for the celebrated John James Rousseau, and in the city where this Scotsman was always uncomfortable and would never receive his due.

There is evidence that Hume's attitude to Rousseau was already coloured by scorn. After all, he was probably the author of the central quip in the King of Prussia letter, and even before Rousseau's departure to Wootton, he had delivered several cutting dissections of his character. There was more than a hint of animosity in all this, attended by the thought that Rousseau's character, his professed desire for solitude, his primitive existence, his 'illness', his 'virtue', was a bundle of affectations. That might explain, for example, Hume's investigation into Rousseau's finances and the evident desire to expose the simple man of feeling as a fraud. Hume's letter urging Mme de Boufflers to contact Rousseau's banker showed his motivation clearly enough: 'For, even if the fact should prove against him, which is very improbable, I should only regard it as one weakness more, and do not make my good opinion of him to depend on a single incident.'

This is why, of all those who read Rousseau's letter delaying the pension, Hume alone took it as a rejection, and on that basis rushed to tell his friends how Rousseau was unaccountable, blameable, extravagant. He condemned Rousseau's extreme sensibility. Rousseau was exhibiting a selfish disregard towards those who had helped him: to Hume, Rousseau's behaviour had provided confirmation of his true nature.

Imagine, then, Hume's state of mind as he opened a letter from Rousseau, anticipating a salute for his extra efforts over the pension. Instead, he was confronted by the 341 words of the mortifying charge levelled by the man to whom he had devoted so much time, and for whom he had, *au fond*, so little time. Moreover, his French coterie had been proved right. Hume's foolish raptures over Rousseau had been shown up for the froth they were. Worst of all, these charges might soon be reproduced in the exile's memoirs, set out with a rhetorical flair that readers would find impossible to resist. But Rousseau had perpetrated something still more provocative. Hume had been hunting for proof that Rousseau was a fraud. Suddenly the quarry had called *Hume*'s virtue in question. *Lye, lye lye*, scribbled the Scot frantically in the margin of the ensuing indictment, simultaneously incensed and terrified. *Lye, lye lye*.

It was at this point that a disjunction in their intellectual personalities ensured that the division between them would be unbridgeable. Rousseau conceived a bold conclusion, and then filled in the details. Hume operated in the other way – starting with the facts, and using these to build a case. So Rousseau imagined the deadly and extensive conspiracy against him, before unearthing his corroborative evidence. Hume, in contrast, went straight to that evidence. By examination of each piece, he sought to discredit his attacker's nightmare thesis, to persuade the public that there were more reasons to disbelieve than to believe it. Rousseau's reliance on intuitive imagination disorientated and enraged his erstwhile benefactor.

All this goes some way to explaining why Hume erupted so violently when he saw Rousseau's allegations, and why he made such frenetic efforts to limit any damage from what was plausibly the most potent and destructive pen in Europe, for he never lost sight of Rousseau's genius. But the unremitting brutality of Hume's reaction put his reputation in Paris more at risk than any claim of Rousseau's: in effect he exchanged roles with his accuser in his search for vengeance. He also demonstrated how little he had assimilated the manners of the salons in which he was fêted. Perhaps he had not been offered the opportunity to study the *Rule of Life* on Mme de Boufflers' bedroom wall.

More perplexing is Hume's persistent mendacity – his utter falsehoods, his economies with the truth, his deviousness.

Before the 'plot' coalesced, these included the false impression he gave that he was ignorant of the King of Prussia letter, his holding back its authorship from Rousseau, then telling him that Walpole had intended it to remain secret; his not forwarding letters to Rousseau from de L'Espinasse and (later) d'Alembert; the exaggeration of his role in winning Rousseau's pension.

The affair of the faux retour chaise is illuminating. Biographers have traditionally skirted over Rousseau's sense of humiliation at being treated as a beggar living on alms, dismissing it as a typical overreaction from the hypersensitive Genevan. At the time, the benevolent Davenport must have been taken aback. Surely this was subterfuge with the purest of motives, for he was both supporting the indigent and concealing the charity.

Hume was just as unlikely to give the ploy a second thought. When it came to the truth, he had an instrumentalist outlook, telling his publisher, Sir William Strahan, in August 1770: 'You see I am a good casuist, and can distinguish cases very nicely. It is certainly a wrong thing to deceive anybody, much more a friend; but yet the difference must still be allowed infinite between deceiving a man for his good and for his injury.'

That attitude, to Rousseau, was an anathema. As so often, there are puzzling inconsistencies in Rousseau's pronouncements, but his gut instinct was to recoil at any form of deception. For Rousseau, a white lie was still a lie, an act that both slighted its target and sullied its creator. Even if Hume was not the originator of the trick over the chaise, his awareness of it, in Rousseau's eyes, made him complicit; his private judgement as to what was in his guest's best interest was both condescending and contemptuous.

In the Fourth Walk of the *Reveries*, where he confesses to having sometimes lied out of shame or embarrassment, he writes, 'The lies we call white lies are real lies, because to act deceitfully in one's interest or that of others is no less unjust than to act deceitfully against the interests of others.' Rousseau saw himself as the apostle of truth: for him, the truth was of paramount importance, for him his 'horror of falsehood outweighed all other things' (*Reveries*).

There were other Hume lies. Following the retour-chaise debacle, and after Rousseau exposed the 'plot', Hume persistently gave misleading information to his supporters: for instance, his assertion that Rousseau had called him *le plus noir de tous les hommes*; the bald statement that he had proof that Rousseau had plotted against him for two months, proof he never produced; the assertion that Rousseau had provided no sign of his distrust of Hume – not so, if we accept that Rousseau mentioned the word 'traitor' in Lisle Street. There were his claims that Conway and Hertford had advised publication and that his French friends had 'extorted' his consent to publish the *Concise Account*; his tricky exchanges with Walpole over the editing of Walpole's letter in the French *Account*; his wrongly describing Davenport as disliking Le Vasseur. An observer in possession of the full facts could have identified at least twelve lies, apart from little embellishments, committed by the Scot. Particularly mystifying are his deceptions of Mme de Boufflers – not only over the Rousseau affair but personal matters such as his plans to return to Paris. Of all people, she was the one who deserved his candour.

Perhaps the moral of the whole sad encounter is that 'while sane men cannot make madmen sane, madmen can make sane men mad.'* In his momentary madness, fury and panic, Hume never grasped the root of Rousseau's complaint: that though Hume had carried out the obligations of a friend in practice, he was constitutionally incapable of doing so in spirit. Rousseau expected his friends to be entirely straight with him, to open their heart, to be motivated purely by love. Friendship required a special form of understanding. He warned Mme d' Épinay, 'My expressions rarely have the usual significance, for it is always my heart that communes with you, and some day maybe you will realize that its language is not that of other hearts.'

The nature of friendship is something Rousseau returns to time after time. In the *Confessions,* he reveals the bar of suspicion potential friends had to hurdle:

> Some friendships . . . are very dear to me. They have often caused me to regret that happy obscurity, when those who called themselves my friends were really such, and loved me for myself, from pure goodwill, not from the vanity of being intimate with a well-known man, or from the secret desire of thus finding more opportunity of injuring him.

Rousseau had a visceral grasp of Aristotle's analysis of friendship in the *Nicomachean Ethics*: 'What is just is not the same for a friend towards a friend as towards a stranger.' Friendship

---

* The authors are indebted for this phrase to Simon Gray.

involves a basket of mutual emotions – respect, trust, warmth, a desire for that person's happiness and success, a desire to be in that person's company – reinforced by action. And friendship is sustained over time. Do not expect friendship to ripen too quickly, Rousseau admonished young François Coindet in 1758. Friendship 'is something that must mature slowly over the years, so that true friends are friends long before they use the word "friend".'

Hume was baffled by Rousseau's fondness for Sultan, 'his affection for that creature is above all expression or conception'. But Rousseau's relationship with the canine gives us some insight into Rousseau's relationship with his fellow humans. Friendship for Rousseau was achievable only by equals, who were independent of each other. A true friend had every claim on his heart but none on his liberty. During Boswell's pilgrimage to Rousseau in Môtiers, Rousseau maintained that a person's attitude to cats was a vital test of character. Those of a despotic nature 'do not like cats because the cat is free and will never consent to become a slave'. A relationship with a dog, too, should not be one of ruler and subject. About the predecessor to Sultan, Rousseau wrote, 'My dog himself was my friend, not my slave: we always had the same will, but it was not because he obeyed me.' As for Sultan, though he was a source of endless trouble, he could never be mendacious, he could never be disingenuous, insincere, hypocritical or patronizing. Sultan was incapable of disloyalty.

Watching Rousseau converse with his lugubrious neighbour Bernard Granville, or botanize in the Dove valley, one might have spotted nothing amiss. But forever scurrying beside the exile was that second dog – the one forewarning of betrayal and conspiracy – its bark echoing in the solitude of Wootton. Although Rousseau's enemies were not chimeras, there was no conspiracy. The 'plot' was the fruit of Rousseau's paranoid imaginings. Yet why did he put Hume at the nucleus of it?

Perhaps it was the simple consequence of Hume's inability to fulfil Rousseau's criteria for friendship. But Rousseau, that apostle of truth and shrewd observer of motivation and personality, could equally have identified some characteristics in his saviour that led him to recoil: some lack of commitment to the truth, a certain looseness in Hume's respect for others. In particular, he may have intuited Hume's fundamental disdain for him. And that lay behind the word 'traitor' on their last evening together, in Lisle Street.

Hume was no plotter. However, the prolonged aggression of his counter-attack (and his final insistence on Rousseau's needing a keeper) was surely fuelled by the knowledge that he was not guiltless: he had contributed to his charge's discomfiture and had acted behind his back. In this light, it is hardly surprising that, once it was over, he would do his best to erase the row from his personal history. Although they had preoccupied a year and a half of his life and demonstrated his benevolence, in *My Own Life* his dealings with so prominent a figure as Jean-Jacques Rousseau merit not one mention.

The image of *le bon David* has endured. That is how Hume is portrayed in philosophy and history books, and by biographers. Of course, in Rousseau's case, he did much to warrant it. But how ironic that his going to Rousseau's aid put that image at risk. And it was precisely *le bon David*'s attempt to preserve his reputation that brought him so close to tarnishing it.

With his rigorous reasoning, Hume had punctured the Enlightenment's inflated claims on behalf of reason. So there was irony, too, in his overwrought response to the assault by Rousseau, the man of sensibility. When, in the summer of 1766, Hume jettisoned a lifetime of moderation, he seemed fixed on demonstrating that reason was indeed the slave of the passions.

Dramatis Personae

Jean-Báptiste le Rond d'ALEMBERT (1717–1783)
The natural son of the salon hostess Mme de Tencin and an eminent soldier, chevalier Destouches-Canon. Abandoned as a baby by his mother in
a wooden box on the steps of the Paris church of Saint-Jean-le-Rond (the
baptistry of Notre-Dame), after which he was named. His father, none the
less, paid for his upkeep and education. A foremost mathematician – he
developed partial differential equations – he became a leader among the
philosophes and a major force in the French Enlightenment. Diderot invited
him to be co-editor of the *Encyclopédie*; he wrote the article setting out its
aims. Socially he was in demand as a jester and mimic. He is also known for
his devotion to Julie de L'Espinasse, to whose aid he came when her aunt and
patron, Mme du Deffand, turned her out.

Reverend Hugh BLAIR (1718–1780)
Edinburgh Presbyterian cleric, and Professor of Rhetoric and Belles-Lettres. Close friend and regular correspondent of David Hume's and a leading figure in the Scottish Enlightenment.

Sir Brooke BOOTHBY (1744–1824)
Born and died in Ashbourne. Translator, botanist, poet and supporter of
Rousseau. A fluent French speaker, he met Rousseau at Wootton in 1766
'in a romantic valley at the bottom of the Weaver hills', and visited him in
Paris in 1774. A famous Wright of Derby portrait has him lying down
reading a copy of Rousseau, thus demonstrating his *sensibilité*. He equally
acquired a reputation for indolence and drunkenness.

James BOSWELL (1740–1795)
Scottish lawyer, writer, diarist, and biographer of Samuel Johnson; also
notable for his perpetual whoring and drunkenness. Son of Lord Auchinleck.

He first met Hume in Edinburgh as a fellow member of the Select Society. In 1764, he visited Rousseau in Switzerland and, at the end of January 1766, notoriously accompanied Rousseau's *gouvenante*, Thérèse Le Vasseur, from Paris to Chiswick.

Marie-Charlotte-Hippolyte de Campet de Saujon, Comtesse de BOUF-FLERS-ROUVEREL (1725–1800)
Married at twenty-one to Édouard, Comte de Boufflers (d. 1764), she soon became the mistress of the Prince de Conti, remaining with him until his death in 1776. Making her home at the Temple, Conti's Paris residence, she was known as 'l'Idole du Temple', but her sensibility, cultivation and accomplishments also gave her the title 'Minerve savante'. Her salon was among the most brilliant of the age. After writing to Hume in Britain in 1761, she entered a relationship with him of passionate friendship; she was the go-between who brought him together with Rousseau, whom she greatly admired and supported until the publication of the *Confessions* in 1770.

John Stuart, Earl of BUTE (1713–1792)
Scottish courtier and politician. Enjoying a closeness to the future George III's mother, Dowager Princess Augusta (she liked his legs), that provoked scandalized gossip, Bute became the Prince's tutor. On George's accession in 1760, Bute was, in turn, a senior courtier, secretary of state and finally first lord of the Treasury in 1762. In 1763, he negotiated the Treaty of Paris to end the Seven Years War. He became the subject of intense public hostility in England and was attacked in John Wilkes's journal, *North Briton*. He resigned in 1763 but was accused of exercising power through the King, from 'behind the curtain', against his successor, George Grenville. Grenville eventually forced the King to dismiss Bute from Court but he remained a bogeyman for Whig politicians. In private life, Bute was a notable botanist.

Étienne-François, Comte de Stainville, Duc de CHOISEUL (1719–1785)
After a brilliant career as soldier and diplomat, he became minister for foreign affairs from 1758 to 1761, then minister for the navy 1761–66, and for war 1761–70, while simultaneously taking responsibility for foreign affairs from 1766. He was seen as the most influential figure in French politics and, in effect, prime minister. He negotiated the Treaty of Paris to end the Seven Years War and avoided total humiliation for France, then concentrated on rebuilding the French navy and reforming the army. A believ-

er in limited monarchy, he was a protector of the *philosophes* and a supporter of the *Encyclopédie*. Rousseau, who regarded de Choiseul as a great statesman, dined with him in 1761 at the Luxembourgs'. De Choiseul facilitated Rousseau's return to Paris in late December 1765 and, concerned at his flouting the *parlement*'s authority, prompted his departure for London on 4 January 1766. When Rousseau returned to France in 1767, Choiseul again ensured that he remained unscathed. When he called for war against England in 1770, Court intrigues forced him into exile and he never regained power.

Louis-François de Bourbon, Prince de CONTI (1717–1776)
Distinguished soldier and Louis XV's private political adviser from 1747 until 1757. In that time he carried out secret diplomacy in Europe for the French King. He then retired to the Temple (his Paris residence as Grand Prior of the Order of Knights of Malta). He was well known as an atheist and supporter of the *philosophes*. After a quarrel with his principal mistress, Mme d'Arty, in 1751, Conti began his long relationship with Mme de Boufflers; however, he was determined not to marry her. Patron of Rousseau after meeting him in 1760. Lost to Rousseau at chess.

Hon. Henry Seymour CONWAY (1719–1795)
Soldier and leading Whig politician, nephew of Robert Walpole and cousin of Horace Walpole, who cared for him deeply. His first career and love was the army (lieutenant-general). He saw active service at Dettingen, Fontenoy and Culloden. He was also a Westminster MP from 1741. He was related by marriage to the third Duke of Richmond, whose sister, the beautiful and wayward Lady Sarah Lennox, married Sir Charles Bunbury. Conway became a political cause célèbre in 1764 when dismissed from his positions both at Court and in the army for voting against general warrants. When Rockingham took over from Grenville in July 1765, Conway was appointed to the heart of his government, becoming secretary of state for the Southern Department (leading the House of Commons, but also responsible for France, Switzerland, Italy, Spain, Portugal and the Ottoman Empire, together with Ireland, and the American colonies). He steered negotiations with the French and managed the charged issue of repealing the 1765 American Stamp Act. In May 1766, he moved to the Northern Department (responsible for relations with the Holy Roman Empire, the Netherlands, Scandinavia, Poland and Russia); when Rockingham fell, he stayed on under Pitt and Grafton. In March 1767, he invited

Hume to become his under-secretary. At this period, Conway voted against his own government on regulating the East India Company and American taxation. He resigned his office in 1768 but remained in the cabinet at the King's request until 1770. He then continued to be heavily involved in American affairs, vigorously opposing war against the colonies. He made his last Commons speech in 1784, losing his seat shortly thereafter.

John CRAUFURD (1742–1814)
Man about town, known as 'Fish'. Friend of Boswell's. In Paris in 1765, he was a favourite of Mme du Deffand's. Much to his consternation, she wrote passionate letters to him on his return to London in 1766. In London, well known as a gambler, he introduced Hume to Almack's club. In 1768, he became an MP.

Richard DAVENPORT (1705–1771)
Owner of Wootton Hall in Staffordshire, which he let to Rousseau in March 1766, as well as his family seat, Davenport, at Calvely in Cheshire and three other properties. Described by Hume as 'a very good, as well as a very rich man', he enjoyed an income of between £6,000 and £7,000 at a time when a gentleman could manage on £300 a year and a tradesman was doing well on £400. By the time he met Rousseau, he was a widower, elderly, lame in one leg and suffering from gout. He looked after two grandchildren, Phoebe and Davies, who got on well with Rousseau.

Marie de Vichy de Chamrond, Marquise du DEFFAND (1697–1780)
Briefly but famously mistress of the infant Louis XV's Regent, Phillipe Duc d'Orléans. In later life, though increasingly blind, she held a salon in Paris at the Convent des Filles de Saint Joseph in rue Saint Dominique, where she was noted for the quickness of her wit and her sprightliness, and the range of talent in attendance. On Monday nights, the cream of Enlightenment Paris came to dinner in her salon decorated in buttercup-yellow silk. Took in her illegitimate niece Julie de L'Espinasse, but ejected her when she proved more popular than her aunt, thus earning the eternal hatred of d'Alembert. Rousseau initially felt sympathy for her handicap, but turned against her, because of, among other things, 'her wild prepossessions', 'her incredible prejudices' and 'her invincible obstinacy'. She corresponded extensively with Voltaire and was smitten by Walpole, with whom she exchanged some 1,700 letters, bequeathing him her favourite black spaniel, Tonton, who was not house-trained.

Mary DEWES (1746–?)
Niece of Bernard Granville and his sister Mary Delany. She enchanted Rousseau when they met at Calwich Abbey.

Denis DIDEROT (1713–1784)
Atheist, novelist, playwright, exponent of radical theories of the stage, innovative literary and art critic, first and principal editor of the *Encyclopédie*, working on it from the prospectus in 1750 to the final plates in 1772. Of relatively humble origin – the son of a master cutler – he was educated at a Jesuit college. The burly Diderot and Rousseau met in the café Procop in Paris in 1741, beginning a friendship that endured for fifteen years.

Sir Gilbert ELLIOT of Minto (1722–1777)
Scottish politician and friend of Hume's. Elliot helped him in the composition of *Dialogues Concerning Natural Religion*. MP for Roxburgh and supporter of Bute, parliamentary orator, Lord of the Admiralty in 1756, Keeper of the Signets for Scotland in 1767, Treasurer of the navy in 1770. His sons were in Paris under Hume's supervision in 1765.

Louise-Florence-Pétronille Tardieu d'Esclavelles, dame de la Live
d'ÉPINAY (1726–1783)
Wife of a dissolute tax-farmer general, from whom she separated. Held a salon in rue St Honoré attended by such *philosophes* as d'Alembert, d'Holbach, and Grimm, who became her lover. An early supporter of Rousseau's, she lent him a property, the Hermitage, when he left Paris. There he wrote *Héloïse*. Sister-in-law of Sophie d'Houdetot's, whom Rousseau loved insanely. Mme d'Épinay parted company with Rousseau in 1757 when he refused to accompany her to Geneva to consult Dr Tronchin: he suspected a plot between her and Grimm to dishonour him.

FREDERICK THE GREAT (1712–1786)
Born in Berlin, son of Frederick William I of Prussia and Sophia Dorothea of Hanover, became King Frederick II in 1740. Practised enlightened bureaucratic despotism at home and bellicose aggression towards his neighbours. Known as the philosopher king, he immersed himself in French culture from an early age, played the flute, and was a patron of Helvétius, Voltaire and d'Alembert. He gave refuge to Rousseau.

DAVID GARRICK (1717–1779)

Actor, producer, dramatist, poet, and co-manager of Drury Lane Theatre. A monument in Lichfield Cathedral bears an epitaph by his friend Samuel Johnson: 'I am disappointed by that stroke of death that has eclipsed the gaiety of nations and impoverished the public stock of harmless pleasure.'

GEORGE III, 1738–1820

Grandson of George II, he acceded to the throne of Great Britain and Ireland in 1760, also becoming Elector, then King of Hanover. In 1761, he married a Protestant princess, Charlotte Sophia, daughter of Duke of Mecklenburg-Strelitz. Abroad, his reign saw Britain win an overseas empire in the Seven Years War, become isolated in Europe, and lose the American colonies. At home, before 1770, the lack of political skills of this hard-working monarch, who 'gloried in the name of Briton', led to a decade of governmental instability in which he could influence the formation and dissolution of seven successive administrations but not find the key to stability. From 1788, he endured bouts of madness that some have put down to the inherited condition of porphyria.

Augustus Henry Fitzroy, Duke of GRAFTON (1735–1811)

Whig politician of a moderate and conciliatory frame of mind. He was secretary of state for the Northern Department in 1765 under Rockingham (conscious of his inexperience, he said he felt like a girl who was going to be married: much pleased with the general idea but much frightened as the hour drew near), resigning in May 1766. Under Rockingham's successor, Pitt 'The Elder' (Earl of Chatham), he was first lord of the Treasury, becoming prime minister when Chatham resigned in 1768, departing in turn in January 1770. He held office in subsequent administrations. While he was quite hard working, he was also indecisive, lacking in leadership, and overly eager to avoid trouble. Walpole wrote of him that 'he thought the world should be postponed to a whore and a horse race'.

Bernard GRANVILLE (1699–1775)

Owner of Calwich Abbey, which he acquired in 1738, and so Rousseau's neighbour in Wootton. An elderly, civilized, urbane, if rather taciturn bachelor, with a love of music and gardens. He spoke good French and maintained a warm relationship with Rousseau. Elder brother of Mary Delany and uncle of Mary Dewes.

George GRENVILLE (1712–1770)
Whig MP from 1741 and brother-in-law of the elder Pitt, under whom he twice served. On Pitt's resignation in 1761, Grenville stayed on under Bute, though his opposition to the Treaty of Paris saw him shunted to the sidelines. None the less, when Bute resigned in April 1763, Grenville succeeded him and, with difficulty, forced the King to dismiss Bute from his private councils. With the attributes of a conscientious technician, he was not to George III's liking. The King complained, 'I would rather see the devil in my closet every day than Mr Grenville.' His administration saw a prolonged battle against John Wilkes, the ultimately unsuccessful defence of general warrants and the introduction of stamp duties on the American colonies in 1765. In July that year, the King finally managed to replace him with the Marquess of Rockingham.

Friedrich Melchior, Freiherr von GRIMM (1723–1807)
An impecunious German baron who became a tutor in Paris to the Duc d'Orléans and entered the inner circle of the *philosophes*. He was notorious for having fallen into a cataleptic fit over an unrequited love. His great contribution to the spread of enlightened ideas was the fortnightly cultural newsletter from Paris known as the *Correspondance littéraire* that he edited from 1753 to 1792. Circulating uncensored among the courts, the sovereigns and nobility in Germany, Scandinavia and Russia, the mix of news, gossip, comment and notes on recent publications is now regarded as invaluable cultural history of the age. He fell out with Rousseau over what he saw as the latter's ingratitude to his lover Mme d'Épinay, but prided himself on not attacking Rousseau in print. Ruined by the French Revolution, he survived only through a pension from Catherine the Great.

Claude-Adrien HELVÉTIUS (1715–1771)
Philosophe whose ambition was to reform society through education. His book *De l'esprit* (*Of the Mind*), published in 1758 and containing an attack on religious-based morality, was banned and burned in France and Switzerland, and led to a temporary suspension of the *Encyclopédie* with which he was associated. So radical was this book that such *philosophe* friends as Diderot and Rousseau rushed to join the critics.

Francis Seymour Conway, Earl of HERTFORD (1718–1794)
Brother of Henry Conway, nephew of Robert Walpole, cousin of Horace

Walpole. Appointed Britain's first ambassador to Paris after the end of the Seven Years War, he took Hume as his private secretary. He left that post on appointment in July 1765 as lord lieutenant of Ireland but then became Lord Chamberlain to and close confidant of George III.

Paul-Henri Thiry, Baron d'HOLBACH (1723–1789)
Immensely wealthy German resident of Paris who provided equally lavish hospitality and financial backing for the *philosophes* and the *Encyclopédie*. He was a participant in the French Enlightenment whose passion for atheism shook even the other *philosophes*. A specialist on applied science, he contributed over four hundred articles to the *Encyclopédie,* on subjects ranging from chemistry to the roots of religion. An admirer and close friend of Hume's, he warned Hume against Rousseau.

David HUME (1711–1776)
Scottish philosopher, essayist, historian, diplomat and saviour of Rousseau.

François-Henri d'IVERNOIS (1722–1778)
Genevan merchant and French refugee who effectively forced his friendship on Rousseau (in spite of the exile's attempt to bore him away), becoming a determined visitor at Môtiers, a walking and botanizing companion, and a regular correspondent thereafter.

Jean-Antoine d'IVERNOIS
Medical doctor and eminent naturalist who taught Rousseau botany on Isle St Pierre. Cousin (removed) of François-Henri.

Samuel JOHNSON (1709–1784)
Poet, essayist, journalist, parliamentary reporter, lexicographer, conversationalist, moralist and clubman. His character and conversation are immortalized in Boswell's *Life.*

Julie de L'ESPINASSE (1732–1776)
Illegitimate offspring of the Comtesse d'Albon and Mme du Deffand's eldest brother, Gaspard. Attracted by her quickness of mind, in 1754 Mme du Deffand took her to assist in her salon, but ejected her in 1764 when she proved too popular with the guests. D'Alembert felt passionately about her – though this was not reciprocated – and set her up in the rue Saint

Dominique; her salon then became a magnet for the younger generation of *philosophes*. She died broken-hearted for love of Comte Guibert and is immortalized in Diderot's *Le Rêve d'Alembert*.

Marie-Thérèse LE VASSEUR (1721–1801)
Rousseau's partner by whom he had five children between 1746 and 1752. A laundry and kitchen maid, she met Rousseau in 1745 at the Paris Hôtel Saint-Quentin where he was staying. They lived together until his death in 1778. Rousseau described his relationship with her as one of 'attachment' rather than love, terming her his aunt, *gouvernante* (housekeeper), and sister. Following Rousseau's death, she was seduced by a much younger man, the thirty-four-year-old valet to the Comte de Giradin, Henri Bally, whom she married in November 1779.

LOUIS XV, the 'Well-Beloved' (1710–1774)
King of France, 1715–74. Great grandson of Louis XIV, inheriting the throne at the age of five under the regency of the worldly, dissolute, but liberal Philippe, Duc d'Orléans. After Louis dispensed with chief ministers in 1744, his court became a place of factional scheming while the King occupied himself with a series of mistresses, of whom the most famous was Mme de Pompadour, and lost almost all France's overseas possessions to Britain. His ineffectual rule led to the decline of royal authority and prestige, and so strengthened the forces of revolution.

Charles-François-Frederic de Montmorency-Luxembourg, Maréchal de France, DUC DE LUXEMBOURG (1702–1764)
Distinguished soldier and protector of Rousseau at his country seat of Montmorency. Provided the coach for Rousseau to escape after the Paris *parlement* issued a warrant for his arrest following the publication of *Émile*. Rousseau thought him 'weak but trustworthy'. His wife, MADELEINE-ANGÉLIQUE (1707–1787), whom Rousseau found charming, was a great supporter of both Rousseau and Le Vasseur. From her salon, she arbitrated on correct style and behaviour – even though earlier, when married to the Duc de Boufflers, she had been notorious for her dissipated habits.

George Keith, 10th EARL MARISCHAL (1692/3–1778)
Scottish Jacobite. Friend of Hume's and a 'father' to Rousseau. Involved in Jacobite uprising of 1715. After its failure, he escaped to the Continent, but

in 1719 fought in the unsuccessful Jacobite attempt to invade with Spanish support and was severely wounded. He was outlawed and his estates were forfeited. Disenchanted with the Jacobite leadership, he wholeheartedly entered the service of Prussia. He won Frederick the Great's favour and was appointed his ambassador to Paris (1751), governor of Neuchâtel (1752), ambassador to Spain (1758). While in Spain, Marischal warned the British government of hostile Spanish plans and by degrees his punishment was rescinded, beginning with a pardon by George II in May 1759, and having the value of his estates returned in 1761 under George III. He visited Scotland but decided to end his days in Prussia. He gave Rousseau refuge in Neuchâtel, but after the attack on Hume reduced contact to a minimum. Rousseau said he was 'wise but he is human' and remained forever grateful to him. The Earl of Chatham (Pitt) visited Earl Marischal some months before the latter's death, when Marischal observed how strange it was that 'one of George III's ministers should come to receive the last breaths of an old Jacobite'. In fact, Chatham died first.

Jean-Charles-Philibert Trudaine de MONTIGNY (1733–1777)
Philosophe. Friend of Hume and translator of his *Natural History of Religion.* Scion of one of the most influential families in France, he was in charge of national finances for roads and transport.

Abbé André MORELLET (1727–1819)
An enlightened economist, conversationalist and writer. Although in holy orders, he became part of the group of atheist *philosophes* who met at d'Holbach's.

Pierre-Alexandre DU PEYROU (1729–1794)
Financier living in Neuchâtel, where he built a new quayside on the lake and gave many of Rousseau's manuscripts to the municipal library. Came from a rich French Huguenot family in Dutch Guyana. Became friendly with Rousseau through their shared joy in rambling and natural history. Suffered from gout. In 1782, he published the first complete edition of Rousseau's works. In his many letters, Rousseau addressed him as 'my dear host', and he addressed Rousseau as 'my dear citizen'.

Margaret Cavendish Bentinck, Dowager Duchess of PORTLAND (1715–1785)
Daughter of the second Earl of Oxford. She was married to the second Duke of Portland and widowed in 1762. She became an insatiable collec-

tor of natural history and fine arts (including the famous Portland vase), but her main hobby was botany, and she knew many of the renowned botanists in England. She was a devoted friend of Mary Delany's sister of Rousseau's neighbour at Wootton, Bernard Granville, and went botanizing with Rousseau.

James PULLEIN (?–1780)
Rousseau's Chiswick landlord. Rousseau described him as an 'honest grocer', though he was probably a man of substantial means.

Allan RAMSAY (1713–1784)
Edinburgh-born portrait painter. With the help of Bute, he rose to be George III's 'principal portrait painter in ordinary' in 1767. (It is recorded that he painted at least 150 pairs of coronation portraits of George III and Queen Charlotte.) He was also a political essayist and classical scholar who became a member of London intellectual society. An Edinburgh friend of Hume's, with whom he (and Adam Smith) founded a debating club, the Select Society, in 1754. That same year, he painted Hume in Edinburgh and in 1766 painted both Hume and Rousseau in London at his studio at 67 Harley Street. An accident to his right arm in 1773 terminated his career.

Charles Wentworth, Marquess of ROCKINGHAM (1730–1782)
Wealthy and powerful Whig politician who became prime minister in July 1765 at the age of thirty-five, although lacking in any previous ministerial experience, principally as a consequence of the King's desperation to rid himself of Grenville. Contemporary comment went that his was 'a ministry composed of the extravagances of youth and the infirmities of age'. His passion for horse-racing also led to the sneer about the men 'called from the stud to the state'. To the surprise of Whig grandees (including himself no doubt), his administration lasted a year and saw the repeal of the Stamp Act, though accompanied by an assertion of the Crown's right to tax the colonies. He was dismissed in July 1766 in favour of Pitt. The defeat in the American war and the fall of Lord North saw him return to office briefly. Historians credit him with beginning the move from faction to party and with defining the Whig party in opposition to the Crown. He brought Conway and Grafton into his administration. He also launched Edmund Burke's career (hiring him as private secretary).

Jean-Jacques ROUSSEAU (1712–1778)
Genevan-born music copyist, composer, novelist, educationalist, essayist, political theorist and controversialist, and precursor of the Romantics.

Adam SMITH (1723–1790)
Moral philosopher and economist. Hume's close friend and one of the brightest stars of the Scottish Enlightenment. When he was received by the Cabinet of Pitt 'The Elder', they rose to their feet: 'We all stand, Mr Smith, because we are all your pupils,' said Pitt. Elected to the Chair of Logic at Glasgow in 1751 and to the Chair of Moral Philosophy the following year. In 1759, he published the *Theory of Moral Sentiments*. In 1763, he was made tutor to the sons of the Duke of Buccleuch and went on the Grand Tour, visiting Voltaire in Ferney and staying in Paris. He returned to Scotland in 1766. In 1776, he published the founding text of modern economics, *The Wealth of Nations*, in which he shattered the dominant mercantilism in favour of free trade.

Tobias George SMOLLETT (1721–1771)
Scottish author of rambling novels and jocund reporter of contemporary scene. Historian, and translator of *Don Quixote*. Had little sensibility for *sensibilité*.

Jean-Báptiste-Antoine SUARD (1734–1817)
Journalist and editor of the *Gazette de France* and *Gazette littéraire de France*. Translator of Hume's account of the falling out with Rousseau.

TRONCHIN family
Among the leading citizens of Geneva, its members included DR THÉODORE TRONCHIN, a physician famous across Europe, seen as the model of the wise and humane doctor, and consulted by nobility and sovereigns. He recommended fresh air and 'a spare diet' but is best known for promoting vaccination against smallpox. He achieved fame by vaccinating the Duc d'Orléans's children; in 1765, the duc invited him to take up residence in France, which he did in 1766. He also wrote a well-known book on the 'dry bellyache'. FRANÇOIS TRONCHIN was on Geneva's governing *Petit Conseil* and was a proponent of action against Rousseau. JEAN-ROBERT TRONCHIN was Geneva's Prosecutor General and author of the attack on Rousseau, *Letters from the Countryside*, in 1763. Théodore's

son, LOUIS-FRANÇOIS, a pupil of Adam Smith's at Glasgow University, was staying in Hume's London lodgings when Rousseau arrived. Rousseau believed he was there to spy on him. The Tronchins were close to Voltaire. Théodore was his doctor. (Théodore also attended Rousseau until they quarrelled in 1757.)

Anne-Robert-Jacques TURGOT, Baron de l'Aulne (1727–1781)
Economist, reformer and statesman. Contributor to the *Encyclopédie* and advocate for policies of internal free trade and laissez-faire, in part as a means of undermining privilege and feudal interests. Regional administrator for Limoges 1761, minister of marine 1774 and controller of finances 1774–76, when his zeal for modernization of the state led to his downfall. His contemporary reputation was for sagacity, penetrating intelligence and profundity. Voltaire said of him, 'I have scarcely ever seen a man more lovable and better informed.' Translated Hume's discourse *Of the Balance of Trade*.

Marie-Madeleine de Brémond d'Ars, Marquise de VERDELIN (1728–1810)
Daughter of impoverished nobleman and close friend of Sophie d'Houdetot's, with whom Rousseau was infatuated. After an uneasy start in 1759, became a sympathetic friend to Rousseau and played a major role in his move to London. Later, they fell out. Rousseau accused her of being a gossip.

VOLTAIRE [François-Marie Arouet] (1694–1778)
Playwright, philosopher, moralist, historian, wit, successful businessman, prolific correspondent, campaigner against superstition and intolerance epitomized in his famous motto, *écrasez l'infame* ('crush the infamous thing'). He was twice imprisoned in the Bastille and spent time in exile in England. In 1764, he anonymously published *Le Sentiment des citoyens*, exposing hurtful secrets about Rousseau whom he met only once, in a salon in 1751.

Horace WALPOLE (1717–1797)
Youngest son of Sir Robert Walpole and cousin of Hertford and Conway. Man of letters, collector, diarist, gardener, originator of the Gothic novel and creator of the Gothic mansion at Strawberry Hill, MP (he spoke only once in the Commons), political mover, wit. His letters, memoirs and journal provide an invaluable guide to eighteenth-century society and politics.

WARENS, Louise-Éléonore de la Tour du Pil, Baronne de (1699–1762)
Swiss baroness, chemist and dedicated proselytizer for Catholicism. On
Rousseau's leaving Geneva, she became his mother-figure and lover. He
admired her remarkable complexion. She died in great poverty.

and . . . in Paris, other *philosophes,* rich patrons, nobles, gentlemen of the
court, confidential servants, men in black, outraged *parlement*arians and
archbishops; in England, postboys, editors, reviewers, anonymous letter-
writers, ministers, MPs, clubmen, bishops and actresses; in Scotland, other
stars of the Scottish Enlightenment, writers, clerics, publishers, hostesses and
landladies; and in Switzerland, radical watchmakers, Genevan oligarchs,
affronted pastors and stone-throwing villagers.

Selected Bibliography

The following is a selected bibliography. Pride of place must be given to three masterpieces of scholarship and erudition, the *sine qua non* of research for any book that covers our subject: Maurice Cranston's epic three-volume biography of Rousseau, Ernest Campbell Mossner's comprehensive biography of Hume, and Ralph Leigh's Olympian edition of Rousseau's complete letters. Unfortunately, just as Rousseau died without having described his English sojourn in the *Confessions*, so Professor Cranston's untimely death occurred before he had completed his chapter covering Rousseau in England.

As well as the works listed below, we have also drawn on documentation from the Chiswick Library, the William Salt Library, the Lincoln Archives, the Royal Library at Windsor, the newspaper archive of eighteenth-century newspapers at the British Library, and the collection of eighteenth-century journals in the London Library.

Ackroyd, P., *London: The Biography*, Chatto & Windus, London, 2000

Acton, Lord, *Essays on Church and State*, Hollis and Carter, London, 1952

Adam Smith, J., *Life Among The Scots*, Collins. London, 1946

Anthorne, R. and S. Williams, *From the Republic of Letters to the Empire of E-mail*, Philosophical Pathways no. 56, Philosophos.com 2004

Baillie, J., *Hume On Morality*, Routledge, London, 2000

Beaudry, C., *The Role of the Reader in Rousseau's Confessions*, Peter Lang, New York, 1991

Berlin, I., *The Age of the Enlightenment*, New American Library, New York, 1956

Birn, R., *Forging Rousseau,* Voltaire Foundation, Oxford, 2001

Black, J., *The English Press in the Eighteenth Century*, Croom Helm, London, 1987

– *Eighteenth Century Britain*, Palgrave, Basingstoke, 2001

Blom, P., *Encyclopédie: The Triumph of Reason in an Unreasonable Age*, Fourth Estate, London, 2004

Boswell, J., *The Journals of James Boswell 1762–95*, Mandarin, London, 1992

– *The General Correspondence of James Boswell 1766–9*, Edinburgh University Press, 1993

– *Letters of James Boswell*, ed. C.B. Tinker, Oxford, 1924

Boyd, W., *The Educational Theory of Jean Jacques Rousseau*, Longmans and Co., London, 1911

Boyd, W., *The New Confessions*, Penguin, London, 1988

Brady, F., and F. Pottle (eds.), *Boswell on the Grand Tour: Italy, Corsica, France 1765–1766* William Heinemann, London, 1955

Braudel, F., *Capitalism and Material Life*, Weidenfeld and Nicolson, London, 1973

– *The Structures of Everyday Life: The Limits of the Possible*, University of California Press, Berkeley, 1992

Braudy, L., *Narrative Form in History and Fiction*, Princeton University Press, Princeton, 1970

Brewer, J., *Party Ideology and Popular Politics at the Accession of George III*, Cambridge University Press, Cambridge, 1976

– *The Sinews of Power*, Unwin Hyman, London, 1989

Brooke, J., *The Chatham Administration 1766–68*, Macmillan, London, 1956

Broome, J., *Jean-Jacques Rousseau in Staffordshire 1766–7*, Keele University Library, Keele, 1966

Buchan, J., *Capital of the Mind*, John Murray, London, 2003

Burton, J., *Life and Correspondence of David Hume*, William Tait, Edinburgh, 1866

Campbell, R., and A. Skinner, *Adam Smith*, Croom Helm, London, 1982

Capaldi, N., *Hume's Place in Moral Philosophy*, Peter Lang, New York, 1989

Cassirer, E., *The Question of Jean-Jacques Rousseau*, trans. P. Gay, Columbia University Press, New York, 1954

Charpentier, J., *Rousseau: The Child of Nature*, Methuen, London, 1931

Churton Collins, J., *Voltaire, Montesquieu and Rousseau in England*, Eveleigh Nash, London, 1908

Cobb, R., *Paris and Elsewhere*, John Murray, London, 1998

Cohen, P., *Freedom's Moment*, University of Chicago Press, Chicago, 1997

Colley, L., *Britons: Forging The Nation 1707–1837*, Yale University Press, New Haven, 1992

Cooper, D., *Tallyrand*, Jonathan Cape, London, 1932

Cranston, M., *Jean Jacques*, Penguin, London, 1983

– *The Noble Savage*, Penguin, London, 1991

– *The Solitary Self*, University of Chicago Press, Chicago, 1997

Craveri, B., *Madame du Deffand and her World*, trans. Teresa Waugh, Peter Halban, London, 2002

Damrosch, L., *Fictions of Reality in the Age of Hume and Johnson*, University of Wisconsin Press, Madison, 1989

Darnton, R., *George Washington's False Teeth*, W. W. Norton, New York, 2003

Davis, N., *Europe: A History*, Oxford University Press, Oxford, 1996

De Beer, G., *JJ Rousseau and his world*, Thames and Hudson, London, 1972

Delaney, M., ed. A. Day, *Letters from Georgian Ireland*, The Friar's Bush Press, Belfast, 1991

Dent, N., *A Rousseau Dictionary*, Blackwell, Oxford, 1992

Ditchfield, G., *George III: An Essay in Monarchy*, Palgrave, Basingstoke, 2002

Dobinson, C., *Jean-Jacques Rousseau: His Thought and Its Relevance Today*, Methuen, London, 1969

Dod's Parliamentary Companion, *The Prime Ministers from Walpole to Macmillan*, London, 1994

Dodd, W., *The Truth of the Christian Religion*, J. Newbery, London, 1765

Douthwaite, J., *The Wild Girl, Natural Man and the Monster*, University of Chicago Press, Chicago, 2002

Duffy, E., *Rousseau in England*, University of California Press, Berkeley, 1979

Dufour, A., *Histoire de Genève*, Presses Universitaires de France, Paris, 1997

D'Épinay, L., *Histoire de madame de Montbrillant*, Gallimard, Paris, 1951

– *Memoirs and Correspondance of Madame D'Épinay*, trans. E. Allingham, Routledge, London, 1930

– *Mémoires et correspondance de Mme d'Épinay*, chez Volland le jeune, Paris, 1818

– *Anecdotes inédites Aux Mémoires de Mme. d'Épinay*, Baudoin Frères, Paris, 1818

Encyclopædia Britannica, Britannica CD Multimedia edition, 2000

Fieser, J., *Early Responses to Hume's History of England*, Thoemmes Continuum, Bristol, 2002

Finlayson, I., *The Moth And The Candle: A Life of James Boswell*, Constable, London, 1984

Fogelin, R., *A Defense of Hume on Miracles*, Princeton University Press, Princeton, 2003

Fortescue, M., *The History of Calwich Abbey*, Warren & Son, 1915

France, P., *Rousseau: Confessions*, Cambridge University Press, Cambridge, 1987

Galiani, F., *Lettres de l'Abbé Galiani à Mme. d'Épinay*, G. Charpentier, Paris, 1881

Gardiner, J., and N. Wenborn, *The History Today Companion to British History*, Collins & Brown, London, 1985

Garrick, D., ed. H. Pedicord and F. Bergman, *The Plays of David Garrick, Volume 1*, Southern Illinois University Press, Carbondale and Edwardsville, 1980

Gerrard, C., *Aaron Hill: The Muses' Projector*, Oxford University Press, Oxford, 2003

Gilmour, I., *Riot, Risings and Revolution*, Hutchinson, London, 1992

Goldsmith, O., *Collected Works*, ed. A. Friedman, Clarendon Press, Oxford, 1966

Gooch, E., *A History of Spalding*, Spalding Free Press, Spalding, 1940

Green, F., *Jean-Jacques Rousseau: A Critical Study of his Life and Writings*, Cambridge University Press, Cambridge, 1955

Greig, J., *David Hume*, Jonathan Cape, London, 1931

Grimm, F., *Correspondance littéraire de Grimm et Diderot*, vol. 5, Chez Furne Libraire, Paris, 1829

Grimsley, R., *The Philosophy of Rousseau*, Oxford University Press, Oxford, 1973

Grosley, P., *A Tour to London or New Observations on England*, trans. Thomas Nugent, Lockyer Davis, London 1772

Hasenson, A., *History of Dover Harbour*, Aurum Special Editions, London, 1980

Hayden, R., *Mrs Delany: her life and her flowers*, British Museum Press, London, 1980

Hoffman, J., *The Marquis: A Study of Lord Rockingham 1730–1782*, Fordham University Press, New York, 1973

Howitt, W., *Visits to Remarkable Places*, Longman, London, 1840

Huizinga, J., *The Making of a Saint*, Hamish Hamilton, London, 1976

Hulliung, M., *The Autocritique of Enlightenment*, Harvard University Press, Cambridge, 1994

Hume, D., *An Enquiry Concerning Human Understanding*, Clarendon Press, Oxford, 1979

– *A Treatise Of Human Nature*, Oxford University Press, Oxford, 1978

– *The History of England*, 1778 edn., Liberty Fund, Indianapolis, 1983

– *Political Essays*, ed. K. Haakonssen, Cambridge University Press, Cambridge, 1994

– *The Letters of David Hume*, ed. J. Greig, vol. 2. Oxford University Press, Oxford, 1932

– *New Letters of David Hume*, ed. R. Klibansky and E. Mossner, Garland, New York, 1983

– *Private Correspondence of David Hume with Several Distinguished Persons Between the Years 1761 and 1776*, Henry Colburn and Co., London, 1820

– *Letters of David Hume to William Strahan*, ed. G. Birkbeck Hill, Oxford, 1888

– *Letters of Eminent Persons addressed to David Hume*, ed. J. Burton, Blackwood, Edinburgh, 1849

– *A Concise and Genuine Account of the Dispute between Mr. Hume and Mr. Rousseau; with the Letters that passed between them during their Controversy. As also the Letters of the Hon. Mr. Walpole and Mr. D'Alembert, relative to this extraordinary affair. Translated from the French*. London. Printed for T. Becket and P.A. De Hondt, near Surry-street in the Strand. MDCCLXVI

Ignatieff, M., *The Needs of Strangers*, Hogarth, London, 1984

Ilchester, Countess, and Stavordale, Lord, eds. *Life and Letters of Lady Sarah Lennox*, John Murray, London, 1901

Inwood, S., *A History of London*, Macmillan, Basingstoke, 1998

Jollimore, T., *Friendship and Agent-Relative Morality*, Garland, New York, 2001

Josephson, M, *Jean-Jacques Rousseau*, Gollancz, London, 1932

Jullian, A. (ed.), *Histoire de Genève des originse à 1798*, Société D'Histoire de Genève, Geneva, 1951

Kelly, C., *Rousseau as Author*, University of Chicago Press, Chicago, 2003

Kolin, A., *The Ethical Foundations of Hume's Theory of Politics*, Peter Lang, New York, 1991

De Koven, A., *Horace Walpole and Mme. du Deffand*, Appleton, New York, 1929

La Fontaine, *Fables*, trans. W. Thornbury, Bibliophile Books, London, 1988

Langford, P., *The First Rockingham Administration,* Oxford University Press, London, 1973

Lee, V., *The Reign of Women: in Eighteenth-Century France*, Schenkman, Cambridge, Mass, 1976

Leigh, J., *The Search for Enlightenment*, Duckworth, London, 1999

Leigh, R. (ed.), *Correspondance complète de Jean-Jacques Rousseau*, The Voltaire Foundation at the Taylor Institute, Oxford, 1978

Lemos, R., *Rousseau's Political Philosophy,* University of Georgia Press, Athens, 1977

Lewis, M., *The Monk*, Oxford University Press, Oxford, 1973

Lewis, W., *Horace Walpole*, Hart Davis, London, 1961

Lucas, F., *The Art of Living – Four Eighteenth Century Minds*, Cassel, London, 1959

Lyons, J., *The Invention of the Self*, Southern Illinois University Press, Carbondale and Edwardsville, 1978

Macaulay, T., *Critical and Historical Essays*, arr. A. Grieve, J. M. Dent, London, 1951

MacDonogh, K., *Reigning Cats and Dogs,* Fourth Estate, London, 1999

Martin, P., *A Life of James Boswell*, Weidenfeld and Nicolson, London, 1999

McDonald, J., *Rousseau and the French Revolution: 1762–1791*, Athlone Press, London, 1965

McKendrick, N., J. Brewer and J. Plumb, *The Birth of a Consumer Society*, Hutchinson, London, 1983

Martin, P. (ed.), *The Essential Boswell*, Weidenfeld and Nicolson, London, 2003

Mason, A., *The Women of the French Salons*, Century, New York, 1891

Maugras, G., *La Marquise de Boufflers*, Librarie Plon, Paris, 1907

Meyer, P., 'Voltaire and Hume's Descent On The Coast of Brittany', *Modern Language Notes*, vol. LXVI, ed. H Carrington Lancester et al. Johns Hopkins Press, Baltimore, November 1951

Miller, D., *Philosophy and Ideology in Hume's Political Thought*, Clarendon Press, Oxford, 1981

Morley, J., *Rousseau*, Chapman and Hall, London, 1878

Mossner, E., *The Life Of David Hume*, Clarendon Press, Oxford, 1980

Mukherjee, S. and S. Ramaswamy (ed.), *David Hume*, Deep & Deep, Delhi, 2000

– *Jean Jacques Rousseau*, Deep & Deep, Delhi, 1995

Mullen, J., and C. Reid, *Eighteenth Century Popular Culture*, Oxford University Press, Oxford, 2000

Nicoll, A., *The Garrick Stage*, Manchester University Press, Manchester, 1980

Nicolson, H., *The Age of Reason*, Constable, London, 1960

Norton, D., *David Hume*, Princeton University Press, Princeton, 1982

Norton, D. (ed.) *The Cambridge Companion to Hume*, Cambridge University Press, Cambridge, 1993

O'Brian, K., *Narratives of Enlightenment – Cosmopolitan History from Voltaire to Gibbon*, Cambridge University Press, Cambridge, 1997

O'Brien, C., *Edmund Burke*, New Island Books, Dublin 1997

O'Hagan, T., *Rousseau*, Routledge, London, 1999

O'Hagan, T. (ed.), *Jean-Jacques Rousseau and the Sources of the Self*, Averbury, 1997

D'Orléans, Duchesse de, et al., *Secret Memoirs of the French Court*, Grolier Society, London (n.d.)

Oxford Dictionary of National Biography, on-line edn. Oxford University Press, Oxford, 2004

Orwin, C., and N. Tarcov (ed.), *The Legacy of Rousseau*, University of Chicago Press, Chicago, 1997

Pares, R., *King George III and the Politicians*, Clarendon Press, Oxford, 1964

Pearson, H., *Johnson and Boswell*, Heinemann, London, 1958

Penelhum, T., *Hume*, Macmillan, London, 1975

Phillipson, N., *Hume*, Weidenfeld and Nicolson, London, 1989

Picard, R., *Les Salons Littéraires et la Societé Françaises 1610–1789*, Brentano's, New York, 1943

Pottle, F., 'The Part Played By Horace Walpole And James Boswell In The Quarrel Between Rousseau and Hume', *Philological Quarterly*, vol. 4, University of Iowa, Iowa City, Iowa, 1925

Porter, R., *English Society in the 18th Century*, Penguin, London, 1991

– *Enlightenment: Britain and the creation of the modern world*, Penguin, London, 2000

– *Flesh in the Age of Reason*, Penguin Allan Lane, London, 2003

– *London: A Social History*, Hamish Hamilton, London, 1994

Reill, P., and E. Wilson, *Encyclopaedia of the Enlightenment*, Facts on
    File, New York, 1996

Riley, P. (ed.), *The Cambridge Companion to Rousseau*, Cambridge
    University Press, Cambridge, 2001

Ritchie, T., *An Account of the Life and Writings of David Hume*, Cadell
    and Davies, London, 1807

Roney, J., and M. Klauber (eds.), *The Identity of Geneva*, Greenwood
    Press, Connecticut, 1998

Rousseau, J-J., *Of the Social Contract*, Harper & Row, New York, 1984

– *Emile*, Everyman, New York, 1993

– *Eloisa*, Woodstock Books, Oxford, 1989

– *Confessions*, Wordsworth Editions Limited, Ware, 1996

– *Les Confessions*, Librarie des Bibliophiles/Flammarion, Paris, (n.d.)

– *Reveries of the Solitary Walker*, Penguin, Harmondsworth, 1979

– *Essay on the Origin of Languages and Writings Related to Music*, trans.
    and ed. J. Scott, University Press of New England, Hanover, 1998

– *Discourse on Inequality*, Oxford University Press, 1994

– *Citizen of Geneva: Selections from the Letters of Jean-Jacques
    Rousseau*, ed. C, Hendel, Oxford University Press, Oxford, 1937

– *Rousseau on International Relations*, ed. S. Hoffmann and D. Fidler,
    Clarendon Press, Oxford, 1991

– *The Confessions: and Correspondence*, ed. C. Kelly, R. Masters and
    R. Stillman, University Press of New England, Hanover, 1995

Sainte-Beuve, C., *Quelques Portraits Féminins*, Éditions Jules Tallandier,
    Paris, 1927

De Saussure, C., *A Foreign View of England in 1725–29*, Caliban Books,
    London, 1995

Schama, S., *Citizens, Chronicle of the French Revolution*, Penguin,
    London, 1989

Schlereth, T., *The Cosmopolitan Ideal in Enlightenment Thought*, University
    of Notre Dame, Notre Dame, 1977

Sennett, R., *The Fall of Public Man*, Faber and Faber, London, 1986

Sheppard, F., *London: A History*, Oxford University Press, Oxford, 1998

Sisman, A., *Boswell's Presumptuous Task*, Hamish Hamilton, London,
    2000

Sloan, K. (ed.), *Enlightenment – Discovering The World in the Eighteenth
    Century*, British Museum Press, London, 2003

Smith, W. (ed.), *The Grenville Papers*, John Murray, London, 1852

Smollett, T., *Humphrey Clinker*, Penguin, London, 1985

Sterne, L., *A Sentimental Journey Through France and Italy*, Chapman and Hall, London, (n.d.)

Storr, A., *Churchill's Black Dog*, Flamingo, London, 1991

Strachey, L., *Landmarks in French Literature*, Williams and Norgate, London, 1920

– *Books and Characters*, Chatto and Windus, London, 1922

Todorov, T., *Frail Happiness*, trans. J. Scott and R. Zaretsky, Pennsylvania State University Press, University Park, Pennsylvania, 2001

Streckeisen-Mouton, M., *J. J. Rousseau: ses amis et ses ennemis*, Calmann-Levy, Paris, 1864

Tarnas, R., *The Passion of the Western Mind*, Pimlico, London, 1991

Thomas, G., Earl of Albermarle, *Memoirs of the Marquess of Rockingham*, Richard Bentley, London, 1852

Tillyard, S., *Aristocrats*, Chatto and Windus, London, 1994

Timbs, J., *Clubs and Club Life in London from the Seventeenth Century*, Chatto and Windus, London, 1886

Tomlinson, J. (ed.), *Additional Grenville Papers 1763–65*, Manchester University Press, Manchester, 1962

Toynbee, P., 'Mme. du Deffand and Hume', *Modern Language Review*, vol. 24, Cambridge University Press, Cambridge, 1924

Trouille, M., *Sexual Politics in the Enlightenment*, State University of New York Press, Albany,1997

Uglow, J., *Hogarth*, Faber and Faber, London, 1997

– *The Lunar Men,* Faber and Faber, London, 2002

Velkley, R., *Being after Rousseau*, University of Chicago Press, Chicago, 2002

Wain, J., *Samuel Johnson: A Biography*, Viking Press, New York, 1974

Walpole, H., *The Letters of Horace Walpole Fourth Earl of Orford*, ed. P. Cunningham, John Grant, Edinburgh, 1906

– *Memoirs of the Reign of King George III*, vol. 3, ed. Derek Jarrett, Yale University Press, New Haven, 2000

– *A narrative of what passed relative to the quarrel of Mr. David Hume and Jean Jacques Rousseau, as far as Mr. Horace Walpole was concerned in it. Works*, vol. 4, London, 1798

– *Horace Walpole's Correspondence with Madame du Deffand and Wiart*, ed. W. Lewis and W. Smith, Oxford University Press, London, 1939

– *Memoirs of Horace Walpole*, ed. E. Warburton, Henry Colburn, 13 Great Marlborough Street, London, 1851

Warburton, N., 'Art and Allusion', *The Philosophers' Magazine*, London 2002

Webster, N., *The Chevalier de Boufflers*, John Murray, London, 1916

Wexler, V., *David Hume and the History of England*, American Philosophical Society, Philadelphia, 1979

Wills, G., *Explaining America*, Athlone Press, London, 1981

Wind, E., *Hume and the Heroic Portrait*, Clarendon Press, Oxford, 1986

Wokler, R., *Rousseau*, Oxford University Press, Oxford, 1995

Woods, L., *Garrick Claims the Stage*, Greenwood Press, Connecticut, 1984

Wright, N., *Spalding, an Industrial History*, Society for Lincolnshire History and Archaeology, Lincoln, 1975

Yolton, J., P. Rogers, R. Porter and B. Stafford (eds.), *The Blackwell Companion to the Enlightenment*, Blackwell, Oxford, 1991

Zonneveld, J., *Sir Brooke Boothby – Rousseau's Roving Baronet Friend*, Uitgeverzij, De Nieuwe Haagsche Voorbung, Den Haag, 2004

Chronology of Main Events

1711, David Hume born in Edinburgh on 26 April 1711.*
1712, Jean-Jacques Rousseau born in Geneva on 28 June.
1758, Rousseau writes *Letter to d'Alembert on the Theatre*, bringing worsening relations with d'Alembert, Voltaire and Diderot. He becomes convinced of a plot against him involving Mme d'Épinay, Grimm and d'Alembert, leading to a severance of relations with them. He moves to Montmorency under the wing of the Duc and Duchesse de Luxembourg and lives at Mont-Louis. He meets Mme de Boufflers.
1759, Rousseau's initial antipathy for Mme de Verdelin warms into fondness.
1760, George III ascends British throne.
1761, Rousseau settles into Montmorency. Mme de Boufflers initiates contact with Hume.
1761–62, Rousseau publishes *La Nouvelle Héloïse*, *On the Social Contract*, and *Émile*. The last part of *Émile*, 'The Profession of Faith of the Savoyard Vicar', brings widespread condemnation from the religious establishment in France and Switzerland.

1762

MAY, In Britain John Stuart, Earl of Bute becomes first lord of the Treasury.
9 JUNE, Warned that the Paris *parlement* has issued a warrant for his arrest, Rousseau goes into exile in Switzerland.
MID-JUNE, Mme de Boufflers informs Hume of Rousseau's plight and that she has advised him to go to England. Hume responds with offer of his house in Edinburgh and first mention of a possible pension for

* 'Old style' – i.e. before 1752 when Britain changed from the Julian to the Gregorian calendar.

Rousseau from George III.

The Geneva ruling council resolves to burn *Émile* and *On the Social Contract* and to arrest Rousseau if he returns to the city. Berne follows suit.

10 JULY, Rousseau moves into Môtiers under the wing of Earl Marischal and Frederick the Great.

JULY, Rousseau resigns his citizenship of Geneva over its refusal to allow his *Letter to Beaumont* (Archbishop of Paris, Christophe de Beaumont) to be published.

1763

10 FEBRUARY, Treaty of Paris concludes the Seven Years War.

APRIL, The earl of Hertford invited to become ambassador to France, and asks Hume to accompany him to act as his secretary.

6 APRIL, Bute resigns as first lord of the Treasury, succeeded by George Grenville.

17 APRIL, Mme de Boufflers travels to England but fails to meet Hume.

AUGUST, Grenville consolidates power. Bute dismissed from Court.

AUTUMN, In Geneva, Prosecutor General Jean-Robert Tronchin publishes anonymously *Letters from the Country*, undermining the opposition *Représentants* (the Party of Liberty).

18 OCTOBER, Hume arrives in Paris as assistant secretary to Lord Hertford.

1764

4 APRIL, Hertford's brother General Conway dismissed from Court and regiment following his vote against general warrants.

3 DECEMBER, Rousseau publishes *Letters Written from the Mountain* in support of the Party of Liberty in Geneva; copies circulated in Geneva throw oligarchy into disarray but ironically the upheaval causes the Party of Liberty to make peace overtures to the oligarchy.

Boswell arrives in Môtiers to meet Rousseau.

DECEMBER, *Views of the Citizens on Letters Written from the Mountain* published anonymously, with scurrilous comments on Rousseau. Voltaire is accepted as having been the author.

1765

FEBRUARY, Grenville introduces Stamp Act for duties on North American Colonies.

MARCH, Alexis-Claude Clairaut informs Hume of Rousseau's misery. Hume responds with a plan to increase Rousseau's income surreptitiously.

3 JUNE, Hume learns of his confirmation as embassy secretary.

10 JULY, Grenville dismissed as prime minister.

13 JULY, The Marquess of Rockingham takes over. In the subsequent reshuffle, Conway becomes secretary of state for the Southern Department and leading Minister in the House of Commons. Hertford is offered lord lieutenant of Ireland, with the Duke of Richmond to succeed him in Paris.

SEPTEMBER, Horace Walpole in Paris for start of six-month visit.

6 SEPTEMBER, Lapidation of Rousseau's house in Môtiers forces him to move on again, to Isle St Pierre.

22 OCTOBER, Hume writes to Rousseau at Isle St Pierre with offer of help to flee to Britain.

29 OCTOBER, Having left Isle St Pierre, and stayed briefly in Bienne, Rousseau goes to Strasbourg, but he is still undecided where to seek refuge.

2 NOVEMBER, Arriving in Strasbourg, Rousseau puts up at La Fleur inn. Here he receives Hume's letter.

9 NOVEMBER, Duke of Richmond arrives in Paris to take up ambassadorship. Hume's post as secretary is effectively terminated.

4 DECEMBER, Rousseau writes to Hume, 'the most illustrious of my contemporaries'. He will put himself under Hume's protection.

9 DECEMBER, Rousseau leaves Strasbourg for Paris.

2 DECEMBER, Walpole dines with Hume, Ossory and Craufurd. At this jovial gathering, the quip is uttered that if Rousseau sought new misfortunes, Frederick the Great could supply all his needs.

16 DECEMBER, Rousseau arrives in Paris, parading next day in the Luxembourg Gardens. He stays first with the widow Duchesne, then in the Temple.

27 DECEMBER, Walpole's King of Prussia spoof letter satirizing Rousseau becomes public knowledge.

1766

3 JANUARY, Making his farewells, Hume is warned by Baron d'Holbach
that he is clasping a viper to his bosom.

4 JANUARY, Hume, Rousseau, Jean-Jacques de Luze and Sultan leave
Paris for London.

4/5 JANUARY, Rousseau hears Hume mutter in his sleep, 'I hold Jean-
Jacques Rousseau.'

10/11 JANUARY, Crossing the Channel from Calais, Hume raises the
possibility of a pension from George III.

13 JANUARY, Rousseau, Hume and Sultan enter London.

18 JANUARY, Hume tells Rousseau that the King of Prussia spoof letter is
in circulation.

23 JANUARY, Rousseau and Hume see Garrick in Drury Lane royal
performance.

28–30 JANUARY, The *St. James's Chronicle* carries a brief report from
Paris of the King of Prussia letter.

31 JANUARY, Rousseau leaves London to lodge with the grocer Pullein in
Chiswick.
Boswell and Le Vasseur set out together from Paris. They begin an
affair on the second night.
(In this period) Rockingham administration in parliamentary battle to
repeal Grenville's Stamp Act.

13 FEBRUARY, Boswell escorts Le Vasseur to Chiswick, where she is
reunited with Rousseau.

1 MARCH, Rousseau sits for portraitist Allan Ramsay at 67 Harley Street.
He meets Richard Davenport, his future landlord at Wootton in
Staffordshire. Sultan runs away, but later reappears.

18 MARCH, Rousseau and Le Vasseur stay overnight with Hume in Lisle
Street before leaving for Wootton in the 'retour chaise'. Rousseau's
version of what occurred between him and Hume becomes central to
his accusations against Hume.

22 MARCH, Rousseau arrives in Wootton. He writes to Hume, designing
the letter to put Hume to the test: is Hume a traitor or not?

3 APRIL, The King of Prussia spoof letter appears in the *St. James's
Chronicle*.

7 APRIL, Rousseau writes to the *St. James's Chronicle* in protest at the
King of Prussia letter. Rousseau's letter appears in the 8–10 April
edition.

9 APRIL, Rousseau writes to Mme de Verdelin with first detailed account of Hume's plot against him.

MID-APRIL, The *London Chronicle* and the *Lloyd's Evening Register* carry a letter (thought to be by Voltaire) to a Doctor Jean-Jacques Pansophe, mocking Rousseau.

17–19 APRIL, In a sequence sparked off by the King of Prussia letter and Rousseau's protest, the *St. James's Chronicle* carries letter from a Quaker 'Z.A.' mocking Rousseau.

2 MAY, Conway notifies Hume that the King has offered a pension of £100 p.a. to Rousseau on condition it is secret.

3–6 MAY, The *St. James's Chronicle* carries letter from 'X' defending Rousseau and criticizing author/s of April letters.

12 MAY, Rousseau writes to Conway explaining that he is too upset to decide on the pension and asking for its delay.

14 MAY, Conway becomes secretary of state for Northern Department.

17 MAY, Hume writes to Rousseau assuming that the pension's secrecy is the problem and hoping he will change his mind on that score. He adds that Walpole is sorry for the spoof letter.

5–7 JUNE, The *St. James's Chronicle* carries letter signed 'V.T.h.S.W.' attacking Rousseau and apparently demonstrating personal knowledge of his time in London.

19 JUNE, Hume writes to Rousseau: if he promises to accept the pension, Conway will ask the King to make it public.

21 JUNE, Hume sends Rousseau a formal note requesting an answer to his offer of 19 June and explaining that as he is returning to Scotland he will be unable to help more.

23 JUNE, Rousseau sends Hume 'the last letter you will receive from me'. He accuses Hume of bringing him to England in order to dishonour him.

26 JUNE, Hume replies to Rousseau demanding particulars of the accusations against him and the name of the 'calumniator' who had made them.

27 JUNE and 1 JULY, Hume writes letters to d'Holbach condemning Rousseau in language of extraordinary violence. Hume also sets about retrieving from Blair and Davenport his earlier letters praising Rousseau.

8 JULY, Hume tells Davenport that Rousseau had plotted the pension refusal so as to cancel all his obligations to Hume.

10 JULY, Rousseau sends Hume a detailed indictment. In it, he describes

how he mocked Hume, giving him three (metaphorical) 'slaps' that Hume did not feel.

22 JULY, Hume sends Rousseau his reply to the indictment. He goes on to annotate Rousseau's indictment in preparation for possible publication. He identifies twelve 'lyes'.

At around this time, Hume's friends in Paris discuss how he should react to Rousseau's charges by publishing his defence.

30 JULY, Rockingham's administration dismissed. The King asks Pitt (Earl of Chatham) to form new government. Conway continues as secretary of state.

2 AUGUST, In a letter to his Paris publisher, Pierre Guy, Rousseau appears to be challenging Hume to publish. News of letter leaks out.

EARLY AUGUST, Hume sends all papers from the Rousseau affair to d'Alembert. Having read Rousseau's long indictment, d'Alembert and other friends tell Hume that his publishing a defence is unnecessary.

LATE AUGUST/SEPTEMBER, London newspapers carry note saying Rousseau has issued a challenge to his enemies to publish. Opinion in Paris now swings back to the desirability of Hume's publishing his account.

9 SEPTEMBER, Hume asks Adam Smith to inform d'Alembert that he has a free hand to edit Hume's account.

OCTOBER, *Exposé succinct de la contestation qui s'est élevée entre M. Hume et M. Rousseau avec des pièces justificatives* published in Paris.

NOVEMBER, Publication of English edition of *A Concise and Genuine Account of the Dispute between Mr. Hume and Mr. Rousseau.*

1767

JANUARY, Jean-François-Maximilian Cerjat in Ashbourne area.

MARCH, Rousseau discusses with Davenport plans to move to London. Davenport revives question of royal pension.

12 MARCH, Rousseau sells his library in preparation to depart.

18 MARCH, Conway informs Davenport that the King has granted Rousseau a pension of £100 p.a.

27 APRIL, Davenport arrives at Davenport Hall and is confined there by gout.

1 MAY, Rousseau leaves Wootton.

5 MAY Rousseau, in Spalding, asks the Lord Chancellor for an official guide for the journey to Dover.

14 MAY, Rousseau leaves Spalding.

18 MAY, Rousseau, in Dover, writes to Conway seeking an agreement on safe passage and accepting his suspicions of Hume were unjust.

22 MAY, Rousseau, Le Vasseur and Sultan arrive in Calais.

1768

29 APRIL, Rousseau marries Thérèse Le Vasseur.

1770

JUNE onwards, Rousseau returns to Paris, completes the *Confessions*, and reads them aloud to rapt audiences until forbidden by the authorities. (The *Confessions* are published posthumously in 1781.)

25 AUGUST 1776, Death of Hume.

2 JULY 1778, Death of Rousseau.

Acknowledgements

We seem to be specializing in knock-down-drag-out clashes between men of titanic gifts. Our previous books focused on a ten-minute argument in 1946 between Ludwig Wittgenstein and Karl Popper, and a two-month battle for the world chess crown in 1972 between the American Bobby Fischer and the Soviet Boris Spassky. This time, we have become involved in a violent eighteen-month relationship in the eighteenth century between two of history's most influential philosophers.

In our earlier works there were dozens of witnesses to the central action, many of whom we were able to interview. Here, our wholly deceased cast live on but only through their books and essays, and their vivid letters, journals and memoirs. Our debts to the quick are therefore less numerous: nonetheless, they are equally heartfelt.

We have to start with Dr Nigel Warburton, to whom we are profoundly grateful. Nigel had penned a fascinating article on the Ramsay portraits of Rousseau and Hume, and when we approached him about this he mentioned that he intended to write a book on Rousseau in England. Hearing of our similar intention, he decided not to write his book but instead to hand over all his notes. Later, he explained that this act of extraordinary generosity was motivated in part by an author who had been equally generous in donating all his research for a book Nigel has written on the architect Erno Goldfinger.

We like to walk the ground. *Wittgenstein's Poker* took us to

Cambridge and Vienna, *Bobby Fischer Goes To War*, to Reyk-javik and Moscow. This time we re-trod Rousseau's footsteps, in Switzerland along Lake Neuchâtel (in Môtiers, Rousseau's expulsion was explained by his predatory lusting after the young women of the village), and in England from London west to Chiswick, north to Staffordshire and east to Lincolnshire. A tour of Strawberry Hill illuminated Horace Walpole through his passion for black rooms lit by a single candle. In Wootton, the Hon Johnny Greenall, who has built a neo-Georgian mansion on the site of Wootton Hall, kindly allowed us to wander around the grounds where we could pause in the remains of 'Rousseau's grotto'. Several miles away, William Podmore, who as a boy had gone with his father to the original Wootton Hall, when it was demolished in 1931, to take possession of the great staircase and the grotto, showed us both purchases – lovingly reconstructed. On David's first trip around Staffordshire, accompanied by the philosopher and writer Jonathan Rée, they were shepherded by Wootton-based artists Simon and Jo Munby through the area's maze of fields and narrow country lanes. In Chiswick, local historians James Wisdom and Val Bott, shared their passion for the area with the present authors over lunch in their Chiswick home. Their tour of Chiswick was so vivid that the eighteenth century village rose up before our eyes, while the busy roundabout on the A40 magically vanished. Carolyn Hammond, at Chiswick Library, prepared the microfiches and rate-books for our perusal and then in her spare time tracked down some fascinating documentation on Rousseau's Chiswick landlord.

John would like to acknowledge two engrossing and scholarly lectures in the Wallace Collection series *Fleshly Olympus*: *Libertine and Liberty: Literature in the Age of Reason* by Professor David Coward, and *Drawing Room to Picture Frame: Women and Celebrity in the Eighteenth Century* by Stella Tillyard.

David would like to thank the staff in the British Library, who make this as pleasant a salt mine as an author could hope for. John would like to salute The London Library: an essential resource in the helpfulness of its staff, the browsing permitted by its open shelves, the breadth of its collection, and the freedom to take out its books, even original volumes of eighteenth-century journals.

We are indebted to our hawk-eyed readers and experts who read all or parts of the manuscript, and identified errors of fact or interpretation. They are, Hannah Edmonds, David Franklin, Peter Mangold, Derek Matravers, Sheena McDonald, Jonathan Rée, Zina Rohan, Neville Shack, Christopher Tugendhat, Maurice Walsh, Nigel Warburton, Andrew Yorke. A few of these readers are now our text-checking veterans, having performed a similarly unremunerated service for the previous books. Simon Gray put aside work on his drama for a comprehensive reading of ours, its meaning and moral.

Our story not only spanned the English Channel, it involved a culture that assumed a knowledge of Latin and its classic works. Several linguists helped with or checked translations in French and Latin and explicated the references in each language: Sara Beck, Hannah Edmonds, Elisabeth Eidinow, Esther Eidinow, Sam Eidinow, Isabel Raphael. In Paris, Catherine and Gerard Hubert zestfully followed up our research requests, as did Christopher Dickson in Switzerland. From Geneva, Alfred Dufour put his deep knowledge of that city's history at our disposal.

The book would not have been possible without the superb professional skills and support of our agent and publishers: at David Higham, Jacqueline Korn, Georgina Ruffhead and Ania Corless; at Faber Julian Loose, Henry Volans, and Jill Burrows; at Ecco, Julia Serebrinsky, Lee Boudreaux, Ghen~a Glijansky, Marty Karlow, and Jane Beirn.

Illustration Acknowledgements

Illustrations in the text are reproduced by kind permission of the following: Private Collection, Ken Welsh / Bridgeman Art Library (Chapter 1: David Hume); National Gallery of Scotland / Bridgeman Art Library (Chapter 1: Jean-Jacques Rousseau); Time Life Pictures / Getty Images; (Chapter 5: Burning at Geneva); Réunion des Musées Nationaux / © Gérard Blot (Chapter 7: Tea in the Salon of Four Mirrors); Scottish National Portrait Gallery / Bridgeman Art Library (Chapter 10: James Boswell); British Library (Chapter 10: Advertisement for lost dog); Hulton Archive / Getty Images (Chapter 16: Hume in Relief); Nigel Warburton (Chapter 17: *Concise Account* title page); Bettmann / Corbis (Chapter 21: Rousseau with Therese); Mary Evans Picture Library (Chapter 22: Rousseau with dog).

Index

Figures in italics indicate captions. 'H.' indicates David Hume, and 'R.' indicates Jean-Jacques Rousseau.